Curriculum and Teaching Dialogue

Volume 7, Numbers 1 and 2

Curriculum and Teaching Dialogue

edited by

Barbara Slater Stern
James Madison University

Greenwich, Connecticut • www.infoagepub.com

Copyright © 2005 IAP–Information Age Publishing, Inc.

All rights reserved. No part of this publication may be reproduced, stored in a retrieval system, or transmitted, in any form or by any means, electronic, mechanical, photocopying, microfilming, recording or otherwise, without written permission from the publisher.

Printed in the United States of America

Curriculum and Teaching Dialogue
AATC Leadership for 2004-2005

President: Cheryl J. Craig, University of Houston
Past President: David Flinders, Indiana University
President-Elect: William Veal, College of Charleston
Executive Secretary: Marcella L. Kysilka, University of Central Florida
Historian: Jennifer Deets
Program Chair—2004: Larry Holt, University of Central Florida
Program Chair—2005: J. Wesley Null, Baylor University

Executive Committee

Pam Brown, Oklahoma State University (07)
Susan C. Brown, University of Central Florida (07)
Jennifer Deets (06)
Alan W. Garrett, Eastern New Mexico University (05)
Robert Gutiérrez, Florida State University (05)

Peggy Schimmoeller, Randolph-Macon Woman's College (06)
Margaret M. Scott, Oklahoma State University (05)
Jeanne Tunks, University of North Texas (07)
Gopakumar Venugopalan, University of Alabama (06)

Publications Chairs and Newsletter Editor

Jeanne Tunks, University of North Texas

Editorial Board, *Curriculum and Teaching Dialogue*

Editor
Barbara Slater Stern
James Madison University

Associate Editor
J. Wesley Null
Baylor University

Editorial Review Board

Lynne Bailey
University of North Carolina—Charlotte

Robert Boostrom
University of Southern Indiana

Monica Brown
University of the West Indies

Susan Brown
University of Central Florida

India Broyles
University of New England

Lynn M. Burlbaw
Texas A & M University

Jennifer Deets
University of Central Florida

Robert Donmoyer
University of San Diego

Moira Fallon
SUNY—College at Brockport

Lyn Forester
Doane College

Doug Ganss
Minnesota State University, Mankato

Jeffrey Kaplan
University of Central Florida

J. Randall Koetting
University of Nevada

Karen Riley
Auburn University at Montgomery

Judith J. Slater
Florida International University

Julia D. Sweeny
James Madison University

Jeanne L. Tunks
University of North Texas

Editorial Advisory Board

Michael Apple
University of Wisconsin—Madison

Thomas Barone
Arizona State University

D. Jean Clandinin
University of Alberta, Canada

Elliot Eisner
Stanford University

William A. Reid
University of Texas at Austin

Steve Selden
University of Maryland at College Park

CONTENTS

The President' Message
Cheryl Craig ... ix

The Editor's Notes: Continuing the Conversation
Barbara Slater Stern ... xi

PART I: WHAT SHOULD WE BE TEACHING?

1. The Failings of No Child Left Behind
   David J. Flinders ... 1

2. The Rationale for Critical Pedagogy in Facilitating Cultural Identity
   Hsuan-Jen Chen ... 11

3. Transcending the Silkworm and Liberal Education
   John Mihelich ... 23

4. Teacher Education Curriculum: What, How and Why
   J.Wesley Null and Chara Haeussler Bohan ... 39

5. Caring for a Troubled Child: Lessons Twenty-Three Years Later
   Sara McCormick Davis ... 51

6. Teaching Reading Strategies to Adult Learners
   Nancy J. Hadley, Marilyn J. Eisenwine and Mary G. Sanders ... 65

7. Educators' Acceptance of and Resistance to Handheld Technologies
   Steven L. Purcell ... 79

PART II: IMPROVING K-12 LEARNING EXPERIENCES

8. Didn't You See What I Meant? Informing Gestures in Teaching and Learning
   Edie S. Gaythwaite — *97*

9. The Nature of Student and Teacher Discourse in an Elementary Classroom
   Violet Dickson — *109*

10. Common ground: An Ecological Perspective of Teaching and Learning
    Christy M. Moroye — *123*

11. The Connection Between Critical Media Viewing and Literacy Skills: An Action Research Study
    Teresa Russell and David W. Nicholson — *139*

12. The Role of Islam and Muslims in American Education: Critical Issues in Teaching and Curriculum
    James R. Moore — *155*

13. Fishbowl Reflections: A High School Teacher's Enlightenment During a Faculty Desegregation Experience
    Judith D. Luckett — *167*

14. Urban Children's Experiences and Teacher Pedagogical Practice: When It's About Race, Do Adult's Care?
    Amy L. Masko — *175*

About the Authors — *195*

PRESIDENT'S MESSAGE

Cheryl Craig

In the Caldecott Honor Book, *The Way to Start a Day,* author Byrd Baylor proposes how fine beginnings should be made:

The way to start a day is this—

*Go outside
and face the east
and greet the sun
with some kind of
blessing
or chant
or song
that you made yourself
and keep for early morning.*

She continues:

The way to make the song is this—

*Don't try to think
What words to use
Until
you're standing there
alone.*

When you feel the sun
You'll feel the song too.
Just sing it.
But don't think you're
the only one
who ever worked
that magic. (Baylor & Parnall, 1977)

As president of the American Association of Teaching and Curriculum, I am delighted to introduce this new issue of *Curriculum and Teaching Dialogue* that Editor Barbara Slater Stern and Associate Editor Wesley Null have so ably put together. My hope is that you will savor the contents of this journal and that the message that each piece conveys will resonate with you in some way. I also hope that the articles will provoke *new day* thinking on your part and that they will offer fresh opportunities for you to mingle theory and practice together. Most of all, may you feel inspired to weave magic in your professional lives in a manner not unlike the authors and editors in this particular issue. I look forward to seeing you at our forthcoming conference in Austin, a meeting for which an unprecedented number of proposals have been received.

REFERENCE

Baylor, B., & Parnell, P. (1977). *The way to start a day.* New York: Simon & Schuster.

THE EDITOR'S NOTES

Continuing the Conversation

Barbara Slater Stern

As I assume the editorship of *Curriculum and Teaching Dialogue*, I first wish to thank Susan C. Brown for her 6 years of excellent stewardship during which she took CTD from its inception as conference proceedings to a twice annual publication. Sue has improved the journal with every volume and I hope to follow the trail she so competently blazed. Next, I want to thank the Executive Committee for entrusting me with the position of editor. I will try to fulfill their expectations over the next 3 years. I promise to give my best effort and to be open to feedback from the membership in AATC's continuing effort to produce a journal that represents the goals and objectives of the organization. I want to welcome J. Wesley Null as associate editor. His expertise will be of great value to the journal for the next 3 years. I also would like to thank those individuals who continue to serve on the editorial board and on the advisory board as well as everyone who volunteered to review articles submitted for publication. Without everyone's help, the journal can not achieve the quality the membership deserves.

It is my intention to seek articles that encompass the range of the curriculum and teaching fields. In addition, I am is interested in reflection/

response essays on articles published; book reviews, especially of member's authorship. I hope to resume featuring articles by conference guest speakers and those who were influenced by their careers. To me the journal is a springboard for continuing conversation about the fields of curriculum and teaching and their relationship to one another.

As I begin my term, *CTD* will be published as a book with both the Spring and the Fall 2005 issues appearing as one volume. It is our hope that this new format will increase subscriptions without compromising the quality of the journal. The Executive Committee and the membership will surely provide feedback on this new format as we seek to increase our circulation. Other changes include initiating electronic submission and review. The forms for submission and review will be available on both the AATC (http://www.unc.edu/~wveal/aatc.html) and Information Age (http://www.infoagepub.com/www/index.html) Websites. Additionally, George Johnson, our publisher, has agreed to house electronic copies of back issues on the Information Age Website. Volumes 1 and 2 have been scanned and are ready for uploading; Volumes 3 is in process. Future volumes will be uploaded to the Website with a 5 year lag. This electronic access will enable broader distribution of our work without compromising volumes that are current and still available for sale.

This edition of *CTD* is divided into two parts. Part I is introduced with a chapter that had its origins in David Flinders' presidential address at the 2004 annual meeting. Flinders addresses the failings of No Child Left Behind by questioning the effectiveness of the accountability demanded by NCLB legislation. That questioning opens the door to questions about curriculum; what should we be teaching? Hsuan Chen makes a case for critical pedagogy to facilitate cultural identity. Chen, a native of Taiwan, argues that critical pedagogy empowers students and leads to social transformation thereby assisting minority groups. John Mihelich argues for the value of liberal education by recounting exchanges between himself and a student who is unhappy with the general education courses that waste time by distracting him from engineering courses and the pursuit of a lucrative career. Teaching students in vocational programs to value the why in addition to the what and the how brings us to Wes Null and Chara Bohan's discussion of the teacher education curriculum. These authors argue forcefully that teacher educators need to have their preservice teachers focus more on the why portion of their future careers. In some respects, that is part of the point in Sara Davis's article "Caring for the Troubled Child." Davis recounts an experience from her early teaching years and explains what it means to her as a teacher educator preparing preservice teachers for their own classrooms. Davis makes the point that critical reflection and learning to listen to the inner voice—knowing the answer is not always *out there* to be found but may rest within the teacher—is an important piece of her teaching teachers.

However, there is always the reality of exams required for teacher licensure. Nancy Hadley, Marilyn Eisenwine, and Mary Sanders are loath to see talented preservice teachers never hired due to an inability to navigate the practical reality of standardized licensure exams. Thus, their chapter focuses on reading strategies for adult learners who must leap this hurdle. Another reality that teachers (and teacher educators) must face is the growth of technology in the business world. Steve Purcell explores educator's views of integrating handheld technologies into their curricula. In short, Part I contains chapters on the what, the why and the how to teach.

Part II looks more directly at K-12 teaching with the goal of improving the learning experiences of students. First, Edie Gaythwaite discusses body language, particularly gestures, that inform teaching and learning. Gaythwaite makes the point that understanding and purposeful use of gesture will improve the classroom climate by reaching out to all learners. Violet Dickson examines student and teacher discourse in elementary classrooms. Dickson is interested in types of teacher talk that either inhibit or encourage student learning. Christy Moroye follows with an ecological look at classrooms. Framing her chapter through the lens of Eisner's connoisseurship and educational criticism, Moroye looks deeply at the classroom focusing on connectedness, contexts, and learning cycles. Then, Teresa Russell and David Nicholson tackle media literacy in a high school English elective. Surely, in our visual age, the use of film to augment literature deserves critical attention. Russell and Nicholson offer advice on how to transfer critical media skills from the elective course to the English literature course making the case that media skills enhance acquisition of literacy skills.

To address critical skill areas for students beyond the English classroom, James Moore makes a case for the inclusion of information about Islam and Muslims in the history curriculum. In addition, Moore focuses on how to teach about religion in history courses, a perennial problem. Given the current political climate and growing Muslim population in the United States, this topic is of immediate importance. This chapter segues into the last two articles dealing with race and racism. Judy Luckett's article is a reflection on her experiences with desegregation in central Florida. As a White teacher assigned to an all African American school, Luckett recounts the problems and achievements of this time. In a more current look at that situation, Amy Masko discusses her action research focusing on urban children's experience with race and adult reactions to these experiences. In some way these two articles complement each other—what did we learn during desegregation and where has it taken us today? Race and racism continues to be problematic in America. Part I opens that issue with its discussion of critical pedagogy to help forge cultural identity and Part II closes with the need for teacher educators to find multiple solutions to these problems. Reader commentary on these chapters is always welcome. You can reach me at sternbs@jmu.edu

PART I

WHAT SHOULD WE BE TEACHING?

CHAPTER 1

THE FAILINGS OF NCLB

David J. Flinders

This chapter argues that No Child Left Behind is based on fundamentally flawed thinking about what accountability is and how it should be used. Following a brief look at the recent history of the accountability movement, the Ten Commandments are used to illustrate the mistaken belief that accountability will serve as a viable means of school reform. In short, accountability may encourage compliance, but not the enhancement of learning. Instead of serving the aims of capitulation, educational scholarship in particular should help us better understand how our society contributes (or fails to contribute) to education and the needs of American youth.

No Child Left Behind (NCLB) is emblematic of today's accountability doctrine in education. The logic of that doctrine is to hold schools in judgment through an array of testing provisions, reporting procedures, bureaucratic mandates, and sanctions for noncomplying schools. In this chapter I argue that such policy is woefully inadequate as a basis for educational reform. The reason for its inadequacy is not that the policy is politically motivated (which it is), not that its mandates are largely unfunded (which they are), not that testing companies have consistently bungled their role (which they have), and not that students find it boring to learn meaningless facts (which they do). Instead, the failings of NCLB are conceptual rather than practical. At the heart of NCLB is fundamentally flawed thinking about what standards-based accountability is and how it should be used.

I will develop this thesis in three parts. The first part introduces a context for today's accountability movement by reviewing its recent history in the United States. The second part uses an historical example to critique the accountability movement and its use of standards. The third part of the chapter proposes not that we reform education but that we educate reform.

THE RECENT CONTEXT AND AN HISTORICAL EXAMPLE

Contemporary accountability policies in education are a legacy of the 1970s and 1980s back-to-basics movement. That movement signaled a broad shift in American educational thinking. As the conservative right took back control of educational issues, the profession at large retreated from social issues to the safety of subject area specializations. With already beleaguered teachers criticized for trying to do to much, broader discussions of educational purpose lost prominence. In 1983, *A Nation at Risk* (National Commission on Excellence in Education, 1983) marked more than a decade of declining SAT scores. That widely-cited report and other reports like it blamed American schools for neglecting their academic mission. This focus on academics made the solutions to our national education crisis seem obvious. With student achievement on the wane, schools needed to improve test scores by raising standards. By the 1990s, the call was for world-class standards. Our nation was to be number one in science, number one in mathematics.

Today standards are once again touted as the solution to a wide range of longstanding problems. From one perspective, however, standards have always been an important part of the Western cannon. Their history, for example, stretches back to Moses and the Ten Commandments. While other illustrations could be cited, including the Code of Hammurabi or the Edicts of Emperor Ashoka, the Commandments are particularly well-known. For this reason, I want to use the Commandments as a practical case in which to ask two questions: Do standards work? And if so, for what purposes or to what ends? The widely assumed goodness of standards has discouraged contemporary educators from asking these questions. Yet few theologians would assume that the Ten Commandments *cause* people to be good. We in education might do well to follow their lead in taking a closer look at our own faith in standards-based reform.

The Commandments also offers an especially strong test case. In research, this type of approach is called a hot house trial because it seeks conditions favorable for success. In the case of the Commandments, for example, they come to us on good authority (the word of God, according to Moses). They are also recognized as part of (or at least compatible with) several major religious traditions. In addition, the Commandments' 3,000 plus year history has allowed plenty of time for what in education we like to call the implementation stage of a new policy. Finally, the Commandments are a high stakes proposition. What is *adequate yearly progress*, for example, compared to eternal salvation?

I am drawing these comparisons intentionally because we should think about what our current education policies would look like in other contexts. What would we think of a church that labeled its practitioners as *failing* based on a single test score, and then refused to provide any sort of guidance on questions of how to improve? In place of guidance, what if this church made condescending threats, withheld its moral resources, and generally sought to penalize those in most need of help? Perhaps a motto for this church might be found in the familiar joke, "Punishment will continue until morale improves." Such is the logic of NCLB.

But the questionable nature of this policy may be particular to NCLB, and not an indictment against standards in general. If standards-based accountability has failed in this specific case but is still sound in theory, then perhaps we can fix the policy. Perhaps we can modify NCLB in order to make it more efficient. The Commandments are again useful in reflecting on this possibility. The commandment "Thou shalt not kill," like many standards, certainly seems unassailable on its face. But any consideration of recent history immediately raises questions. If anything, a moral prohibition against killing seems almost hypocritical in light of the past century's vast bloodshed—a century that included the horrors of the First World War, the Nazi genocide, Dresden, Hiroshima, the Soviet Gulag, Vietnam, Cambodia, Rwanda, and Bosnia (for a much longer list, see Glover, 1999). History does not offer a particularly encouraging track record when it comes to the effectiveness of this Commandment, or the effectiveness of others. On the other hand, historical arguments may miss the point. The purpose of the Ten Commandments may never have been to instruct us on how to behave morally or ethically. After all, they come to us in such a succinct form that the best they can do is telegraph abbreviated meanings of what we take to be right and wrong. They are historically equivalent to today's television sound bites. As such, the Commandments eschew complexity, emotions, and human motives—all of which seem unavoidable in considering what constitutes moral behavior. Put another way, the Commandments are not particularly good *teachers* of morality, except perhaps for the very young.

Nevertheless, this shortcoming does not discount other possible functions. While the Commandments do not provide anything like a detailed instruction manual, they may still serve as springboards for deeper ethical discussions. They may also serve as a way to affirm shared values, or as a basis for strengthening community life, or as important symbols of our humanity. None of these functions depend on the Commandments being followed blindly and without thought. On the contrary, to take them as absolute rules or as *the* measure of moral behavior may actually undermine their moral authority. Compliance is not the same as virtue, and following rules is not the same as being moral. Yet, this is the mistake that the Department of Education (DOE) has made with standards-based accountability. Rather than approach standards as opportunities for discussion, reflection, and learning, the DOE has taken up standards as a means of control. In the department's roadmap for implementing NCLB (http://www.ed.gov/about/reports/strat/plan2002-07/index.html), for example, its number one objective is to link federal funds to accountability for results. In more specific terms, the DOE seeks to withhold recourses from schools that do not conform to an increasingly rigid set of standards, thereby rewarding compliance over merit. However, just as people cannot be made morally good by holding a gun to their heads, schools cannot be made educationally good by threats of closure.

This problem of top-down school reform is one of the key findings of recent research on accountability. In one of the most comprehensive studies to date, Carnoy, Elmore, and Siskin (2003) found that a common response to accountability among high schools is what they term "compliance without capacity." Referring specifically to low income schools that were also low achieving prior to accountability policies, Elmore (2003) concludes that: "These schools essentially did what they thought the law required, with a minimum of alteration in their basic way of organizing and delivering instruction—and, not surprisingly, produced little in the way of improved performance" (p. 200).

HOW TO MAKE STANDARDS WORK

While standards-based accountability has not been studied as widely as needed, the early findings of research should serve as a wake-up call for those who have rushed to capitulation. Like individual schools, much of the educational literature first responding to NCLB sought to specify what the law required and how to comply (see, for example, Mann & Shakeshaft, 2003). More recent publications have acknowledged practical problems and design flaws in the NCLB provisions. Many worry, for example, that the *failing* schools soon to be denied funding are often among the nation's poorest schools to begin with. In this respect, NCLB is designed to function as a Robinhood law in reverse—stealing from the poor to give to the rich.

But even without such design flaws, the heart of NCLB would remain unchanged in its assumptions that standards and assessment should be designed not to help schools but to control them. This controlling or strategic use of standards, which is now unquestioned by the DOE, simply contradicts our basic tenets of good teaching. Many teachers still believed that what is taught should determine the knowledge and skills on which students are tested. NCLB reverses that relationship. What is tested now determines what is taught. Moreover, this remote control of classroom teaching is not an ancillary consequence of NCLB but its stated aim. On this count we have reached a new level of bureaucratic shortsightedness.

If we assume the DOE's point of view that standards-based accountability is the best way to whip schools into shape, then the success of NCLB depends ultimately on teachers following both the approved content standards and methods of teaching. Under these conditions, professional judgments become a liability rather than asset. Stopping to think before conducting a scripted lesson, making adjustments in process, taking advantage of teachable moments, or building on student interests—all such pedagogical moves only increase the variance across classrooms and increase noncompliance. Thus, blind and unthinking obedience is the only way to make standards work. Yet such a cure for whatever ails our schools is worse than the disease.

Fortunately, no one has yet found a way to stop classroom teachers from thinking. Regardless of past efforts (many of us can recall the teacher-proof curricula of the early 1960s), no one has been able to eliminate the need for teachers to make their own decisions about how to carry out a given lesson—including the need to decide what content is most relevant to the students and the situations at hand, how a lesson is to be paced, where and when repetition is called for, how to motivate a particular class, and so on.

WHAT TO DO?

If expecting teachers to perform like trained seals is not the answer to the nation's difficult educational challenges, and if standards prove to be an inadequate basis for helping schools do a better job, then what are we to do? On the one hand, we should appreciate that different individuals are often positioned in unique ways to advocate for education. But at the same time, we can unite some of our efforts by recognizing that current debates over public education represent only half the story. On the pro-education side of the debates are those who insist that schools are essential to meeting urgent social ends—a strong economy, a literate workforce, an informed citizenry, a lower crime rate, greater social equity, and so forth. Another group argues that schools have failed in just about any service to society that one could name. Both groups ignore that the relationship between society and our schools is a two-way street. If schools are to provide for society, society must provide for schools. Some politicians may respond that society already provides for schools by supplying educational funding. The veracity of that claim needs to be challenged, and NCLB itself offers a ready example. While the backers of this legislation demand that schools accomplish Herculean tasks, they have consistently promised funding without any serious intention of providing it. On this score, NCLB follows a growing list of legislation that either underfunds its educational mandates, or does not fund them at all, expecting others to pick up the tab. Ironically, the same politicians what shun responsibility for their own actions are often those most vocal in demanding that others be held accountable.

Yet money is not the only issue. Even if our schools were adequately funded, education has always required more than four walls, a chalkboard, and an overworked staff. What, then, should schools ask of society? They might begin by asking that all children have homes. Today 750,000 American children are reported to be homeless (NSCAHH, 2004). Schools might also ask that children be adequately fed, and that they receive basic health care. They might ask that families have employment opportunities and the types of affordable housing that would lessen student mobility and reduce the problems of having to move children from school to school two or three times a year. All of these basic needs are found to be among the strongest predictors of educational achievement (Barton, 2004; Rothstein, 2004), which is not a claim that can be made for standards-based accountability. But even without the educational benefits, we should ask on moral grounds alone that children be well cared for. Any educated society should expect as much.

Schools should also ask that their teachers and staff be shown basic levels of respect. NCLB is particularly worrisome on this point. In conveying distrust and contempt for classroom teachers, NCLB dissuades people form entering the profession and encourages others to leave. Richard Ingersoll (2004) notes that between 40 and 50% of new teachers leave teaching within the first 5 years of their careers. For this reason, he argues that the teaching profession is best thought of today as a "leaky bucket" (p. 144).[1] Referring specifically to NCLB, Ingersoll writes: "If the new accountability measures only serve to increase pressure on teachers without providing commensurate increases in their autonomy and resources, then they may end up simply driving even more teachers out of the occupation" (pp. 145-146). The problems of retention are further suggested by the fact that three to four times as many credentialed teachers exist than there are vacant teaching positions (Darling-Hammond, 2004, p. 251), and many schools still find it difficult to fill these positions.

Such concerns over standards-based accountability underscore the need for more research on this topic. Educational researchers have conducted relatively few careful studies of accountability to date. However, those studies that have examined school and classroom practices seem to confirm many of the concerns raised by the skeptics of NCLB. The goal-displacement of compliance strategies was mentioned earlier as a central finding of the Carnoy et al. study (2003). Their study also found that the modest and temporary gains in test scores associated with high-stakes accountability fail to be corroborated by other measures of student achievement, this suggesting that accountability produces better test takers rather than any increase in real learning.

Other studies of accountability include Linda M. McNeil's (2004) research on high-stakes accountability in Texas. While the Texas system was originally proposed to reduce inequities between White and Latino students, the effects have been the just the opposite. In particular, McNeil argues that poor and minority schools not only receive less funding under the Texas accountability system, but also that they have shifted "already scarce resources into the purchase of test-prep materials" (p. 281). Another study conducted by the Council for Basic Education (von Zastrow & Janc, 2004) echoes McNeil's findings more broadly. Surveying four states, this research found that schools with high minority populations suffer disproportionately from accountability in having to reduce support for the arts, foreign language, and elementary social studies (pp. 7-8).

Those who study the achievement gap between ethnic and social groups are beginning to reach a consensus that standards-based accountability will have little if any effect on such entrenched and persistent inequalities.[2] Yet early research cannot be regarded as conclusive in part because it has focused mostly on test scores and randomized trials. Such research is not in a good position to explain *how* or *why* educational reforms lead to a given outcome. "To determine that," says Denis Phillips "you need finer-grained qualitative studies" (quoted in Hass, 2004, p. 4).

The implication of needing to look more closely at educational programs is that we cannot limit our research to the simple-mindedness of accountability. Because strong and enduring relationships between adults and children are more likely to make a difference in student achievement than threats of school closure, we kneed to know more about the models of schooling that encourage such relationships. We need to know more about how students become genuinely engaged in their studies, and how teachers can encourage such engagement. We need to know more about the conditions that help students direct their own learning, formulate their own questions, and cultivate their personal talents. We need to know more about what forms of teaching and curriculum help students assume multiple points of view, see beyond their own self-interests, and make connections between what they study in school and their lives outside of the classroom. No amount of testing students will answer these important questions. If anything, testing sidetracks us into insisting that otherwise good teachers spend time specifying particular standards for every lesson, every activity, and every student assignment done in every classroom. Such policies may assure standardization, but not high standards.

CONCLUSION

In John Dewey's 1929 pedagogic creed, he wrote that, "All reforms which rest simply upon the enactment of law, or the threatening of certain penalties, or upon changes in the mechanical or outward arrangements, are transitory and futile" (p. 294).

In this chapter I have argued that NCLB is a futile education policy for the very reasons that Dewey noted more than 75 years ago. When threatened with certain penalties, schools respond only by changing mechanical and outward arrangements, thereby removing education still further from the lives and interests of students. I have also suggested two general strategies in response to current policies. The first strategy is to exercise more skepticism than we have in the past about the impulse to control others that is so brazenly expressed in NCLB. The second strategy is to use research to better educate reform.

With the recent re-election of NCLB's most staunch supporters, the task of educating reform seems especially daunting in today's political climate. Government oversight continues to plunge scholarship into ever deepening shadows. Yet this darkness does not make our work irrelevant. On the contrary, if the aim of research is to help us see more clearly, then we might think of today's scholarship as important beacons of light. In dark times, beacons are *more*, not less relevant to finding our way. If we lose direction today it is because would-be school reformers are so determined to take light rather than shed it.

NOTES

1. "Having *experienced teachers* with at least five years of experience," another researcher (Barton, 2004) writes, "makes a difference in student achievement" (emphasis in the original).
2. See, for example, the November 2004 theme issue of *Educational Leadership* (Vol. 62, No. 3).

RERFERENCES

Barton, P. E. (2004, November). Why does the gap persist? *Educational Leadership, 62*(3), 8-13.

Carnoy, M., Elmore, R., & Siskin, L. S. (2003). *The new accountability: High schools and high-stakes testing*. New York: RoutledgeFalmer.

Darling-Hammond, L. (2004). Conclusion: Schools that work for all children. In C. Glickman (Ed.), *Letters to the next president* (pp. 239-253). New York: Teacher College Press.

Dewey, J. (1929, December). My pedagogic creed. *Journal of the National Education Association, 18*(9), 291-295.

Elmore, R. (2003). Accountability and capacity. In M. Carnoy, R. Elmore, & L. S. Siskin (Eds.). *The new accountability: High schools and high-stakes testing* (pp. 195-209). New York: RoutledgeFalmer.

Glover, J. (1999). *Humanity: A moral history of the twentieth century*. New Haven, CT: Yale University Press.

Hass, B. (2004, Fall). The brouhaha surrounding scientifically-based research. *Stanford Educator*, 1-2, 4.

Ingersoll, R. (2004). Revolving doors and leaky buckets. In C. Glickman (Ed.), *Letters to the next president* (pp. 141-147). New York: Teacher College Press.

Mann, D., & Shakeshaft, C. (2003, January). In God we trust; all others bring data. *School Business Affairs, 69*(1), 19-22.

McNeil, L. M. (2004). Creating new inequalities: Contradictions of reform. In D. J. Flinders & S. J. Thornton (Eds.), *The curriculum studies reader* (2nd ed., pp. 273-284). New York: RoutledgeFalmer.

National Commission on Excellence in Education. (1983). *A nation at risk: The imperative for educational reform*. Washington, DC: U.S. Government Printing Office.

NSCAHH. (2004). *Hunger and homelessness facts*. Retrieved on May 18, 2005, from http://www.nscahh.org/hunger.asp?id2=15769

Rothstein, R. (2004, November). The achievement gap: A broader picture. *Educational Leadership, 62*(3), 41-43.

von Zastrow, C. & Janc, H. (2004). *Academic atrophy: The condition of the liberal arts in America's public schools*. Washington DC: Council for Basic Education.

CHAPTER 2

THE RATIONALE FOR CRITICAL PEDAGOGY IN FACILITATING CULTURAL IDENTITY DEVELOPMENT

Hsuan-Jen Chen

In this chapter I argue that critical pedagogy can facilitate subordinate groups' cultural identity development by examining its philosophical and theoretical orientations. Built on critical theory, critical pedagogy recognizes the existence and constraints of the larger societal context and power relations. Emancipatory in nature, critical pedagogy is more inclined to consider the plight of subordinate groups in developing a positive cultural identity. Critical pedagogy aims at student empowerment and attempts to bring about social transformation.

INTRODUCTION

Culture is embedded in various human activities and social relations (McLaren, 1998). Human beings do not exist in a vacuum. Instead, they live together in groups to facilitate their survival needs. Since interaction with others is an inevitable part of human activities, various social and power relations exist. Power can be defined as the ability to impose or exert one's will on another, as well as the degree of respect one receives in society. As dominant groups possess power to make their culture the mainstream, the degree of adaptation their members need to make is relatively low. On the contrary, subordinate groups possess less power and need to make more adaptation to be accepted in the mainstream (Marshall, 2002). One's cultural identity is closely related to one's position in the power relations.

Cultural identity can be defined as self-perception of one's position in different dimensions of life, such as race, social class, gender, religion, age, sexual orientation, and physical and mental ability (Tatum, 1997). Cultural identity is multidimensional because of the complexities of human activities. An individual usually fulfills multiple roles in life. Within each dimension, there are dominant and subordinate groups. The dominant groups are "systematically advantaged by the society because of group membership" (Tatum, 1997, p. 22); vice versa, subordinate groups are systematically disadvantaged. Based on this notion, each individual is likely to be dominant in certain dimensions and subordinate in others. Tatum (1997) proposed that the dimension that stands out as one's major identity is usually the one that reveals subordinate status. For example, for a White, middle class, gay person, his sexual orientation may stand out as his major identity. This is a result not only of subjective individual choice but because of the larger sociocultural context. Because we perceive ourselves based on how others judge us, identity formation reflects individuals' interaction with the external environment, that is, the historical and social contexts (Berger & Luckman, 1967; Erikson, 1968; James, 1997; Laing, 1969; Tatum, 1997). One's position in power relations plays a decisive role in one's interaction with the world and her cultural identity development (Darder, 1991; Giroux, 1983; McLaren, 1998). For example, because subordinate groups are often portrayed negatively or as inferior in the dominant culture, it becomes difficult for these groups to develop a positive cultural identity (Marshall, 2002).

Although some people may live their whole lives without examining their perception of self, one's identity still exists and can greatly impact one's belief system, choice of life, and career. A positive sense of self, or identity, enables one to view one's group or community positively, which facilitates the cultivation of healthier citizens with stronger self-esteem. This is beneficial for society since individuals will exert their full potential and contribute more to their families and communities. On the other hand, a negative identity is detrimental to both individuals and society.

Through explicit and implicit curriculum, schools participate in shaping students' cultural identity. As institutions of the dominant culture, schools typically help maintain the existing social structure by transmitting dominant cultural ideologies to students (McLaren, 1998; Spring, 2000). As a result, the inequity between dominant and subordinate tends to be reproduced. This situation places educators in danger of helping social reproduction if they do not become aware of the connection among schools, power relations, and cultural identity. The notion of social reproduction is important in the discussion of cultural identity. Social reproduction happens because of the dominant culture's ability to control power relations. Power suggests status. Status reflects back to individuals. The dominant groups gain and maintain their power; the subordinate groups remain so. Self-identity, in this framework, is influenced by what is reflected back to us by the larger, dominant society.

In this chapter I will argue critical pedagogy as a possible solution to subordinate groups' cultural identity development because it recognizes the existence of power relations. To provide the rationale for critical pedagogy, I will first define critical pedagogy and illustrate its connections with critical theory. I will then develop the rationale based on critical theory's philosophical and theoretical orientations, including: (1) its views of reality (individuals as part of the structure); (2) its epistemological views (knowledge as a result of the power relations); and (3) its emancipatory nature (reflection and understanding of social structure as the beginning of possible social transformation). By examining these underlying assumptions of critical theory, I will argue that critical pedagogy is a powerful tool for cultivating positive cultural identity for subordinate groups.

DEFNITION OF CRITICAL PEDAGOGY

According to McLaren (1998), critical pedagogy, known as "the new sociology of education" or "critical theory of education" (p. 163), comprises a large body of literature that demonstrates critical pedagogues' enthusiasm in analyzing the impact of race, gender, and socioeconomic relations on students from historically disenfranchised groups. Critical pedagogues take an interest in exploring the theoretical constructs of their critical thinking. They attempt to explore the connections between these theoretical constructs and democratic schooling (Darder, Baltodano, & Torres, 2003). Although critical pedagogy is not made up of a homogeneous set of ideas, critical pedagogues do share one common objective, that is, "to empower the powerless and transform existing social inequalities and injustice" (McLaren, 1998, pp. 163-164). This common objective shows that while critical pedagogues recognize the existence of racial, class, and gender barriers, they do not view these barriers as completely insurmountable. Rather, examining and understanding these barriers is considered the first step to transforming them. Critical pedagogues are hopeful for the possibilities of social transformation.

The term *critical pedagogy* first appeared in Henry Giroux's publication in 1983, *Theory and Resistance in Education*. Yet, the origin of its central notions can be traced to progressive educational movements in the early 1900s (Dewey as a representative; Darder et al., 2003). These aspirations facilitate the link between "the practice of schooling to democratic principles of society and to transformative social action in the interest of oppressed communities" (Darder et al., 2003, p. 3). This link between schooling and society illustrates why critical pedagogues perceive politics and power as central to the understanding of how schools work. In other words, schools need to be perceived as part of the social and political framework that constitutes the dominant society. As a result, the work of critical pedagogues focuses on subjects such as the political economy of schooling, the representation of texts, and the construction of student subjectivity (McLaren, 1998).

Critical pedagogy draws its foundations from critical theory. Ashley and Orenstein (2001) identified critical theory as one of three major sociological theoretical orientations (i.e., positivism, hermeneutics, and critical theory). Critical pedagogues are usually also critical theorists. As suggested by Greene (2003), conceptions in critical theory can be traced to classical Greece. They are modern constructs, which became a central part of human understanding only after the Enlightenment (Ashley & Orenstein, 2001). Critical theory often is associated with the Frankfurt School, a group of social science scholars at the University of Frankfurt in Germany. The Frankfurt School scholars included the melding of the philosophies and theories of Kant, Hegel, Freud, and Marx (Webb, Metha, & Jordan, 2000). At the heart of the Frankfurt School is the analysis, scrutiny, and critique of all ideologies. Although often identified as a sociological theory, critical theory also is known as a philosophical school, unique in its ontological, epistemological, and axiological assumptions (Noddings, 1998). By understanding critical theory as critical pedagogy's major philosophical and theoretical orientation, I will identify several underlying assumptions of critical theory to establish a rationale for critical pedagogy as one possible solution to the hegemonic force that subordinate groups face for their cultural identity development.

VIEWS ON REALITY

Critical theorists view individuals as entities who function in society. They also recognize existing power relations as an important force that affects individual development. Rather than viewing elements which are involved in one phenomenon in isolation, critical theory situates these elements within the larger societal context. For example, in studying human behaviors, critical theory would take into consideration the family, community, and/or society that human beings act upon (Ashley & Orenstein, 2001). Critical theory contrasts with positivism in the sense that the former is more holistic whereas the latter is reductionistic. Reductionism is referred to the way of analysis that focuses on elementary units. Such an approach is valuable in science as greater control can be exerted over a specific phenomenon. While reductionism fails to seize how the elementary parts are influenced by the larger context, critical theory is capable of accounting for the influences from the larger context (Ashley & Orenstein, 2001).

While acknowledging the existence of a larger context that individuals act within, critical theory also acknowledges power relations in society. Individuals are viewed as agents that function within a social structure. MacLeod (1995) stated,

> Structure and agency are inseparable. Individual agents ... are always structurally situated, and thus human agency is itself socially structured. Social structures reach into the minds and even the hearts of individuals to shape their attitudes, motivations, and worldviews. Structural determination is thus inscribed in the very core of human agency. (p. 255)

Situated within the network of power relations, individual agents are confined by various structural constraints such as racial, class, and gender barriers. For example, the American educational system reveals the impact of the structural determinant of social class on the educational resources. While school budgets come from property taxes, higher and lower social class schools frequently receive drastically different resources (Olsen, 1997). Additionally, the hidden curriculum creates another layer of structural constraint on individual inclination (agency) because it usually values the cultural capital of the higher class students and depreciates the cultural capital of those from lower classes (MacLeod, 1995). When individuals are involved in the schooling process, they cannot escape from the structural constraint of the hidden curriculum.

The conception of structure and agency reflects critical theory's understanding of the nature of reality. Positivism, which models itself after the natural sciences, views reality as neutral and controllable. Consequently, positivists are interested in generalizing universally applicable rules to predict and control human behaviors (Ashley & Orenstein, 2001). Both hermeneutics and critical theory view reality as subjective. These viewpoints also recognize that reality is perceived differently by individuals, depending on social and historical context. The difference between hermeneutics and critical theory is that hermeneutics attempts to understand reality by seeing things from the subjects' perspectives with no attempt to bring about changes. Hermeneutics seeks reciprocal understanding and communicative interaction. On the other hand, critical theory takes a step further by recognizing that individuals are not equal due to their various positions in the power relations. Additionally, in critical theory, human communicative interaction has to be analyzed within the framework of power relations (Ashley & Orenstein, 2001).

Each theoretical orientation represents a different way of perceiving the world and human nature. Critical theory recognizes power relations and views individuals as functioning parts of the whole social structure. Because cultural identity development is largely impacted by power relations, critical theory is most effective in providing a hopeful framework for analyzing subordinate groups' cultural identity development.

EPISTEMOLOGICAL VIEWS

The second underlying assumption of critical theory has to do with its view of knowledge and the role of school in the shaping of knowledge. Critical theory views knowledge as a result of power relations and questions constantly the legitimacy of all forms of knowledge. Critical theorists do not view schools as a neutral or apolitical entity (McLaren, 1998). Thus, the knowledge presented and valued in the school curriculum should not be viewed as truth, but simply constructed by the dominant groups in order to maintain legitimacy of their dominance in the power relations (McLaren, 1998). By the same token, major philosophical works are not truth but works constructed at various points in history to secure the dominant groups' sense of legitimacy and power (Gutek, 1997). Critical theorists question the legitimacy of the knowledge students acquire in school by asking who controls how we know and what we know (Webb et al., 2000).

Critical pedagogy scholars, such as McLaren (1998), argue that schools serve the interests of the wealthy and the powerful, while simultaneously disconfirming the values and abilities of those students who are most disempowered in our society already, for example minorities, the poor, and women. The pitfall is that schools reproduce the values and privileges of the dominant culture, which perpetuates the existing power hierarchy. For example, in a Eurocentric curriculum where stories and histories of subordinate groups are omitted, their lack of representation in the dominant culture may lead subordinate groups to perceive their ancestors' status in the history as less important or negative. In this case, it becomes difficult to foster a positive cultural identity. The historian Ronald Takaki (1993) used the image of mirror to describe the horror of such an omission, which is like looking into the mirror but cannot see one's own reflection. Therefore, including multiple perspectives in the curriculum becomes crucial for attaining a better understanding of an event (Greene, 1995; Spring, 2000). Additionally, Ladson-Billings (1994, 1995, 2000) also suggested, in her notion of *culturally relevant pedagogy*, the importance of utilizing students' culture as a vehicle for learning. By inviting students' family to be guest speakers or to conduct various workshops, teachers create opportunities for students to learn about heir own culture in school. This way, the gap between home and school can be diminished. Also, while the subordinate culture is included as part of the curriculum, learning could become more meaningful for the students from subordinate groups.

By recognizing that power relations affect what knowledge a person has access to, critical theorists advocate holding a skeptical attitude toward knowledge. Such a skeptical attitude could facilitate a healthy development of subordinate groups' cultural identity. When subordinate groups become conscious of how the dominant groups devalue them through societal institutions, critical pedagogues believe that they may be more likely to question what they learn in school and subsequently avoid internalizing negative messages about their culture. The epistemological views of critical theory are intimately associated with the critical pedagogues' advocacy for raising consciousness as the first step in transformation.

EMANCIPATORY NATURE

The third underlying assumption of critical theory is its emancipatory nature. Critical theory is morally passionate (Ashley & Orenstein, 2001). It is concerned with the well-being of mankind and inquires about how we should live. As a result, issues such as the subordinate groups' cultural identity and its relation to power relations would concern critical theory, but not necessarily the other two theoretical orientations. As a pedagogy that bases itself on critical theory, critical pedagogy is thus more inclined to confront the barriers for cultivating a positive cultural identity. In addition, critical theory is action oriented. McLaren (1998) maintained that critical pedagogy commits itself to the forms of learning and action undertaken in solidarity with marginalized groups. By questioning what is taken for granted about schooling, critical pedagogy commits itself to emancipatory practices by creating space where students can work toward social and personal transformation.

In *Pedagogy of the Oppressed*, Paulo Freire (2000) illustrated the notion of liberation as a necessity to break down the relationship between the oppressor and the oppressed. Freire argued that the oppressed are dehumanized because their vocation of becoming more fully human is distorted by the oppressors. He posited that dehumanization is "not a given destiny but the result of an unjust order that engenders violence in the oppressors, which in turn dehumanizes the oppressed" (p. 44). The oppressors also dehumanize themselves when they dehumanize others by violating their rights and preventing them from being more fully human. Freire held that only the oppressed can free their oppressors by freeing themselves. The oppressors are incapable of freeing others or themselves as the oppressive class because they are dehumanized themselves. Liberation only can be initiated by the oppressed. There are two stages involved in the process of liberation. The first stage is characterized by the consciousness of the oppressed. At the second stage, the reality of the oppression has already been transformed so that the pedagogy of the oppressed becomes the pedagogy of all people in the process of permanent liberation.

Empowerment is essential for emancipation, which is laden with the expectation of social transformation. Webb et al. (2000) indicated, "The educational theory of social reconstructionism has two predominant themes: (1) society is in need of change or reconstruction, and (2) education must take the lead in the reconstruction of society" (p. 116). If societal power relations remain stable and even reinforced by the educational process, then the power relations are in need of changes. Critical theorists support the idea that education can be used as a vehicle for creating possibilities for social transformation. By being empowered, students expand their ability of functioning in society, which greatly increases possibilities for them to work toward social transformation.

Giroux (1992) defined empowerment as cultivating the ability to think and to act critically. Giroux stated,

> This notion has a double reference: to the individual and to society. The freedom and human capacities of individuals must be developed to their maximum but individual powers must be linked to democracy in the sense that social betterment must be the necessary consequence of individual flourishing. (p. 11)

In other words, individual empowerment coincides with social transformation. It would eventually move beyond the individual level and impact society.

Several suggestions have been made by critical theorists concerning student empowerment. For example, Freire (2000) posited that students should not be controlled or manipulated in learning, but should take initiatives and become involved in their own learning. In the process of facilitating student empowerment, teachers first have to respect, care about, and believe in their students (Webb et al., 2000). This requires teachers' understanding of themselves and their students as cultural beings. Teachers need to understand how the various social dimensions (e.g., race, social class, and gender) affect who they are as well as who their students are. Classroom teachers are viewed as capable of playing a more active role in bringing about change (Giroux, 1988). Also, students should be encouraged to become involved in the social issues that confront the community and society. Rather than only reading and studying about problems of the poor or the disenfranchised, the students could spend time in the community becoming acquainted with and more aware of problems within the community and their possible solutions (Webb et al., 2000). Examples of this would be expressing concerns about community issues by actions such as writing to newspaper editors (Ladson-Billings, 2000) and other service learning projects (Dudderar & Tover, 2003; Freeman & Swick, 2003).

Critical theorists advocate student empowerment as a way of enhancing the possibilities of emancipation and social transformation. Once empowered, an individual develops different worldviews. He acts on the world differently. For instance, when a person develops racial consciousness, that person also develops the ability to detect a racist act. This increases the possibility for the person to address racism. Yet the ideal of empowerment encounters several obstacles due to the structural constraints such as power relations. One major obstacle is fear of freedom by the oppressed group. Freire (2000) explained, "The 'fear of freedom' afflicts the oppressed. This is a fear that may equally well lead them to desire the role of oppressor or bind them to the role of oppressed" (p. 46). Because the oppressors set the only model of living with which the oppressed are familiar, the oppressed tend to become the oppressors themselves. Thus, in large part due to the oppression they face, the oppressed come to internalize the belief system of their oppressors. Nowhere is this more evident than their undervalued impression of themselves. Freire (2000) stated,

> Within their unauthentic view of the world and of themselves, the oppressed feel like "things" owned by the oppressor. For the latter, *to be* is *to have*, almost always at the expense of those who have nothing. For the oppressed, at a certain point in their existential experience, *to be* is not to resemble the oppressor, but *to be under* him, to depend on him. Accordingly, the oppressed are emotionally dependent. (p. 64)

Believing that they know nothing, the oppressed are usually emotionally dependent on the oppressors. The internalization of the oppressors' belief system is one of the greatest obstacles to liberation or empowerment, because "oppressive reality absorbs those within it and thereby acts to submerge human beings' consciousness" (Freire, 2000, p. 51). This discussion about the mentality of the oppressed also illustrates the difficulty for both dominant and subordinate groups to develop a positive cultural identity. By making the dominant culture the norm, dominant groups have justified their way of living. Within this framework of power relations, dominant groups are dehumanized as their sense of self is built upon a false sense of superiority with limited understanding of other cultural groups. While the dominant culture is the norm, the subordinate culture is not. Consequently, subordinate groups have to become aware of how power relations function against them so that they will not blindly be convinced that they are less valuable than the dominant groups. Such awareness is crucial for the development of a positive cultural identity.

Freire held that oppression is functionally realized through education for *domestication*. Education for *domestication* is the opposite of education for emancipation. Hence, transforming education for *domestication* into experiences of education for empowerment requires reflection and action on the part of the oppressed. By the same token, if the emotional dependence on the oppressor is an obstacle for liberation, then the oppressed have a long struggle before they head toward independence. They have to be able to reflect on themselves and rediscover their ability to act. To build up their ability to reflect, "students have to become literate about their histories, experiences, and the culture of their immediate environment" (Freire & Macedo, 2003).

Critical theory's advocacy for social and personal transformation reflects its action-oriented nature, which is necessary in order to resolve the oppressor-oppressed contradiction. Freire (2000) stated, "the oppressed must confront reality critically, simultaneously objectifying and acting upon that reality" (p. 52). A perception of reality without critical thinking thus should not be viewed as a true perception because it will neither steer a transformation of reality nor bring about liberation. To avoid suffering from oppression, the oppressed have to reflect and act on the world to bring about change (Freire, 2000).

Freire (2000) believed that the struggle of liberation should come from the *conscienzação* of the oppressed. By *conscienzação*, Freire referred to the action and reflection of people on their world to transform it. Self-reflection plays an important role in fostering the consciousness. Yet it is even more important to move beyond consciousness and take actions to change the status quo. The whole process empowers and emancipates the oppressed. Applied to the context of learning, empowered students would no longer depend on teachers to tell them how to act and what to learn but take initiatives in learning and take responsibilities for their actions. On the societal level, this empowerment can be transformed into more social actions and eventually bring about social transformation. As we understand the process of critical theory, it is equally important to recognize that the whole process described above is a constant struggle because various barriers, such as racial, social class, and gender barriers, do exist.

CONCLUSION

Based on critical theory's philosophical and theoretical orientations, critical pedagogy is more likely than other instructional theories to recognize cultural identity as a complex mental construct affected by the interplay between self and the external environment. Critical pedagogy recognizes the existence of structural constraint and power relations in society, as well as the impossibility for school knowledge to be neutral. This recognition enables critical pedagogues to consider subordinate groups' plights in the unequal societal power relations. Aiming at student empowerment, critical pedagogy hopes to bring about personal and social change. The beginning of student empowerment is fostering students' self-reflective ability in order to raise self-consciousness. Student empowerment is especially valuable for subordinate groups. While their ethnic cultures and languages are being omitted, distorted, or degraded in the dominant culture, a positive sense of self is difficult to attain. If subordinate groups could recognize how individuals function within the social structure and how school knowledge is impacted by societal power relations, they would be able to identify the forces that help formulate their images in the dominant culture, detach themselves from those images, become empowered, and even turn the newly attained power into action. Such self-reflection and self-consciousness will contribute to positive cultural identity and social transformation.

REFERENCES

Ashley, D., & Orenstein, D. M. (2001). *Sociological theory: Classical statement* (5th ed.). Boston: Allyn & Bacon.

Berger, P. L., & Luckman, C. (1967). *The social construction of reality.* Garden City, NY: Anchor Books.

Darder, A. (1991). *Culture and power in the classroom: A critical foundation for bicultural education.* Westport, CT: Bergin & Garvey.

Darder, A., Baltodano, M., & Torres, R. D. (Eds.). (2003). Critical pedagogy: An introduction. In *The critical pedagogy reader* (pp. 1-21). New York: Routledge-Falmer.

Dudderar, D., & Tover, L. T. (2003). Putting service learning experiences at the heart of a teacher education curriculum. *Educational Research Quarterly, 27*(2), 18-32.

Erikson, E. H. (1968). *Identity, youth, and crisis.* New York: W.W. Norton.
Freeman, N. K., & Swick, K. J. (2003). Perservice interns implement service-learning: Helping young children reach out to their community. *Early Childhood Education Journal, 31*(2), 107-112.
Freire, P. (2000). *Pedagogy of the oppressed* (30th anniversary ed.). New York: Continuum International.
Freire, P., & Macedo, D. (2003). Rethinking literacy: A dialogue. In A. Darder, M. Baltodano, & R. D. Torres (Eds.), *The critical pedagogy reader* (pp. 354-364). New York: RoutledgeFalmer.
Giroux, H. A. (1983). *Theory and resistance in education.* New York: Bergin & Garvey.
Giroux, H. A. (1988). *Teachers as intellectuals: Toward a critical pedagogy of learning.* Westport, CT: Bergin & Garvey.
Giroux, H. A. (1992). *Border crossing: Cultural workers and the politics of education.* New York: Routledge.
Greene, M. (1995). *Releasing the imagination: Essays on education, the arts, and social change.* San Francisco: Jossey-Bass.
Greene, M. (2003). In search of a critical pedagogy. In A. Darder, M. Baltodano, & R. D. Torres (Eds.), *The critical pedagogy reader* (pp. 97-114). New York: RoutledgeFalmer.
Gutek, G. (1997). *Philosophical and ideological perspectives on education.* Boston: Allyn & Bacon.
James, N. C. (1997). When Miss America was always White. In A. Gonzalez, M. Houston, & V. Chen (Eds.), *Our voices: Essays in culture, ethnicity, and communication* (2nd ed., pp. 46-51). Los Angeles: Roxbury.
Ladson-Billings, G. (1994). *The dreamkeepers.* San Francisco: Jossey-Bass.
Ladson-Billings, G. (1995). Toward a theory of culturally relevant pedagogy. *American Educational Research Journal, 32,* 465-491.
Ladson-Billings, G. (2000). But that's just good teaching! In J. Noel (Ed.), *Notable selections in multicultural education* (pp. 206-216). Guilford, CT: McGraw-Hill.
Laing, R. D. (1969). *Self and others.* Harmondsworth, England: Penguin Books.
MacLeod, J. (1995). *Ain't no makin' it: Aspirations and attainment in a low-income neighborhood.* Boulder, CO: Westview Press.
Marshall, P. L. (2002). *Cultural diversity in our schools.* Belmont, CA: Wadsworth/Thomson Learning.
McLaren, P. (1998). *Life in schools: An introduction to critical pedagogy in the foundations of education* (3rd ed.). New York: Longman.
Noddings, N. (1998). *Philosophy of education.* Boulder, CO: Westview.
Olsen, L. (1997). *Made in America: Immigrant students in our public schools.* New York: The New Press.
Spring, J. (2000). *The intersection of cultures: Multicultural education in the United States and the global economy* (2nd ed.). Boston: McGraw-Hill.
Takaki, R. (1993). *A different mirror: A history of multicultural America.* Boston: Little, Brown and Company.
Tatum, B. D. (1997). *"Why are all the Black kids sitting together in the cafeteria?" and other conversations about race.* New York: Basic Books.
Webb, L. D., Metha, A., & Jordan, K. F. (2000). *Foundations of American education* (3rd ed.). Upper Saddle River, NJ: Merrill.

CHAPTER 3

LIBERAL EDUCATION AND TRANSCENDING THE SILKWORM

John Mihelich

As a teacher, I maintain a commitment to the principle of a liberal education both to teach students the content of my disciplines and to enhance their lives and cultivate good citizens. However, I struggle to help students make sense of the tension between pragmatic economic concerns and the goals of a liberal education. Through examining a case study in this chapter, I demonstrate how in a mentoring relationship I navigated this tension in the life of one student, Alex. The case involves the question of how to get young students engaged in their educational process and, in particular, how to get them invested in the classes they take as part of a general core curriculum, the foundations for a liberal education. I begin by describing the core curriculum changes in my institution that reflect an increasingly popular trend toward interdisciplinary and liberally infused core curriculums. After discussing the particular core course that Alex was engaged in, I comment on the challenge I posed to students early on in the semester and the dialogue that ensued between Alex and me. The case illustrates well-reasoned student resistance to a liberal education and provides some suggestions for helping students think critically about the tension between pragmatic concerns and the opportunities offered by a liberal education.

INTRODUCTION

Generally, a required core curriculum at the university level is intended to foster a liberal arts education through both providing the foundations for a successful career and enhancing the capacity of individuals to reflect on, create, and sustain democratic ideals of freedom. The goals of a liberal education vary, ranging from the noble notion of helping students develop their full human potential (Gregory, 2003) to the end of fostering more concrete skills such as the ability to think critically and, with such skills, to make sound, civil, and just decisions (Vallentyne & Accordino, 1998). Generally, scholars agree that a liberal arts education provides students with an ability to grow intellectually and morally and to see their experience within a broader historical and cultural context (Fox-Genovese, 2002; Thomas, 2002). Although some see the compatibility between a liberal arts education and the marketplace (Durden, 2003; Fellowes, 2003), others have noted the tension between the values and goals of a liberal arts education and the instrumentalist, practical demands of the employment market, careers, and financial stability (Axelrod, 2002; Cornwell & Stoddard, 2001).

As products of and actors within a cultural realm, students' negotiate this tension and the possible conflict of values as they develop their approach to education and make difficult decisions about majors, coursework, and effort expenditure within a particular educational setting. A recent survey reveals this negotiation as 73% of freshman said they attended college to "to be able to get a better job" while 59.9% of freshman said they were in college "to gain a general education and appreciation of ideas" ("The Nation," 2000). For these students, the primary purpose of higher education is a means to an end, viewing the university as a credentialing bureaucracy granting them access to higher wage and status jobs. However, a large percentage of students also maintained the goal of cultivating their minds more broadly. As a teacher, I struggle to help students make sense of this tension as I maintain my commitment to the principle of a liberal education both to teach students the content of my disciplines and to enhance their lives and cultivate good citizens. My commitment to a liberal education finds perhaps its fullest expression in my interdisciplinary core course designed for incoming freshmen. Despite my commitment, however, I am challenged by the larger context in which I operate, the bureaucracy of an institution itself part of the cultural process of higher education that increasingly is forced to employ a marketplace model. In this chapter I use a case study to demonstrate how I navigated, through a mentoring relationship based on an ethic of benevolence or *care*, the tension between pragmatic economic concerns and the goals of a liberal education in the lives of students (Borowiec &

Langerock, 2002). The case study provides suggestions on how others equally committed to a liberal arts education might respond to such tension.

The case involves a problem many of us encounter on a regular basis: how to get young students engaged in their educational process and, in particular, how to get them invested in the classes they take as part of a general core curriculum, the foundations for a liberal education. This chapter will focus on one sustained engagement with a student, for whom I will use the pseudonym Alex, over the course of a year. I begin by describing the core curriculum changes in my institution that reflect an increasingly popular trend toward interdisciplinary and liberally infused core curriculums. After discussing the particular core course that Alex was engaged in, I comment on the challenge I posed to students early on in the semester and the resulting dialogue that ensued between Alex and me. The case provides an illustration of well-reasoned student resistance to a liberal education and suggests one approach for helping students think critically about their resistance and about the opportunities offered by a liberal education.

THE LETTER: CLAIMING AN EDUCATION

The University of Idaho recently revised its core curriculum in an effort to retain incoming students and to help infuse a sense of connection across disciplines and between students' personal lives and their classroom learning. As one step in the process, we developed a group of year-long interdisciplinary core courses each with a focus on a particular topic on which the humanities and social sciences can and have provided substantial analysis and exploration. Alex was enrolled in my core class called "Time Warps: Religion, Science, Technology, and Cultures of Time." This course, offering credit in both social science and humanities, engages students in a critical analysis of the dominant contemporary U.S. culture of time, including historical, structural, cultural, and psychological frameworks with cross-cultural comparison.

To facilitate reflection and critical thinking about both the educational process and the engagement of students with it, I developed, drawing from Adrienne Rich (1979), an assignment concerning how students can claim their education rather than simply receive it. The assignment is prefaced with a reading of William Cronon's 1998 essay about the value of a liberal education, a lecture and discussion about the history of public education and its common current forms, and a critical analysis of those forms. We then watch a brief segment from the Pink Floyd video "The Wall" followed by a discussion of comments the artists explicitly and implicitly make through music video. Finally, I hand students a letter explicating what it means to claim an education, what I expect of them, and what I pledge to offer.

The contents of the letter are firmly grounded in a liberal education and a belief in the emancipatory possibilities of education. After introducing students to the university at the outset of the letter, I make the bold promise: "If you devote your energy toward the intellectual pursuit of a liberal arts education, if you 'claim' your education and strive to understand the links between intellectual pursuit and personal life, your reality and your self will be transformed in the process of becoming more 'free.'" I then quote Rich's (1979) distinction between receiving and claiming an education:

> The first thing I want to say to you who are students, is that you cannot afford to think of being here to receive an education; you will do much better to think of yourselves as being here to claim one. One of the dictionary definitions of the verb "to claim" is: to take as the rightful owner; to assert in the face of possible contradiction. "To receive" is to come into possession of; to act as receptacle or container for; to accept as authoritative or true. The difference is that between acting and being acted-upon. (p. 231)

I reveal that my pedagogical goal is to create a learning environment in which claiming one's education becomes a real possibility, and, thus, becomes an avenue toward claiming one's personal life, toward knowing one's self, and, ultimately, toward contributing to the betterment of humanity. To further explicate claiming an education, I discuss how exercising a sense of curiosity, accepting educational challenges, and developing an ability to think critically are all vital components. Because students often misunderstand *critical* to mean *negative* and *criticizing*, I explain that thinking critically involves questioning and evaluating knowledge and ideas, both those they possess and those presented. I acknowledge the ease of passively receiving an education but caution them from doing so because of the potential loss of intellectual freedom: the desire and ability to think clearly, to articulate ideas, to reform values, to create self-discipline, and to act intentionally. In my letter to students, I encourage them to:

> develop a general curiosity about the world. Rather than accepting "pat" answers or accepting the world as it has been handed to you, a person who claims her or his education develops and pursues a sense of wonder about social life. That person confronts what he or she currently knows by questioning the known, pursuing answers, entertaining possibilities, exploring without fear of discovery, demonstrating humility, respecting knowledge,

and listening. When you engage in these activities you are becoming "intellectually free."

While I emphasize students' responsibility to claim their education, I also acknowledge my own responsibility as a teacher to provide them with opportunities to claim an education, to believe in the importance of what I teach, to recognize the privilege of my job that entails learning and teaching, and to expose them to information, perspectives, questions, and a range of possible answers to critique and reflect on. I also note my responsibility to demonstrate the relevance of course material to their daily lives. Rejecting the "banking model of education" (Freire, 1972), I explain that my job is to fuel their curiosity, not to fill them with facts.

I then ask students to create a well-crafted essay in response to my letter, commenting on their past educational behavior and aspirations and how they might better claim their education. Following their assignment, we discuss the issue further in class. Although student essays varied, most explained how they had previously claimed their education during high school and specific steps on how they would continue to do so. Several students honestly noted that they had never claimed their education, writing about the ease and even the benefits of receiving one (e.g. not having to work hard). Alex's essay in response to my letter and to the curriculum itself is representative of common student resistance to a liberal curriculum. Our correspondence can apply broadly to students with the same critical inquiry—an inquiry that should not be feared or disdained but encouraged and addressed with enthusiasm.

ALEX'S RESPONSE

Alex was attending the University of Idaho on an academic scholarship and had joined the honors program (this particular section of my time core course was an honors section). He was particularly skilled in math and science and had a sarcastic edge to his personality, often displayed through witty comments and responses in class. Not possessing an abundance of humility, Alex began the course with noted skepticism. He was an engineering major and not shy about sharing his thoughts about the course and life in general with the rest of the class. However, he also exhibited a degree of curiosity concerning both the course content and how I would react to his behavior and attitudes. As the assignment and the course unfolded, Alex thoughtfully raised significant questions about the value of a liberal education both in the classroom and in his response essay, although, as we will see, he maintained his skepticism. He also was particularly interested in what I would have to say about his essay and argument. I crafted a lengthy response to his essay, drawing from course readings and lectures. He then responded again, and we sustained a dialogue about the values of humanities and social science courses and the knowledge and value he might gain from claiming a liberal education.

Alex submitted his essay via an email attachment, but, before I had a chance to read the essay, he sent me this email:

> I want you to tell me if you felt in any way offended by my letter. I thought about it a little, and it is probably rather "different" from what you expected. Maybe I shouldn't have come down on humanities/soc sci this hard. I just wanted to show you exactly what I think so that you, as a doctor (not MD though :)) can diagnose me and treat my condition (refusal to accept hum/ss). Alex.

In retrospect, I viewed Alex's email as an attempt to determine the boundaries of our relationship and to negotiate power. As noted by hooks (1994) the classroom is a site of political and personal struggle over knowledge and power. Students learn all too often that, given their subordinate role, providing the *right* answer is preferential to challenges. Alex's humor was also infused with meaning, noting the difference between a medical doctor and a doctorate of philosophy, but his last line indicated a willingness to reflect on the limitations of his interest.

After this interaction with Alex, I returned to his letter determined to address his issues with liberal education, his educational engagement, and his expectations of me as a teacher. In his assigned letter, Alex contemplated the notion of claiming one's education and concluded that claiming one's education simply meant to question it. Alex shared his history of such questioning during high school:

> Claiming an education, as I understand it now, thanks to your letter, involves questioning information. The more I think about it, the more I realize I actually tried to claim my education in high school. I often engaged in long discussions with teachers, stayed after class, participated in academic events outside of class.

Alex discussed numerous admirable and successful extracurricular academic endeavors that demonstrated his enthusiasm for math and science. Among those was challenging himself with problems from his math teacher, sometimes "for extra credit, others just for fun." Alex recalled:

> I still remember and physically posses ... my best proof ever.... It took me over a month of hard work ... to finally get it. But in the process, I learned that there is a strong positive correlation ... between the amount of time I spent on a challenging problem and the joy I feel when I solve it.

Alex also argued he had claimed his education in English because he "wrote a lot of papers out of class, but again, most of them were technical papers on scientific topics." However, he recognized some limitations in his educational pursuit in stating, "The problem is that I am not a well-rounded student, so I can claim (pardon the pun) that I claimed my education only in the areas of science and mathematics." While Alex took advanced placement humanities and social science courses in high school, he argued he did not claim his education in these fields because he "figured I will never need any of that stuff for my career, so I just sat through classes and learned whatever I was expected to learn."

Alex carried this attitude to college, noting that he understood the rationale for university core requirements, but adding, "I still hate these requirements. If I didn't have to take Core 101, I wouldn't be in your class right now. I don't see what's so interesting about learning about time and its social effects." Alex also confessed his feelings about such courses:

> I fear them.... My worst school experiences are associated with them.... Right now, I realize that grades don't mean a thing—they are just rough estimates of one's knowledge, understanding, and ability. Pretty much the only reason I still somewhat care about grades is that I need scholarship money and I want a high-paying job in the future.

Alex concluded with a rationale for why he has little interest in claiming an education in humanities and the social sciences. He argued that the time and work required to do so would be costly although "in the math/sci/engr areas, however, I don't mind spending (not wasting) time and doing efficient and useful work."

While Alex provided little analysis of the structural constraints on his interest and curiosity, it is noteworthy that his need for strong grades to remain eligible for scholarship funds limited his quest for knowledge to fields he felt competent in. Alex's interest in a "high paying job in the future" reflects the value of the dollar in a consumer driven economy and the reality that his family is not a financial resource for him. His words reveal the discourse of economics. Ironically, even his view of time reflects the construction of time as a commodity, a topic we would later study in the course. Thus, in many ways he was making a reasonable choice to pursue disciplines in which he knows he is likely to be successful, and his letter reveals the inherent conflicts between a liberal education and the marketplace. Alex ended his letter with a challenge, or a thinly veiled plea:

> I bet that nearly all students in our core class will write letters saying how good they (the students) are about claiming their education and how they will positively enrich themselves, that kind of BS, pardon me. Well, I ques-

tion the validity of your arguments in the letter. I am telling you this right now so that you ... can see what I am talking about and try to change me, if you strongly believe I should. For instance, maybe you can somehow make me appreciate humanities and social studies ... if you want to teach me to claim my education in these fields that I currently have no interest in, then you will attempt to do what's better for me, in your opinion (that's your goal as a teacher, according to the letter).

I took the challenge to heart, and thought about the silkworm.

THE SILKWORM LETTER

In one segment of the time warps course, we explored how time is managed and shaped to various ends. We studied the historical development of *clock time* and the mechanisms to control time, and work, for efficiency and financial purposes. In my response to Alex, I linked this content to our dialogue. I provide my response in its near entirety for cohesion purposes:

Alex: It sounds like you had and created many opportunities in HS to enhance your educational experience, at least in math and science. I understand your interest in these subjects, and I commend you on the work you have done thus far. I also understand your reluctance to devote your energies to your learning in the fields of the social sciences and humanities, and your honesty is appreciated. However, I believe you do already have an interest, as partially indicated in your "love" for your HON math class ... and the connections between math, history, science and psychology you are learning about. In addition, I think you are very curious about your world in general which makes you intrigued by the HUM and SS, even if you don't "value" the pursuit of knowledge or the expenditure of energy in these fields.

Your understandable lack of willingness to apply your energy in the HUM and SS parallels a more general pattern concerning the lack of interest on the part of many students to pursue knowledge outside math and the sciences or engineering, or outside of any of their fields of choice for that matter. I will focus here on the neglected exploration of the humanities and social sciences, and I'll build on the discussion from class. Since my perspective basically sees people, particularly young people, largely as products of their culture, I treat this "problem" as a cultural phenomenon. I do not claim that people are "determined" by their culture, but the values, beliefs, and behaviors that people learn and adopt are largely taken from the realm of culture. The values and beliefs tend to be aligned with, and both cultivated and constrained by, the patterns of whatever particular culture they encounter in depth. Therefore, I think the key to understanding this "problem" lies with the "value" placed by our culture on the type of study involved in the social sciences and humanities and the knowledge it can generate.

The prevailing "material ethic" and "work ethic" in our culture are largely responsible for the placement of value on the math/sciences/business over SS and HUM. These "ethics" can be directly linked to capitalism, along with other things like Protestantism (although not as clearly). The goal of capitalist enterprise is to generate profits. Outside of very small businesses, the generation of profit depends on the level of production provided by wage/salaried workers. Controlling and maximizing the production of human workers presents a problem for management. A silkworm produces silk at a predictable rate depending on controllable conditions. One could "employ" a silkworm, control conditions, and depend on the worm's instincts to ensure predictable production. Humans pose a more difficult problem when they work for wages. A human is not as predictable as a silkworm when it comes to production. Thus, for maximum benefit for the employer, humans must be persuaded or encouraged by a variety of means to produce, as a worker, with as much efficiency as possible. Efficiency is encouraged through the implementation of technology, like the clock and the assembly line, through the inducement and promise of rewards, and through cultivating values.

In the case of rewards meted out in a capitalist realm, the question of what behaviors are to be rewarded presents itself. If the rewards are coming from the economic realm, they will correspond with those behaviors that enhance efficiency, and, thus, profit. However, "reward" is relative, for something to be perceived as a reward, it must be valued by the recipient, and, thus, the question concerning what form the reward shall take arises. Since values are culturally constructed, culture strongly influences what individuals value. For a variety of reasons, U.S. culture, over time, has come to emphasize individual material accumulation. Individuals, then, learn to value material rewards above other forms, and we all learn the "language" of individual material gain. Coupled with our cultural values surrounding "hard work," and the ideology that associates hard work with material gain, U.S. workers are not only controlled by technology, their efficient production is also controlled by their cultural beliefs and values. They respond well to rewards in the form of money and will endure much sacrifice to obtain these treasures. As a side note, the responsibility for the inefficiency often charged to U.S. industry often lies with profit-taking decisions on the part of corporate elite, not the inability of workers to be efficient.

The control of the production (work output) of white collar workers, those occupations often filled by college graduates, relies on material rewards, recognition for individual achievement, and the promise of further rewards and recognition in the form of advancement up the employment "ladder." Furthermore, particularly with white collar workers, the problem of management not only presents itself in terms of work, but also in dealing with the human potential for creativity. Employers depend on the creativity of their workers, to one degree or another, for development and innovation. Thus, for maximum efficiency and benefit to the employer, human creativity must be encouraged but also channeled and directed toward particular ends, and, in the economic realm, those ends are toward production. In other words, the closer the workforce is made to resemble a silkworm, in both work and creativity, the better it is for those who benefit most from economic production. Increase the quality and quantity of production, and profits will increase (of course, this depends to some degree on the "market," but workers are also employed to control the variables of the market). U.S. culture has taken a form that produces the kind of individuals amenable to the control of production in a capitalist system.

The link between "value" and rewards and math and the sciences in our society is directly related to the "services" a "worker" can provide to the economic system upon graduation. As U.S. culture intersects with education (education in the sense of broadening one's mind and human potentialities—claiming a liberal education), achievement and knowledge/expertise in math and the sciences is assumed to most directly relate to an increase in production quantity and quality, which lead to efficiency and profit, which, in turn, lead to rewards for workers. Those fields, thus, are considered more "worthy" of effort and expense. This is especially emphatic when one talks about fields such as engineering, chemistry, biology, computer science, agriculture, etc. These fields are more directly related to financial rewards in life after college, not because they "better" cultivate the individual, but because they are better for business.

It is no mistake that U.S. public education early on emphasized basic academic skills—reading, writing and arithmetic, and behavior patterns ranging from an achievement oriented reward system and competitive "grading" based on that achievement to conditioning according to a clock and bell system. These were the skills that most prepared students (future workers) for the employment sector. When we turn to "higher" education at the college level in the third millennium, the same principles carry over. The clock and bell system are not as important both because students (future workers) have already learned that pattern and because many of them will have "white-collar" jobs that don't rely so much on the time clock. However, the emphasis falls on basic skills directly applicable to the workplace, most evident in the sciences and math along with business and forms of "practical" training. Also at the college level, achievement recognition is intensified in the form of competitive grading which incorporates the "work ethic" so valued in those who work for wages/salaries.

Although other forms of skill and knowledge do apply to the workplace, such as those that give rise to some of the personal qualities Cronon claims "embody the values of a liberal education" including the ability to listen and hear, read and understand, converse with anyone, write clearly and persuasively, problem solve, respect rigor as a way of seeking truth, and to practice self-criticism (1998, p. 76), it is not often expedient to cultivate these skills and knowledge nor is it always readily apparent, let alone quantifiable, how to do so or how they apply. Also, the potential for these forms of skills and knowledge to lead to a decline in production is great enough to prevent their emphasis in our culture at large. A decline in production can affect the profitability of a company and can also affect the student's future ability to materially support her or his self and family. It is much more expedient and economically efficient, both on a personal level and a capital level, to encourage students, particularly the students we have identified as the "best and the brightest," to invest ALL of their energy into those types of knowledge that directly apply to enhancing material gain. Any energy diverted to work or creativity toward other ends is energy "wasted." The material and work ethics are not concerned with the development of individuals. They are concerned with the development of individual workers/producers. The goal is the silkworm, not the moth. The cost to the life of the individual in terms of development or life-enhancement is of no concern, because material gain is what "matters," and the rewards (wages and material security) are assumed to compensate for the "sacrifices" made by individuals.

The costs may be great, however, as we cultivate students (future workers) highly trained in technical knowledge and procedures but sorely lacking in the diversity of thought, experience and personal qualities cultivated through an exploration of the meanings and knowledge historically generated through the fields of the HUM and SS. Whether exploring social issues or matters of the "soul," the search for understanding and experience in the humanities and the more humanity-oriented areas of the social sciences is intended to enhance the human experience in a balanced and introspective manner. The neglect of this kind of exploration can threaten one's ability to support her or his self or family in non-material ways and even, in the long run, affect the ability to support materially. The neglect of this kind of exploration, an exploration that is certainly not limited to study in college although college study can enhance the exploration, constrains the student/worker and leaves her or him underdeveloped in ways that are both hard to explain or to put a finger on and, perhaps because of that, unrecognized by our culture at large. The neglect might even stifle productivity in the long run. Further, we rarely address the issue of how this kind of intellectual development might affect the development and application of the knowledge and technologies generated in the realm of mathematics and science. In short, the total emphasis on the exploration of math and science, with very little service given to other areas, best prepares students to contribute toward the aim of material gain. It best prepares them to maximize their material output and all but assures the predictability of their work. The values associated with the material and work ethics in our culture move humans, including and perhaps especially our "best and brightest," as close as possible, at this point of human engineering, to silkworms. The costs to individual development and experience are great, but individual humans unfortunately often are deemed expendable, as has often been the case historically, in the pursuit of the larger cultural aims, however "good" or "evil" they may be.

We are all embedded in a cultural web and are necessarily conditioned by it. However, we are not necessarily stuck in a specific place on that web and have the potential even to begin to weave our own particular significances into the form of that web. But we must be freed, we must be able to think outside the confines of the web, and we must turn to other forms of thought to enable our freedom and prevent our "freedom" from being merely an expression of narcissistic gratification or rage. We do this through obtaining wisdom and training in whatever forms we come across in our exploration. Through those forms, which take effort to encounter and digest, we form and reform and reflect upon ourselves. In this process, we have some agency in who we are as humans and begin to cultivate our potential above the instinctual level of the silkworm. We may even find the opportunity to impact society in constructive ways. The most powerful human "instinct," a propensity to learn, compels us to adopt the forms of knowledge and understanding directly presented to us through culture without question or confrontation. That "instinct," however, can be expanded to include the questioning and confrontation that helps form a more conscious pursuit of what lies in the spaces within and beyond the cultural web. This is what claiming your education is about, and the humanities and social sciences, along with our vast knowledge in math and science, can provide "tools" with which to think. But we must put forth the effort and discipline to understand those tools, particularly if our culture doesn't emphasize or value them. I encourage you to put forth that effort and cultivate your humanity.

I'm not suggesting you reject practical considerations involving your means to provide financially for yourself in the future or even that you think about changing fields of study. I certainly don't suggest that you abandon your love for math and science. I only suggest that, while you have the opportunity now and when you have the opportunity in the future, you tend also to other aspects of your intellectual development. If you claim your liberal education, you can develop broad, integrated knowledge, the kind of knowledge enhanced with some study in the HUM and SS. This knowledge can be related to the development of your full potential as a human being. Embrace your love for math and science, but aspire to transcend the silkworm while retaining the "awe" for the worm itself. John.

The evening after I handed my comments to Alex, I received the following response via email:

Wow, that was very well-written! I greatly appreciate your reply. It matters a lot to me. I am glad to know that you actually care about your students, unlike many other professors. I understand the "math" behind capitalism and MSE (math sci engr). It makes perfect sense. Your discussion reminded me of the Matrix episode we just watched, in which Morpheus says, "There are fields, endless fields, where human beings are no longer born, we are grown." I am grown to become a silkworm ... how "nice." Well, I did choose the engineering field because of the money, but that's not the only reason. I also used to be interested in Comp Sci and Chemistry.

Alex labeled himself a silkworm, stating that he likely would not major in engineering if it were not for the potential income associated with the field. He notes the world has "become polluted with structural organization in pretty much every aspect of the world. Money causes tons of problems." Positioning himself as a cultural product, he begins to identify the structural constraints that prevent him from pursuing and developing other interests:

> Another example: college. The chance to enrich myself in the HUM and SS is currently being taken away from me! I know that many UI engineering majors don't finish their degrees in 4 years. Well, I am on the 4-year route and I simply cannot afford to take optional HUM and SS courses.

The engineering major is structured in such a way that students have constrained curricular choices, but Alex also avoided such classes, fearing potential financial consequences:

> I am also scared ... when it comes to 100% optional stuff, I am scared. All those English and biology honors courses—I'd be able to fit them into my 4-year plan, but I am scared to take those courses.... Why am I scared? Because this "work ethic" crap in the educational system punishes us for taking risks, such as the risks of taking those "scary" courses. The punishment would be a lower GPA, if I don't succeed to my fullest potential, or if my potential simply isn't high enough in those fields. Lower GPA, in turn, punishes me financially, because that's what they look at for determining scholarship awards. Unfortunately, my family is going through extremely difficult financial times right now, so the lack of scholarships would ruin everything for me ... so, as a chain reaction, I am forced to try to get a high GPA, I am forced to stay away from scary courses, I am forced to stick to MSE courses (which are relatively easy for me) and play it safely.

Alex recalled how he earlier wrote that he liked challenges and this explained his presence in the honors college. After our correspondence he wrote:

> now that I think about it, I am not that much different from some people I know who cheated' the system and got easy A's. I am kind of doing the same. The difference is that they took easy courses in all kinds of disciplines, while I simply limit myself to the fields I excel at. I am still not as bad as those other students, because I indeed challenge myself in those fields, but the problem is that I do attempt to stay away from "scary" stuff.

Alex also revealed that perhaps he was fooling himself about his lack of interest and willingness: "Another thing that I was thinking is that perhaps, my lack of willingness to explore HUM and SS is actually an illusion. Maybe that's what I WANT to believe. Maybe I am in the state of denial and try to deny my curiosity? Honestly, I don't really know."

At this point, Alex was clearly open to critical thought about liberal education and about his own thoughts, fears and abilities. While he was grasping for understanding, I think he had taken a step toward liberal education and begun a precarious journey of self-exploration.

CONCLUSION: A LIBERAL EDUCATON OUTSIDE OF THE CLASSROOM

As Alex and I clarified and talked with one another through email and conversations, we developed a relationship of honesty and care. Alex often stayed after class to chat with me about course material or the larger issues of his educational pursuits and goals. In many ways, my relationship and the dialogue with Alex is an illustration of a liberal education in practice. Our ongoing correspondence occurred out of a sense of curiosity, and perhaps frustration, and out of a sense of ethics and the moral contract that exists between teachers and students (Ayers, 2003).

Ultimately, Alex decided to drop the second semester of the core class, though we continue to correspond. But convincing Alex to stay in the yearlong course was never my objective. I wanted to understand and empathize with the numerous issues he faced, some personal, some cultural, and some institutional. I wanted him to have a broader basis from which to make his decision to pursue, or not, liberal education in my course or any other on campus. I wanted him to gain from the decision-making process, which was at times agonizing for him. I wanted him to gain from having a professor invested in his education. Mostly, I wanted him to get the most out of his educational opportunity. I know I gained much from the interaction.

One of the main things I learned more about from corresponding with Alex was the difficult realities that young students face, particularly those from working-class families. Such students have less capital to leisurely pursue liberal arts courses. They are often on a strict time schedule and financial budget to obtain an educational credential that can help them become socially mobile. I was also reminded of the potential in young adults to question and engage critically in the world, if given the opportunity to do so. As mentioned earlier, Alex, while unusually honest, is representative of many of my students' struggle with integrating an efficiency model of education with the liberal arts. Because I presume my students are typical of others nationwide, this case study suggests scholars who seriously embark on teaching the liberal arts must provide better opportunities for honest dialogue. Direct discussions, readings, and assignments like my own "claiming your education" letter and response are good avenues that can evoke such opportunities.

Key values in a liberal education are growth, enlightenment and liberation. While I have no objective assessment evidence of Alex's intellectual growth, his final email suggests his heightened ability to question and evaluate his early disregard for the humanities and social science. Like Alex, I wondered how honest other students were to my initial "claiming one's education letter," and suspected their answers were written under the veil of subservience, obedience, and indoctrination. So often we expect students to engage liberal arts education, and our manifestations of core curriculum, and even dismiss them as less than serious students if they do not. In doing so we both miss an opportunity to explicitly teach those who do not readily adopt our requirements and expectations, and even fail to question and challenge those students who do. Although there certainly are limitations on our time and on our explanatory capacities, and certainly no guarantee that our efforts will be successful, in either example I think we miss an opportunity. Even the students who appear to accept the value of liberal arts education may not really understand it. They may think they do or simply act like they do as a means to achieving the necessary grades for graduation. We need to open the dialogue about liberal education with students. They do not read our journals and all too often do not share our educational values. That should not surprise us, nor should we expect it. But, perhaps if we create the opportunity, we can assist the silkworm in her or his emergence from the cocoon and transcend a silkworm existence through liberal education.

REFERENCES

Axelrod, P. (2002). *Values in conflict: The university, the marketplace, and the trials of liberal education*. Montreal, Quebec, Canada: McGill-Queen's University Press.

Ayers, W. (2003). Who in the world am I? Reflections on the heart of teaching. *Curriculum and Teaching Dialogue, 5*(1), 1-7.

Borowiec, J., & Langerock, N. (2002). Creating empathetic spaces. *Curriculum and Teaching Dialogue, 4*(2), 79-87.

Cornwell, G., & Stoddard, E. W. (2001). The future of liberal education and the hegemony of market values. *Liberal Education, 87*(3), 6-16.

Cronon, W. (1998). "Only connect?": The goals of a liberal education. *American Scholar, 67*(4), 73-80.

Durden, W. (2003). The liberal arts as a bulwark of business education. *Chronicle of Higher Education, 49*(45), B20-21.

Fellowes, P. (2003). From books to business: The value of a liberal education. *Chronicle of Higher Education, 49*(25), B16-17.

Fox-Genovese, E. (2002). Liberal education in the university: Prospects and pitfalls. *Journal of Education, 183*(3), 39-47.

Freire, P. (1972). *Pedagogy of the oppressed*. Harmondsworth, England: Penguin.

Gregory, M. (2003). A liberal education is not a luxury. *Chronicle of Higher Education, 50*(3), B16-17.
hooks, b. (1994). *Teaching to transgress: Education as a practice of freedom.* New York: Routledge.
The Nation: Students. (2000). *Chronicle of Higher Education, 47*(1).
Rich, A. (Ed.). (1979). Claiming an education. In *On lies, secrets, and silence* (pp. 231-236). New York: W. W. Norton.
Thomas, N. (2002). In search of wisdom: Liberal education for a changing world. *Liberal Education, 88*(4), 28-34.
Vallentyne, P., & Accordino, J. (1998). *Teaching critical thinking about ethical issues across the curriculum. Liberal Education, 84*(2), 46-52.

CHAPTER 4

TEACHER EDUCATION CURRICULUM

What, How, and Why

J. Wesley Null and Chara Haeussler Bohan

In this chapter, we introduce the phrase teacher education curriculum to focus specifically on the question of what curriculum prospective elementary and secondary teachers should study. Then, we organize teacher education curriculum into three components: what to teach, how to teach, and why to teach. Finally, we argue that professional educators should seek to integrate what to teach and how to teach, so that renewed attention can be focused on the forgotten question of why to teach.

Teacher education can be an ambiguous concept. Teacher education *curriculum*, on the other hand, is a bit more specific. Our goal is to focus on this more specific subject of teacher education *curriculum*. Discussions of teacher education abound in contemporary news reports and research studies. Specific discussions of teacher education curriculum, however, are less common. Or, if questions of teacher education curriculum are addressed, only two aspects of curriculum for the education of teachers are discussed: what to teach and how to teach. Although what to teach and how to teach are no doubt important pieces of teacher education curriculum, we will argue that *why to teach* matters just as much, if not more, than the other two.

We want to be clear about the terms we use. Clear understandings of what *teacher education* is and who should be considered a *teacher educator* make investigation into this field complex. Furthermore, the deeply contextual nature of schools for the education of teachers compounds the study of teacher education. The manner in which prospective teachers have been educated at specific institutions has been influenced heavily by the specific nature of the institutions where this practice takes place. Moreover, programs for the education of teachers have reflected not only the nature of particular institutions, but also the requirements mandated by state departments of education across the country (Allison, 1998).

Other factors, such as the problematic dualisms between liberal education and professional education, subject-matter content and professional knowledge, pedagogy as an art and pedagogy as a science, and the relative value of practice teaching experiences also color the story of teacher education curriculum in the United States (Borrowman, 1956). Differences between curriculum for elementary teachers and curriculum for secondary teachers complicate the picture even further. Perhaps the level of controversy and complexity surrounding the education of teachers demonstrates its significance.

We hope to provide a clearer way of thinking about teacher education. To do so, we want to introduce the phrase teacher education *curriculum*. We hope the three-part philosophy of teacher education curriculum described will be useful to others who study and practice in this field. The phrase *teacher education*, as commonly used in university language and research, typically represents a process-based affair that takes place only after a student has mastered his or her subject matter. This widespread understanding of teacher education leaves unquestioned numerous important assumptions that must be examined. For example, teacher education curriculum cannot and should not be reduced to how to teach. The narrowing of teacher education to nothing but process, or how to teach, reduces our profession to a technician mindset that is destined to drain the life from our vocation. Stripped of the topic of why to teach, our field becomes embroiled in useless wars between what to teach and how to teach.

To battle this problem, those who teach teachers should understand more fully how teacher education curriculum has evolved beginning when normal schools were created in the United States in the 1840s (Barnard, 1851). This larger historical perspective on teacher education curriculum is useful and necessary. However, we seek, rather, to clarify curriculum for the education of teachers by focusing on the phrase *teacher education cur-*

riculum rather than only teacher education. This more specific focus on teacher education curriculum can help teacher educators to understand their role more clearly. This emphasis on curriculum also allows us to recognize the significance of teaching *why to teach*, in addition to the more commonly recognized topics of what to teach and how to teach.

A teacher education curriculum is a curriculum that results in the education of a teacher. That is the goal of this curriculum. Teacher education curriculum has purpose. Teaching children and youth is (or at least should be) an end in and of itself to those who design, teach, and administer a teacher education curriculum. A teacher education curriculum, moreover, is distinct from a curriculum that results in the education of a professor, lawyer, physician, journalist, political pundit, or engineer. The commonplace term for someone who graduates from college and then begins to work with children and youth in a public school classroom is a *teacher*. This commonsense term is what we mean by teacher in the three-word phrase *teacher education curriculum*. Teacher education curriculum also represents an institution (Reid, 1999). The recognition of teacher education curriculum as a single institution, meaning a group of people who work together toward a common goal, helps us to avoid numerous philosophical pitfalls that have weakened the profession of teaching for many years.

Since the creation of normal schools in the United States in the 1840s, three pieces of teacher education curriculum have existed to varying degrees and in different amounts within the contexts in which they have developed. The first piece of teacher education curriculum is liberal or general education. Liberal education refers to aspects of the curriculum that provide students with knowledge of the various conventional disciplines. Obvious examples of liberal education courses include English literature, mathematics, history, and biology. Virtually all arguments for teacher education curriculum made during the last 150 years claimed that prospective teachers should complete at least some coursework in liberal or general education.

Many figures from the history of American education have emphasized the what piece of teacher education curriculum. Critics of teacher education curriculum, for example, often have bought into the dualism that separates *what to teach* from *how to teach*. These critics claim that prospective teachers have not spent enough time studying the *what* aspect within teacher education curriculum. One well-known critic from the 1950s, Arthur Bestor (1953), for example, made many of these points in his widely-known book, *Educational Wastelands*. Bestor, a professor of history at the University of Illinois, claimed that educational theory had focused so exclusively on process, or how to teach, that the traditional subjects had been forgotten, if not downright disparaged. In Bestor's typical style of separating what to teach from how to teach, he argued:

> A reorganization of teacher training and certification requirements along the lines here outlined would correct some of the gravest abuses in the present situation. It would bring to an end the aimless accumulation by experienced teachers of credits in pedagogical courses.... And it would end the preposterous overemphasis upon pedagogy that produces teachers who can talk glibly about how to teach, but who know too little about any given subject to teach it satisfactorily. (Bestor, 1953, p. 136)

Throughout the book, Bestor disparaged coursework on how to teach in favor of coursework on what to teach. More importantly, however, he completely ignored the question of why to teach.

Bestor's omission of why to teach, nonetheless, makes sense. He was an historian. Underlying his complaints about teacher education curriculum in the 1950s was a deeper question about the purpose of higher education in general. Throughout the twentieth century, institutions of higher education consistently marginalized moral commitments, for example the education of teachers, in their quest for intellectual status through research (Reuben, 1996). The story of the last 100 years of higher education has been one in which research has trumped teaching almost every time (Cuban, 1999). Bestor's purpose at the University of Illinois was not the education of teachers. His purpose was to conduct historical research and to train future historians. The purpose of his department of history, moreover, was not to educate teachers. No department within a college of arts and sciences (other than a department of education), would (or currently does) identify the education of teachers as its purpose.

Like other historians and liberal arts professors, however, Bestor played an essential role in the task of educating teachers, primarily secondary teachers. His role, however, was limited to the what aspect of teacher education curriculum. Since he had no experience teaching children and youth in public schools, Bestor was not qualified to teach the how dimension of teacher education curriculum. Moreover, since he was a research-minded historian, Bestor was far removed from teaching prospective teachers the subject of why they should teach as well. As a professor of history, his ideal was to produce historians, not teachers. Teaching, at any level, to Bestor, was a means to the end of becoming an historian. Teaching children and youth was not an end in and of itself to professors like Bestor. The curriculum for Bestor's department of history was what we should call a *historian* education curriculum, not a *teacher* education curriculum. This distinction matters. Nevertheless, Bestor's *Educational Wastelands* provides a clear representation of a researcher from the past who emphasized the what piece of teacher education curriculum, albeit at the expense of how and why.

The second piece of teacher education curriculum is professional education. Curriculum within institutions created for professional education arose in the United States during the nineteenth century (Goodlad, Soder, & Sirotnik, 1990; Herbst, 1991). These institutions—whether they were normal schools or schools, colleges, or departments of education within universities—were created because of the desire to educate all American children and youth and not only a small, elite percentage of the population (Barnard, 1851). Courses that comprise the professional education component of teacher education curriculum, therefore, always have presupposed democracy. As a result, battles over democratic education have been closely related to battles over the meaning of professional education in general and teacher education curriculum in particular. Even though professional educators of the late nineteenth and early twentieth centuries may have agreed that democratic education and professional education were desirable, they often disagreed vehemently with regard to the nature of the curriculum they thought should comprise the professional education component of teacher education curriculum (Monroe, 1952).

A few examples of professional education courses that were created during the late nineteenth and early twentieth centuries are instructive. These courses, which represent different philosophical perspectives on teacher education curriculum, include history of education, philosophy of education, teaching of history, teaching of mathematics, general methods of teaching, educational psychology, educational science, and principles of teaching. Professional education curriculum was created to provide prospective teachers with a foundation for their profession, a sense of moral purpose for their vocation, a repertoire of lessons on how to teach students from a variety of cultural backgrounds, and an understanding of the science of education. Many psychologists from the late nineteenth century believed this last goal, the development of a science of education, would "fix the problems" of American education (O'Donnell, 1985; Robinson, 1995).

A central issue for contemporary teacher educators to consider is the question of how professional education should be defined. One way to define professional education remains closely tied to the liberal arts disciplines. This *integrationist* approach defines democratic education as the task of providing liberal education to as many young Americans as possible (Bagley, 1928; Learned et al., 1920). Professional educators, from this perspective, are the individuals who take it upon themselves to spread knowledge of the conventional disciplines more widely throughout the American populace. Thomas Jefferson (1778) articulated an integrationist pedagogical vision in his aptly titled "Bill for the More General Diffusion of Knowledge" (Milson, Bohan, Glanzer, & Null, 2004). Jefferson wrote the bill when he was trying to create public education in the Commonwealth of Virginia. In his introduction, Jefferson set forth why diffusing knowledge more generally was essential if democracy were to flourish:

> [E]xperience hath shewn, that even under the best forms, those entrusted with power have, in time, and by slow operations, perverted it into tyranny; and it is believed that the most effectual means of preventing this would be, to illuminate, as far as practicable, the minds of the people at large, and more especially to give them knowledge of those facts, which history exhibiteth, that, possessed thereby of the experience of other ages and countries, they may be enabled to know ambition under all its shapes, and prompt to exert their natural powers to defeat its purposes. (Jefferson, 1778, p. 1)

Jefferson, of course, supported democratic education. His conception of democratic education, however, retained the ideal of liberal education for as many young Americans as possible. Both what and how are critically important from the integrationist perspective to which Jefferson adhered. Later integrationists, such as William C. Bagley and Isaac L. Kandel, argued that the integration of what and how is one of the most central philosophical issues for professional educators to face (Bagley, 1934; Kandel, 1943).

On the other hand, another definition of professional education takes the opposite view from the integrationists. Instead of integrating what and how, the *technicians*, many of whom draw on psychology to make their claims, strictly separate what and how in order to focus exclusively on the how piece of teacher education curriculum. Professional educators, from this perspective, are to become efficient technicians who possess expertise in how to teach. Typically, professional educators of this sort are not supposed to focus on what to teach or why to teach. Instead, their expertise lies in understanding how people learn. They also are to be experts in training teachers how to teach using the latest, most efficient methods of teaching.

Many prominent educational psychologists from the early twentieth century espoused this technician approach. Perhaps the most prominent was Edward L. Thorndike of Teachers College, Columbia University. Thorndike, a universally recognized psychologist, wrote scores of books and published hundreds of studies that influenced the profession of teaching in numerous ways (Clifford, 1968). Perhaps the clearest description of the psychology that supported this technician approach to teacher education curriculum can be found in Thorndike's 1906 book *Principles of Education Based on Psychology* (Thorndike, 1906). Thorndike's goal was to describe how people learn so that he and others could make the instruction that teachers provide more *efficient*. In Thorndike's words:

> The teacher confronts two questions: "What changes to make?" and "How to make them?" The first question is commonly answered for the teacher by the higher school authorities for whom he or she works. The opinions of the educational leaders in the community decide what the schools shall try to do for their pupils.... How most efficiently to make such changes as educational aims recommend, is a question usually answered under the headings "Principles of Teaching," or "Methods of Teaching," or "Theory and Practice of Teaching," or "Educational Psychology." This book will try to answer this latter question—to give a scientific basis for the art of actual teaching rather than for the selection of aims for the schools as a whole or of the subjects to be taught or of the general result to be gained from any subject. Not the *What* or the *Why* but the *How* is the topic. (Thorndike, 1906, pp. 1–2)

As Thorndike stated clearly in this introduction, his focus was squarely on how to teach, not what to teach or why to teach. Why to teach, in fact, was ignored completely by Thorndike. Teachers, to him, were not supposed to focus on what or why, but only on how. Even with regard to the question of how to teach, however, Thorndike was to be the expert, not the teachers.

Although a number of the professional educators who originally placed their faith in technician psychology later began to doubt their earlier convictions, the technicians no doubt contributed greatly to the campaign to establish education as a scientific discipline (Null, 2003). In addition to Thorndike, Werrett Wallace Charters of the University of Chicago also espoused technician psychology (Charters, 1912; Charters, 1927; Charters & Waples, 1929). As the twentieth century progressed, the integrationist philosophy of teacher education curriculum gave way to the technician approach. This change in teacher education curriculum philosophy took place as the normal schools and teachers colleges (which were founded for the single purpose of teaching teachers), abandoned the education of teachers as their single purpose. Instead, teachers colleges began to transform themselves into research universities as opposed to teaching institutions. During the last 10 to 15 years, however, the integrationist philosophy of professional education has become revitalized (Bullough, 2001; Shulman, 1987).

Curriculum for the education of teachers, however, cannot be contained entirely by questions of what to teach and how to teach. The third and final piece of teacher education curriculum is perhaps the most difficult to grasp. Remarkably, contemporary discussions of teacher education within policy circles almost completely ignore this final aspect of curriculum for teaching teachers. In addition to what to teach and how to teach, prospective classroom teachers must and should learn *why to teach*. Without a solid sense of the purpose behind why they are entering the teaching profession in the first place, prospective teachers will not last for any considerable length of time in American classrooms. The lack of attention to questions of why to teach is evident in the shocking statistics which reveal that almost 50% of new teachers leave the profession within 5 years (National Commission on Teaching and America's Future, 2003).

This problem is most evident in programs like Teach for America, which often draw on students who have little commitment to the profession of teaching beyond 1 or 2 years. Put simply, prospective teachers who complete a curriculum such as Teach for America may have learned what to teach and even some how to teach, but they have not learned *why to teach*. Long-term commitments to working with and for children, which our profession so desperately needs, cannot be cultivated if prospective teachers only learn what to teach and how to teach. More substance is required if our profession is to have the long-term viability that American democracy demands.

The why to teach dimension of teacher education curriculum, however, is difficult to measure. This difficulty with measurement, nonetheless, does not mean that questions of purpose and commitment are not critically important. Few people who enter the profession of teaching do so because they are motivated by money or by the social standing they will hold in their respective communities. Other factors motivate young people to enter the profession of teaching. Undergraduates who choose education as a major (as contrasted, for example, with fields like chemistry, economics, or business) often enter the field because they have a desire to serve others.

One contemporary author, Parker Palmer (1998), has addressed many of these ethical questions in his widely popular book, *The Courage to Teach*. Palmer stresses that teachers should view their work as a vocation, rather than only as an occupation or job. By using the word vocation, Palmer draws attention to the idea of teaching as a calling. In doing so, he emphasizes the moral foundations that support the teaching profession, which Palmer believes keeps teachers motivated in the face of sometimes daunting challenges. Palmer argues that teachers should learn a curriculum that cultivates all aspects of their humanity. In his words:

> This book is for teachers who have good days and bad days, and whose bad days bring the suffering that comes only from something one loves. It is for teachers who refuse to harden their hearts because they love learners, learning, and the teaching life. When you love your work that much—and many teachers do—the only way to get out of trouble is to go deeper in. We must enter, not evade, the tangles of teaching so we can understand them better

and negotiate them with more grace, not only to guard our own spirits but also to serve our students well. (Palmer, 1998, pp. 1–2)

With words such as these, Palmer is teaching teachers why to teach.

Palmer urges teachers to think deeply about the internal motivations that inspired them to enter the teaching profession in the first place. As much as anyone else in our contemporary culture, he helps those who teach teachers to develop the why to teach dimension of their teacher education curriculum. The reintroduction of why to teach into curriculum for the education of teachers can help schools, colleges, and departments of education to address the deeper questions of purpose and ethics. Thinking deeply about purpose also gives our profession power. Moral challenges will become increasingly prominent during the postmodern twenty-first century that stretches out before us. After events like Columbine and Enron, morality is on the minds and hearts of all Americans. Consequently, those of us who teach teachers should find ways to address these deeper questions, which often motivate students to come to us in the first place.

CONCLUSION: WHAT ABOUT WHY TO TEACH?

To establish its proper place within American democracy, the profession of teaching must re-establish powerful institutions for the education of teachers (Shen, 1999). Individuals within these institutions, moreover, must learn to integrate what to teach with how teach, while at the same time focusing renewed attention on why to teach. The last 50 years of increasing emphasis on modern research within institutions of higher education have so marginalized teacher education curriculum that integration within the current landscape of higher education will be difficult. For our profession to be filled with the kinds of individuals we need and should have, however, education faculty and liberal arts faculty will have to unite in order to serve the common good by teaching teachers. What to teach and how to teach should be viewed as equal aspects within teacher education curriculum. Once this balanced approach is recognized, liberal arts and education faculty can focus on the equally if not more important question of why to teach.

Public education should be served by thoughtful, well-educated teacher educators from the ranks of both liberal arts and education faculty. Who is a teacher educator? We believe a teacher educator is someone who has thought deeply about all three pieces of teacher education curriculum that have been discussed in this chapter. Teacher educators recognize that institutions of higher education, both public and private, must reaffirm their commitments to K–12 public education. They can do so by teaching teachers. A person who is a teacher educator, moreover, takes the education of teachers as his or her primary purpose as a faculty member within an institution of higher education. These individuals can and should come from the ranks of both liberal arts and education faculty.

Rarely, however, do we find professors from the various specialized disciplines who see the education of teachers as their primary purpose as professors. Such individuals have become increasingly rare during the last 100 years. Institutions of higher education have emphasized specialized research to such an extent that professors in the arts and sciences disciplines cannot survive the tenure gauntlet if they take teaching or the education of teachers seriously. This problem cannot be solved easily. It can, however, be addressed by education faculty *and* liberal arts faculty who join together, commit themselves to teaching teachers, and then challenge other faculty within higher education to do the same. The future of public education rests in the hands of higher education faculty who teach a curriculum to future teachers that includes what to teach, how to teach, and why to teach. Future teachers of American youth deserve this more substantive understanding of teacher education curriculum.

REFERENCES

Allison, C. B. (1998). *Teachers for the South: Pedagogy and educationists in the University of Tennessee, 1844–1995*. New York: Peter Lang.

Bagley, W. C. (1928). The problem of teacher training in the United States. In I. L. Kandel (Ed.), *Educational yearbook of the international institute of Teachers College, 1927* (pp. 571–606). New York: Teachers College Bureau of Publications.

Bagley, W. C. (1934). *Education and emergent man: A theory of education with particular application to public education in the United States*. New York: T. Nelson.

Barnard, H. (1851). *Normal schools and other institutions, agencies, and means designed for the professional education of teachers*. Hartford, CT: Case, Tiffany.

Bestor, A. E. (1953). *Educational wastelands*. Champaign–Urbana: University of Illinois Press.

Borrowman, M. L. (1956). *The liberal and technical in teacher education: A historical survey of American thought*. New York: Teachers College Press.

Bullough, R. V. (2001). Pedagogical content knowledge circa 1907 and 1987: A study in the history of an idea. *Teaching and Teacher Education, 17*(6), 655–666.

Charters, W. W. (1912). *Methods of teaching: Their basis and statement developed from a functional standpoint*. Chicago: Row, Peterson.

Charters, W. W. (1927). *How to teach ideals*. New York: Macmillan/Methodist.

Charters, W. W., & Waples, D. (1929). *The commonwealth teacher-training study*. Chicago: University of Chicago Press.

Clifford, G. J. (1968). *Edward L. Thorndike: The sane positivist*. Middletown, CT: Wesleyan University Press.

Cuban, L. (1999). *How scholars trumped teachers: Constancy and change in university curriculum, teaching, and research, 1890–1990.* New York: Teachers College Press.

Goodlad, J. I., Soder, R., & Sirotnik, K. A., Eds. (1990). *Places where teachers are taught.* San Francisco, CA: Jossey-Bass.

Herbst, J. (1991). *And sadly teach: Teacher education and professionalization in American culture.* Madison, WI: University of Wisconsin Press.

Jefferson, T. (1778). Bill for the more general diffusion of knowledge, A bill introduced to the commonwealth of Virginia.

Kandel, I. L. (1943). *The cult of uncertainty.* New York: Macmillan.

Learned, W. S., Bagley, W. C., McMurry, C. A., Strayer, G. D., Dearborn, W. F., Kandel, I. L., & Josselyn, H. W. (1920). *The professional preparation of teachers for American public schools* [Bulletin No. 14.]. New York: Carnegie Foundation.

Milson, A. J., Bohan, C. H., Glanzer, P. L., & Null, J. W. (2004). *Readings in American educational thought: From Puritanism to progressivism.* Greenwich, CT: Information Age.

Monroe, W. S. (1952). *Teacher–learning theory and teacher education, 1890–1950.* New York: Greenwood Press.

National Commission on Teaching and America's Future. (2003). *No dream denied: A pledge to America's children.* Washington, DC: Author.

Null, J. W. (2003). *A disciplined progressive educator: The life and career of William Chandler Bagley.* New York: Peter Lang.

O'Donnell, J. M. (1985). *The origins of behaviorism: American psychology, 1870–1920.* New York: New York University Press.

Palmer, P. (1998). *The courage to teach: The inner landscape of a teacher's life.* San Francisco: Jossey-Bass.

Reid, W. A. (1999). *Curriculum as institution and practice: Essays in the deliberative tradition.* Mahwah, NJ: Erlbaum.

Reuben, J. A. (1996). *The making of the modern university: Intellectual transformation and the marginalization of morality.* Chicago: University of Chicago Press.

Robinson, D. N. (1995). *An intellectual history of psychology.* Madison, WI: University of Wisconsin Press.

Shen, J. (1999). *The school of education: Its mission, faculty, and reward structure.* New York: Peter Lang.

Shulman, L. (1987). Knowledge and teaching: Foundations of the new reform. *Harvard Educational Review, 57*(1), 1–22.

Thorndike, E. L. (1906). *The principles of teaching based on psychology.* New York: Mason Press.

CHAPTER 5

CARING FOR A TROUBLED CHILD

Lessons Twenty-three Years Later

Sara M. Davis

Storytelling has the power to change ideas and develop practice. It is used in this chapter to theorize about the connection of teacher development with reflection on a particular experience. This chapter tells the author's teacher story which has developed over the past 23 years. Meaning is examined by using themes of care and women's ways of knowing as analytical frames. Reflection on personal development is shown to have connections to teacher identity. Implications for teacher education are discussed.

INTRODUCTION

The following story has unfolded over the last 23 years in sometimes expected but often surprising ways. It is a story that I've told many times, but it is just now beginning to help me connect my own development as a teacher with educating others to become teachers. I begin by simply telling the story. I then take the perspective of who I was as a beginning teacher in order to reflect on teacher education. "Women's ways of knowing" (Belenky, Clinchy, Goldberger, & Tarule, 1986) is used as one frame for analysis and issues of care help make sense of issues affecting teacher education. I also argue that certain issues in teaching are more complicated than can be imagined. I tell this story because I know that "one's own experiences are also the possible experiences of others" (van Manen, 1990, p. 54). By describing my ongoing story with Brian I might be able to support the reflection of other teacher educators on their own lived experiences and how those experiences can inform their practice.

This story started as a critical incident in my early teaching career, became a story used as an example of the complexities and emotional tugs of teaching and now has evolved into what Micheline Stabile describes, as "rupture." Stabile goes on to describe the cycles of heuristic inquiry as starting with "resting in one's own experience" and then moving on to an "engagement cycle" where a "rupture" creates a "discontent and unrest in practice" (2001). When this story took place I had started my fourth year of teaching and had already experienced the thought changing and practice provoking experience of going from teaching in a private, upper income preschool to teaching in the lowest socioeconomic elementary school in a large urban district. This in itself was enough to shake my early theories of what teaching was all about and my ability to meet the demands placed on urban teachers.

EARLY WARNINGS

I had just started my fourth year of teaching, my third in a small, impoverished, inner-city elementary school. It was the second or third day of school and the August heat had seeped into the high-ceilinged room. I had given my second graders a writing assignment as one of the last activities of the day. They were supposed to copy a poem from the board so I could assess their handwriting. Everyone was fairly quiet as they started, but suddenly Brian, a tall, chubby-faced boy with African American and Native American heritage, wadded up his paper and threw it violently to the floor. I don't remember what he said or exactly how I responded at the moment other than being surprised at the intensity of his reaction. I asked him to stay after school for a few minutes so we could talk.

Brian sat on a chair, and I sat on the edge of a table next to him. He stared into space as I talked. "Was the assignment too hard? Were you having trouble finishing? Is there something you want to tell me about what you were doing?" As I talked, trying to get some response from him, tears started running down his cheeks. This touched me; I put my hand on his shoulder and back and patted him as I tried to assure him that we could work on this together, that it wasn't the end of the world. Brian reached up slightly and put his arms around my neck, I leaned over to hug him, trying to comfort a very sad little boy. The next thing I knew he was nuzzling my neck. I glanced down at his face and his eyes were half-mast. This made me very uncomfortable; the moment seemed to take on a very different meaning. I quickly pulled his arms from my neck and stood up. I didn't want to reject him, so I left my hand on his shoulder, but I was holding him at a distance. He still hadn't really said anything that could explain his earlier behavior or what he had just done. As I patted him on the shoulder, I said in as positive a tone that I could manage, "Well, you go on home Brian, and I'm sure tomorrow will be a better day." He reached around me with both hands to hug me and still not wanting to make him feel rejected, I hugged him back. It was a rather open hug, with me creating space between us. However, he managed to place both hands on my bottom and run them up and down, sliding my dress and slip together. I practically jumped away from him then and he immediately sprinted out the door. I followed, but in the school hall he walked as far away from me as space permitted.

I watched him leave the building and then went quickly to the principal's office where I told her that I had just had a very discomforting moment with one of my second graders. "I've never had an experience like this, I don't know what to make of his behavior!" She was puzzled, too, and suggested that I speak with his first grade teacher to see what she had done with Brian the previous year. The conversation with the first grade teacher was not very helpful or revealing. She had not had any physical experience with him similar to what I described, but she had had several instances where he had thrown temper tantrums or run away from school. I asked her what she had done about it, and she told me that for one thing, she let Brian be the line leader all the time. I thought that probably wouldn't go over well with the other children in the class, but thanked her anyway.

Brian's behavior the next day provided no clues. He swaggered into the classroom with his usual loud, joking manner. The inappropriate touching did not repeat; however, at least once a week he would argue with me to the point of totally disrupting the class and becoming physically violent. Two or three times a month he would fly into a rage for no apparent reason, throwing his chair and tipping over his desk. He was very big for his age so physically controlling him was difficult. I would go get one of the first grade teachers down the hall who was taller than I, and between the two of us, we would escort him down to her room where he could cool off before returning to my class.

Years of busing had effectively diversified ethnicities represented in my classroom. Native American, African American, Asian, and Caucasian children made up the class of 27, but the culture of poverty was the overriding influence. I felt this made it imperative that I do home visits with the families of the children in my class, but calling parents and asking for the opportunity to visit them was sometimes met with suspicion. However, I found that if I offered to take their child out for dinner and then bring them home, that was fine. It framed the experience as a social occasion and was warmly accepted. So began the practice of taking children to my house for dinner or out to eat. Brian's parents were not living together, but they did live close to each other, and I was able to get their written permission to take Brian out to eat.

When it was Brian's turn we went to MacDonald's, which turned out very well because he had not been to MacDonald's often so it was a huge treat. He was so excited to go home and tell his Mom all about the visit that we hurried to return to his house. The door was unlocked and I walked into a dark and rather dingy room where his mother sat on a couch. Brian bounded into the room, showing his mom the toy he had gotten from the restaurant and bubbling with excitement. I had never seen a woman as obese as Brian's mother, which seemed to explain one of the reasons I had never seen her at school. She was quietly smiling and told me several times how grateful she was that I had taken Brian out for dinner and how excited he had been about the adventure. She reminded him to thank me, which he did happily.

His behavior at school did not noticeably improve. I spent hours after school each week setting up different activities with the express purpose of responding to his need for meaningful activities and structure. I went through a variety of classroom management approaches, from trying to build classroom community using class meetings to behavior modification plans specifically aimed at curbing his outbursts. Our half-day, once a week counselor was of little help; completely overwhelmed with the number of children she was expected to see and the accompanying paperwork expected by the system.

Often, I brought my concerns about Brian's behavior to other faculty. One topic of discussion that I visited more than once was the possibility that Brian may have been sexually abused. In the early 1980s there had not been a great deal of published information for teachers about physical child abuse. The advice from other faculty was mostly anecdotal, but we often talked about how Brian's behavior seemed to be that of a child exposed to inappropriate media or older teens' behavior. For the most part we thought it might have been simply the lack of parental guidance and supervision—that maybe he was watching adult entertainment on late night television. Many discussions with my colleagues provided sympathy, suggestions, and support; but no one had any easy answers.

POSSIBILITIES

One bright and hopeful spot for Brian involved a Federal school grant that focused on nutrition. The program enabled us to plan and prepare meals with our classes. An empty classroom had a stove, refrigerator and all the cooking utensils needed for a class to come in and cook. We made breakfast on one occasion and egg rolls on another. One of the teachers at school worked weekends at an up-scale restaurant in town and the chefs came to our school once to make omelets for lunch, complete with parsley garnish. Brian's engagement during the cooking activities was much higher than during any of our more traditional school experiences. Brian told me on more than one occasion that when he grew up he would be a chef. I thought this probably a realistic goal for a child in his environment and found myself hoping that somewhere along the way, someone would be able to give him the opportunity to pursue a cooking career.

REALITIES

Unfortunately, opportunities for positive experiences in Brian's life turned out to be extremely brief. By the time he was 15 years old he was in the juvenile system for the gang rape of a 12-year-old girl who testified against him and four other boys. Three years later, at the age of 18, he was summarily released. According to his attorney, his family was not too eager to have him back, but the juvenile system had had enough of him so they put him on a bus in a snow storm and sent him "home." Shortly after getting home he ran into his former kindergarten teacher and was obviously pleased to see her, telling her that he had a job and was in school. She was glad to see him too, but didn't realize that "job and school" meant that he had just been released. Since he had been a juvenile at the earlier trial, no one knew that he had been in jail.

Two weeks later he entered the Pilot Center building, a neighborhood recreational program and park connected to the elementary school grounds. After waiting for the supervisor to leave, he assaulted Marie Scott, a 21-year-old elementary education major, beating her to death with his hands, a golf club and a coat tree. Police described it as one of the worst crime scenes they had ever investigated. He was arrested for her death 2 days later. With the testimony of other kids who hung out at the Pilot center, there didn't seem to be much doubt as to his guilt.

I wasn't watching television news when he was arrested. I had left the inner city several years earlier and was teaching in a suburban school district, but I still kept in touch with faculty. I got a phone call from one of the teachers I had worked with asking me if I had seen the news. I said I hadn't and that's when she told me that they had arrested Brian for the murder of the OU student. I was shocked and got off the phone quickly to tell my husband what the call was about. He jokingly asked, "What did you do to that guy?" I started to cry, and of course my husband tried to console me with explaining the intent of his remark was to emphasize how little impact a second grade teacher could have on someone like Brian. I was just as surprised as he was by my reaction. I don't think I had realized up to that moment that I had invested an awful lot of myself into trying to make a real difference in a little boy's life and that it was very easy to imagine positive outcomes for him.

REPONSIBILITIES

Brian's trial in 1990 was over quickly. He didn't express any remorse or responsibility for the crime, only smirked at cameras following him down the courthouse halls. He claimed that he and others had taken part in raping Marie Scott, but that he hadn't hit her. The jury took a little under 2 hours to condemn him to death and if that was appealed, life in prison. I watched the trial and outcome unfold on television with a sense of sadness for lives lost, both his and the victim's. When a local independent paper ran a front-page story condemning the juvenile system for releasing Brian I bristled at the tone of the story, which seemed to objectify him. It was certainly understandable that emotions would run high because of the nature of his crime, but without a sense of who he was and where he came from I felt society was being shortchanged. I wrote an emotional letter to the paper pointing out that many people had tried to reach out to him and his family and maybe, if we had had more resources, his future and his victim's could have been different. My point was that society doesn't put a lot of money into keeping these things from happening. My letter was not published and the whole experience became part of my professional reflections shared with anyone who had a passing interest in the case.

BACK TO THE FUTURE

I have told my story about Brian many times over the years, always referring to it as one of those moments in your career when you learn about yourself and gather educational wisdom. I thought this chapter was long over when early in October of 2002 I was contacted by the state's public defender. She wanted to know what I remembered about my experiences with Alfred Brian Mitchell. It seems that in the previous year the woman in charge of the FBI Crime Lab in Oklahoma City had been fired for among other things, giving false testimony in several trials, Brian's case being one of them. He now had another opportunity to appeal his death sentence. Another change in the case was his own brush with death 2 years earlier when an emergency appendectomy went wrong and he almost died. He started telling the truth about his responsibility in the coed's death. One of the things he was now telling those who would listen was that he had been sexually abused as a child. The public defender followed up on names given to her by the family and by Brian about a few teachers who seemed to care about him and my name came up. My family and I had moved to Portland, Oregon where I had taken a position as an assistant professor in early childhood education since completing a doctorate in education, so I was not easy to track down, but they prevailed.

As I told my story about Brian to the public defender I could tell she was surprised at how much I remembered and the impact he had had on my life. At the end of my story she asked if I could testify to all of this for a jury. So, 21 years after agonizing over the behavior of a little, chubby-cheeked boy in my second grade class, I was sitting on a witness stand recounting all that I remembered about my experiences with him. The memories of him at 7 and a half years old were hard to reconcile with the 29-year-old sitting at the defendant's table. One point I hoped to make in my testimony was that society let a child down and set him on a fatal trajectory.

I received a phone call 2 weeks later from the public defender, telling me that the jury had just returned with another death sentence after deliberating for over 6 hours. She assured me that I was probably her best witness, that I had spoken from my heart, and that my testimony was probably the reason that two jurors voted for "life" before changing to "death" on a revote.

PERSONAL MEANINGS AND BROADER ISSUES

So, is that it? Is his life essentially over along with his victim's? Marie Scott's mother started volunteering at the park center where the murder happened; trying to understand what drew her daughter to work with children in one of the poorest neighborhoods in Oklahoma City. Marie Scott had been a senior elementary education major and, for all we know could have gone on to care about a child just like Brian.

When he walked out of the door of my second grade classroom I can't say I was extremely sorry to see him go. I breathed a sigh of relief that I didn't have to deal with him anymore, that he could go make life difficult for his third grade teacher. Little did I know that it wouldn't be the last time I would feel unable to make the kind of difference I would have liked to make. As a young and inexperienced teacher, my idealism came up against some harsh realities of life. My belief system was to operate on the immediacy of the classroom. I truly thought that if I cared enough, the children in my care would blossom and bloom, becoming generous little learners who came to our safe and accepting classroom to escape the big, bad world.

WHAT DOES IT MEAN TO "CARE"?

Max van Manen writes, "Nowadays the word 'caring' is being over-used by social work, medical, legal, educational, and counseling professionals. And this occurs at a time when we no longer seem to know what it means to really care" (1990, p. 58). He goes on to say that the teacher's role is "not [taking] the place of the child but rather [being able to prepare] such place wherein and whereby the child is empowered to be and to become" (1990, p. 59). Van Manen's ideas on this resonate in the abstract, but may not go far enough for teachers in real classrooms.

In order to enter into these relationships of care with children, teachers must have the space and freedom to respond to the contextual, emotional, and cultural needs of the child. Unfortunately, we are not living in a time of agreement about this. Educational policymakers are moving away from encouraging teachers to form meaningful relationships in the classroom with calls of greater quantitative responsibility and accountability.

As the push for more academic accountability is made for political reasons, professional bodies have taken stands on the need for more responsive teachers. We seem to have learned more about teaching and learning and the place of the child in the ecological elements of his/her world, yet political ideology continues to claim that narrowly defined units of knowledge must be taught in effective and efficient ways by *highly qualified teachers*, as measured by the use of standardized tests. The Federal government has chosen to ignore the professional organization statements arguing against the wholesale standardized testing of young children. In his State of the Union Address, President Bush said, "The only way we can be sure children are learning is by testing them" (2001).

Nel Noddings (1984) argues for themes of care and against the political when she writes about the importance of children believing that they are cared for and that they are capable of caring for others. She defines a component of a caring relationship as one where there is a mutual awareness of caring; it must be two sided. At the time I was dealing with Brian, I was not sure at all that his perception or his family's perception was one of being cared for. However, that's how they characterized it 21 years later. In the course of events surrounding my decision to testify, the testimony and the after effects, I have returned many times to what it was that I did 21 years earlier that resulted in this perception of care.

Noddings (1984) makes the point that caring happens without a rational thought process; that you act in the moment based on who you are and what you want to give of yourself. I remember making a few rational and thoughtful decisions based on my education and belief system. But the day-to-day interactions with Brian necessitated many more actions that had not been thought out and had to be made in the moment.

In my fourth year of teaching, the passion for caring was strong, but the means for acting on it was not. One of the first things made clear to me by my principal was that I was inexperienced and should follow her instructions to the letter if I wanted to survive. My conversations with more experienced teachers revolved around how to maintain control in my classroom, not how to develop relationships of care. In the inner-city school, opportunities for conversations with parents were few and understanding for the lack of parental involvement was not explored by the system.

It is at this point in the analysis of what this story means to me that I have found it useful to use different ways of knowing (Belenky et al., 1986). As described by Janice McDrury and Maxine Alterio the voices are characterized as:

- Silence: The process of attempting to find a voice; a growth from being silent to finding a voice and being assertive.
- The Listening Voice: Received knowledge that focuses on listening to the voices of others, which results in a rigid, unimaginative and narrow perspective where events are prescribed rather than interpreted.
- The Inner Voice: Subjective knowledge that involves a quest for self, a knowing of self by gaining an awareness of attitudes and values that are held, concerns that are felt and an alertness about the context within which actions occur.
- The Voice of Reason: Procedural knowledge that enables examination and comparison to occur along with a sense of connectedness through which a sense of the whole is retained. And,
- Integrating the Voices: Constructed knowledge that involves the successful integration of information from the various ways of knowing and an ability to incorporate the wisdom of experience into practice realities (McDrury & Alterio, 2003, pp. 118-119).

NEW TEACHERS AND THE SILENT VOICE

One of the first things my principal, an older woman with many years of teaching and supervision experience, told me was, "You are basically a new teacher. You need to follow the curriculum programs as they are written." The fact that I had two teaching credentials, had worked as a junior editor for a popular basal reading series publisher and had 2 years of teaching experience did not count. My experiences were not referenced, but at the same time, there was no offer to support my learning. My background was not unlike many of my student's backgrounds who are currently in our graduate education program at Portland State. I had had rather diverse experiences, but still needed a support system. The principal made a huge difference in how I saw myself operating within the system. Any hope of having a voice was essentially stifled and silenced.

The Silent Voice is also described as a denial of self and needing an external authority. The power of the principal to force me into listening to her voice of authority was fairly complete. She operated in a system that gave her ultimate authority and she chose to use it to maintain control.

I believe new teachers always struggle with finding their voice, but in supportive environments they are more apt to develop one sooner and be able to extend this power to their students. Unfortunately, my experience resulted in my inability to speak out as strongly as I could have or should have about my suspicions of child abuse.

THE LISTENING VOICE

In my struggle with Brian I turned to the voices of *authority*; my father, a cognitive psychologist, and my principal. I looked for information and knowledge from these experts—neither of whom really had to deal with Brian all day, every day. I believed that if I created a classroom that worked for Brian there would be a huge transformation because, after all, there are best practices that must work for all children. I was very aware of Developmentally Appropriate Practice and worked diligently to bring those practices into my classroom.

Of course, none of these sources of knowledge were enough. Everyday I felt a sense of foreboding and dread. Everyday I thought that somehow if I could just work a little harder at finding out how to deal with Brian's behavior I could change his life.

Now we have a federally mandated system that forces teachers into being recipients of received wisdom. We don't seem to trust that they will develop ways of being with children that will result in a better classroom life for everyone without being accountable.

THE INNER VOICE

This voice includes dichotomous thinking; that truth is out there as a personal, private idea. As a young, fairly inexperienced teacher, it gave me some comfort in a way to think that the right answer was surely out there. Even though I had no idea how to access this truth, it gave me hope of finding it someday.

By the time I had Brian in class I had had 2 years of experience with the children from the immediate inner-city neighborhood and their families. I was beginning to look to my colleagues for their perceived wisdom more than I looked to the principal or others, but I was still looking for answers outside of my experience. I was still being told that there were people who knew more and that my curriculum was more important than the relationship I had with Brian.

It wasn't that my colleagues did not care what was happening, but they were working just as hard at keeping their spirits up and not being overwhelmed by a system that had turned to Mastery Learning and nine pages of evaluative forms to be filled out every week. Their advice usually included sympathetic statements, but the bottom line was generally, "I'm glad he's not in my classroom."

This is one area that I feel we do a fairly good job with in our graduate teacher education program. We spend a lot of time and energy in a variety of classes discussing the idea of truth not being a thing to be discovered. However, the message new teachers get even more strongly though is that, yes, there is *truth* with a capital T. There are standards that must be followed, there are best practices that are scientifically based, there are materials that must be used and there's no room for investigations. I remember longing for someone who could come into my classroom to give me a subjective, noncritical perspective about Brian. I thought if there was such a person, the truth could be known at last.

THE VOICE OF REASON

Procedural knowledge was definitely lacking in my early teaching experiences. My student teaching and first year teaching experiences were in early childhood classrooms that matched my education in family relations and child development so seamlessly that there was little reason to question anything.

There is an ongoing debate over what kinds of classrooms preservice teachers should be placed in for student teaching. Our program is constantly on the look out for good, cooperating teachers. Our students tell us that they want the best teachers for their student teaching so they can learn the best ways of doing things. I believe that if I had more experiences in my teacher education program, involving more problems to be solved, I would have had a stronger conviction in my role as a teacher in the inner city. This may support the thinking behind professional development schools or more infusion of faculty out in the field. Preservice teachers need to be presented with problems and issues in a supportive environment; one in which it is safe to take risks. Then problems they encounter could push them outside of their comfort zone for a deeper, richer reflection on practice.

Because my procedural knowledge had been developed in environments that were not problematic, I entered a different educational culture little prepared for the problems I would encounter there. One piece of procedural knowledge I felt I had was the relationship of care to learning.

FINAL THOUGHTS: THE INTEGRATED VOICE

Who I am now is not who I was when Brian was in my second grade classroom. Years of experiences in different classrooms and school districts, a variety of professional development opportunities, two academic degrees and many mentors have now shaped my practice and redefined who I am in the lives of children and my adult students. Parenthood has added another dimension of who I am and what I want for children in classrooms. When I think back on my career and development as a teacher, the many voices I have identified seem to converge on this moment. By interrogating these voices I can begin to understand what is important to me in teacher development. From this perspective many threads come together and I can tell my story to different audiences and search for meaning. Part of that meaning has become what my responsibilities as a teacher educator might be. I can analyze my development through this particular story to guide my role in developing others to teach. Jane Danielewicz writes: "What makes someone a good teacher is not methodology, or even ideology. It requires engagement with identity, the way individuals conceive of themselves so that teaching is a state of being, not merely ways of acting or behaving" (p. 3).

I can see the development ahead for my preservice teachers, maintain a focus on whom they might become and not get mired in the here and now emergencies and anxieties of program completion and licensure applications.

Of course this is my personal story, and the chances that something like this will happen to others exactly as it happened to me are small. But the stories of others will have their own Brians and their own opportunities to be more than just the transmitters of knowledge.

How do we facilitate new teachers' ability to enter into caring relationships with their students? I think it means that we make reflection explicit and critical. They need to look deeply at all the components of education with their focus on how those components either support their relationship with their students or keep them at a distance. Reflection is defined as not only reflecting on how well lessons are planned; but also it becomes using personal development to reflect on the relationships between the teacher and the student. It means supporting our student's abilities to take everything they know, dialogue with others, write about their ideas, feelings and plans and then come back to a support group at some point in their development to ask questions and continue the process, because it *is* a process.

My experiences with Brian still resonate with me even though there have been many children since him that have added to my stories and my understandings of who I am in the lives of children. There has to be the recognition that time is a necessary part of development, that looking for ways to start people on this journey of teaching and relationship building is an ongoing endeavor.

I will continue to examine my story for what it may tell me about my development as a teacher. Hopefully, this knowledge will allow me to help my students develop their own voices, understand their capacity to care in educational relationships, and have a positive impact on children's lives.

REFERENCES

Belenky, M., Clinchy, B., Goldberger, N., & Tarule, J. (1986). *Women's ways of knowing: The development of self, voice and method*. New York: Basic Books.

Danielewicz, J. (2001). *Teaching selves: Identity, pedagogy, and teacher education*. Albany: State University of New York Press.

McDrury, J., & Alterio, M. (2003). *Learning through storytelling in higher education: Using reflection and experience in to improve learning*. London: Kogan Page.

Noddings, N. (1984). *Caring, a feminine approach to ethics and moral education*. Berkeley, CA: The Regents of the University of California.

Stabile, M. (2001, April). *From rupture to resolve through practice-based heuristic inquiry: A think piece*. Paper presented at the meeting of the American Education Research Association, Seattle, Washington.

van Manen, M. (1990). *Researching lived experience*. Albany: State University of New York Press.

CHAPTER 6

TEACHING READING STRATGIES TO ADULT LEARNERS

An Interactive Approach Addressing Standardized Testing

Nancy J. Hadley, Marilyn J. Eisenwine, and Mary G. Sanders

The purpose of this chapter is to describe an ongoing research project establishing the efficacy of an interactive approach in an attempt to assist struggling college students with reading comprehension skills for the purpose of passing their state certification exams. The contructivist activities and classroom experiences are part of a final course students complete while doing their student teaching. Preliminary findings suggest that this approach provides needed assistance for struggling readers.

INTRODUCTION

Some university students reach their final year of preservice teacher training lacking skills needed to be proficient, critical readers. They have successfully completed the bulk of their undergraduate courses, mastered the required content, and demonstrated a talent for teaching children. However, they have not developed targeted comprehension strategies to the degree necessary to pass their licensure test to become a certified teacher. For example, two candidates who initially failed the Praxis, a standardized test used in many states to screen teacher candidates for state licensure, were subsequently voted teachers of the year in their respective schools (Wakefield, 2003). These promising teachers require tactical skills to avoid the traps laid for them in standardized tests.

Proponents of standards-based tests tout the ability of the tests to require students to practice critical thinking skills in applying knowledge of the standards to the classroom situations presented. In many cases, it is not that the student has failed to master the required content; it is that the student is unable to maneuver the intent of the question. The traditional preparation approach of learning facts, interpreting these facts, and then applying them in the test situation is no longer enough to ensure success on this type of test. The students must not only have a mastery of the facts but must learn how to be successful in the standardized testing game.

For Texas educators, the State Board for Educator Certification (SBEC) has specified standards to form the basis for the Texas Examinations of Educator Standards (TExES) that constitute the licensure tests for teachers in Texas. The TExES tests present a formidable hurdle for both students and professors, not because the students fail to master the standards, but because the tests are presented in a multiple-choice maze designed to sabotage the test taker. Students, particularly at-risk students, get lost in the labyrinth of verbiage presented in the standards, test frameworks, and competencies. They fall prey to test questions that are designed to trick them. These students have difficulty connecting the standards (and the content represented by the standards) to specific questions that capitalize on diversion and misdirection in an intimidating, high-stakes environment.

At a state university in Texas, preservice teachers attend a seminar-type course in which pertinent content is reviewed while test-taking strategies are rehearsed during their student teaching semester. A large percentage of these preservice teachers fail the pretest for the state teacher certification exam each semester. Struggling students seem to bog down in their attempts to understand scenarios, dissect questions, and traverse the complicated sentence structures employed in both the questions and answers.

Professors involved in teaching the course found that the review of content should be expedited and simplified, not only in the interest of time, but also for some of the students to succeed in passing their certification exams. As a result, professors have developed a study guide that employs an interactive approach to empower students by actively engaging them in constructivist activities that focus on key content and test-taking strategies (Hadley & Eisenwine, 2004). Rather than the directors of learning, professors assume the role of facilitators of instruction, coaching students in creating schemes to organize, simplify, and master the content. Students become partners in the process and own the learning. Ownership and success empowers students to be able to disseminate comprehension strategies as future educators. Those who have struggled are uniquely qualified to empathize with at-risk students and equip them with tactics to avoid the semantic minefields of standardized testing.

PURPOSE

This chapter describes an ongoing research project establishing the efficacy of an interactive approach in an attempt to assist struggling preservice teachers with reading comprehension skills for the purpose of passing their state certification exams.

TESTING

From the beginning, professors suspected reading ability was a mitigating problem for passing teacher certification exams. To diagnose possible reading problems, one professor, who practiced as a school diagnostician, suggested administering the Woodcock Diagnostic Reading Battery (WDRB), a well-standardized and acceptable measure of reading ability (Woodcock, 1997). This individual diagnostic reading test covers a wide range of reading levels, providing norms as well. It is a comprehensive, single-subject test designed for adults and children. The test yields age and grade equivalents.

The WDRB is used in diagnosing specific weaknesses that may be interfering with learning. A Passage Comprehension Subtest portion of the WDRB contains 20 items and requires reading a sentence or short paragraph, then supplying the missing word (modified "cloze" technique). The examiner records 1 or 0 indicating the accuracy of each answer as the test progresses. The reliability measure of internal consistency is .89 and test-retest is .89. Concurrent validity is acceptable as demonstrated by adequate correlations between the WDRB and other achievement tests, including the Peabody Individual Achievement Test, Basic Achievement Skills Individual Screener, Kaufman Test of Individual Achievement, and Wide Range Achievement Test-Revised. The test sample for validity contained 916 adults enrolled in college (Sattler, 2001).

Students tested in the current study were volunteers who had previously failed the pretest for the TExES Pedagogy and Professional Responsibilities (PPR) Test. A total of 22 undergraduates in their final semester of preservice education participated in the study. The sample included elementary, middle school, and high school teacher candidates.

THE EVOLUTION OF THE APPROACH

The interactive approach utilized by the professors has evolved over a period of many years of working with struggling students attempting to pass the state teacher certification exam. In particular, the main author of this chapter analyzed teacher certification exam practice test questions for 6 years to isolate pertinent content and develop test-taking strategies geared toward students who experience difficulty. While utilizing other test preparation materials in teacher education courses, she became frustrated with the volume of information overwhelming students. To provide more specific test review information, the professor discovered that backloading the curriculum by aligning the test with targeted materials produced a more effective test preparation tool (Steffy & English, 1997). In the process of constantly field testing methodology and interviewing students who *just don't get it*, the primary author has refined effective tactics for struggling students.

Statistics also indicate that after failing the actual TExES exam for the first time, a downward spiral occurs for the student. The number of times they must take the test in order to pass increases inordinately. After taking the test, students are not informed as to specific questions missed, so they do not know which questions they answered correctly and which questions they answered incorrectly. Furthermore, they may encounter the exact same questions on subsequent exams. Multiple test-takers begin to recognize test scenarios and answer choices. Struggling students become confused as to how they should answer correctly. Naturally, their self-esteem and confidence decline. In order to avoid this downward spiral, students must be actively engaged with condensed content and test-taking strategies before encountering the test for the first time.

For students to be successful with standardized testing, they must make connections between their knowledge of the standards and the test. Even students who are able to memorize test content are often unable to make necessary connections when answering test questions. Past experiences of the authors in helping students pass certification exams have indicated that active engagement helps them make critical connections. These connections are facilitated through constructivist experiences. Concerning constructivist experiences, Callahan, Clark, and Kellough (1995) note that students build their knowledge not from "previously established steps" but by "student manipulation" of curriculum materials (p. 17). The authors have developed successful activities that actively engage students in the construction of their own knowledge resulting in improved test scores. This study guide contains a compilation of constructivist experiences for students and test-taking strategies that assist students in organizing knowledge of the standards and competencies into a form that can be applied to the question stems presented on the TExES (Hadley & Eisenwine, 2004). An active approach results in the empowerment of the students in making the necessary connections between knowledge and test-taking skills.

INTERACTIVE EXPERIENCES TO IMPROVE COMPREHENISON

According to research, comprehension can be taught to struggling students who are not likely to create effective strategies on their own (Barry, 2002; Fielding & Pearson, 1994; Pressley, 1998; Song, 1998). As a result of the trial and error process over a number of years, the interactive materials evolved into a set of selective constructivist experiences for students. These experiences include the reading strategies listed below.

Condensing Content

Simplifying the content for review purposes constituted the first step in the progression of learning experiences. Professors scrutinized sample test questions and developed an outline of relevant content containing preferred researched-based practices from the practice tests. The assumption was that if the students had access to an abbreviated version of the critical material, better test results would occur. This proved successful for higher achieving students, but many students still failed the practice tests. Providing the materials did not necessarily mean that all students would benefit from them. Some students made notes on the outlines and highlighted key phrases, whereas others displayed no evidence of manipulating the materials at all. After interviewing both successful and unsuccessful students, it was apparent that unsuccessful students were less likely to devise effective learning strategies on their own. A highlighting exercise in the interactive materials encourages the students to make the condensed materials their own.

Condensing the content for struggling students also entails shortening the content into bulleted phrases which depict relationships among ideas. When combined with boldface font highlighting important phrases, this shortened visual representation helps students to maneuver the maze of words they encounter. Because struggling students are often overwhelmed with long reading passages and have few comprehension strategies in place, they benefit from this bold and bulleted approach.

Vocabulary

The review outline was then supplemented with strategic vocabulary lists derived from having the students highlight unfamiliar words throughout the practice tests. Traditionally, research has shown that there is a relationship between students' vocabulary and their understanding of what they read (Francis & Simpson, 2003). It is important to note that poor performing students highlighted both content specific as well as general vocabulary words. Students were instructed to define the words. However, students were not specific enough in their definitions for the vocabulary lists to be effective. Therefore, definitions were later included with the vocabulary lists. These lists were created from student-generated lists to target the struggling students. During this phase, students were held accountable for the material with vocabulary tests and tests over the outline.

To supplement vocabulary testing, a flashcard exercise in the interactive approach encourages students to write vocabulary words missed on a pretest on cards with a mnemonic device of some sort on the back of the card to help them remember the meaning. This idea is similar to one presented by Francis and Simpson (2003) using more elaborative information on concept cards. Students enjoy using the flashcards during classroom sponge activities, and all students benefit from the original and creative memory aids displayed.

To further augment vocabulary-building, students are given a list of commonly used verbs generated by students circling unfamiliar words on pretests. Students are tested over these words as well, helping them to internalize the vocabulary. They are also asked to create a list of abbreviations and acronyms used throughout the materials, requiring them to review the materials as a whole. The emphasis on both content-related and general vocabulary words in the interactive materials targets the struggling students and boosts their comprehension of the materials.

Modeling

Students also practiced test-taking strategies geared for deciphering scenario-type questions. According to Song (1998), reading strategy training can be effective in improving the reading proficiency of college students. The professors modeled strategies for interpreting the intent of the question and the appropriateness of each of the choices. Students engaged in full class discussions on their thought processes for determining the correct answer, utilizing the *think aloud* technique. Gains made by low reading proficiency students were particularly impressive, using strategies such as modeling and "think-alouds" (Song, 1998). The interactive materials contain steps in a question dissection process, and professors model the process during classroom discussions. Through practice, the students develop successful inner speech defined by Vygotsky as the internal dialogue that takes the place of the teacher's questions and prompts, guiding the learner through similar problems (Vygotsky, 1962). All students seemed to benefit from this strategy and rated this activity as a valuable one during course evaluations in previous semesters.

Summarizing and Inference

Although test scores improved, there remained students who failed the practice tests. Many students continued to have difficulty deciphering the main point of the questions even with access to the outline of key content, vocabulary lists, and modeling techniques. Therefore, the next step in the evolution of the study approach involved students analyzing practice question stems and corresponding correct answers.

Because the certification exam is divided into competency areas, professors asked students to analyze questions within a competency to determine what correct answers might look like. In groups, students analyzed multiple questions within a competency and summarized both the question and the correct answer. Summarization is a "powerful study strategy" because of the connections made by students in grouping ideas into "interrelated hierarchical networks or schemata" (Friend, 2001, p. 321). The groups were then asked to look at all the questions within a competency, as well as the correct answers. Inference is also a valuable reading skill for struggling students to acquire.

Cooperative learning groups are often helpful in reinforcing strategies students need to practice (Friend, 2001). Professors grouped students based on pretest scores, making sure that a low-, medium-, and high-achieving student comprised the group. High achieving students took the lead in these activities, and low-achieving students participated with less initiative. Although the low-achieving students seemed to benefit from the exercise, they still had trouble arriving at a summary on their own. They tended to memorize associations developed by the group and depended on the recall of those associations when working on their own. The interactive materials contain both a practice test analysis exercise and a synthesis exercise which require the individual student to identify correct and incorrect answer possibilities for each competency. These exercises aid all students in constructing key associations which should facilitate identifying correct answers on the test.

Elaboration

According to Friend (2001), the strongest study strategies are the ones that incorporate elaboration in which the student creates associations for the knowledge to be learned. Locating the correct answer requires the student to first determine what the question is asking, then associate preferred research-based practices to the specified classroom situation in the question. The state-developed teacher competencies define those classroom situations, and the certification exam presents them for the test-taker to determine the appropriate best practice represented in the answers. Because the language of the competencies is echoed in the practice questions themselves, the next step in the evolution of the study approach entailed teaching the students to relate the language of the competency to certain keywords in order to develop associations between the competency and research-based practices.

The main author developed a chart for each competency with the competency statement in one column and keywords and phrases representing research-based practices in a corresponding column. The chart provided an organizational structure for related ideas. Connections or links between related ideas help students to recall and apply information (Friend, 2001). Key phrases located in both columns were highlighted and written in a boldface font to facilitate quick recall.

Professors made charts available to the students with the expectation that the students would use them as study aids. Once again, the higher achieving students benefited greatly from the charts, highlighting them with colored markers and making notes on them from the outlined materials. However, many of the lower achievers did not have anything on their charts, and they did not show initiative in utilizing the charts. Color-coding is a strategy recommended by special education professionals for college students with learning disabilities (Vogel & Adelman, 1993). The interactive materials require students to highlight these charts with different colors to aid in recall. Professors learned to encourage more active engagement in constructing meaning for struggling students.

Predictions

To engage students more actively in the process of finding correct answers, it became apparent that they needed to be able to identify both good and bad practices in general terms. This required that students be immersed in the learner-centered philosophy of the test. Although the students were informed of the learner-centered philosophy underlying the test, it became evident that low-achieving students were not able to recognize learner-centered, constructivist practices in general, much less be able to determine which learner-centered practice was the best solution to a specific classroom situation. Therefore, students are asked to summarize each learner-centered proficiency and predict "Do's and Don'ts" for each proficiency in an exercise from the interactive materials. Predicting is a higher-level thinking skill often promoted as a reading strategy (Pressley, 1998). This activity helps all students recognize possible correct answers and eliminate incorrect ones before reading the question.

Additionally, students are required to predict whether or not a specified practice is recommended or not recommended after studying a list of research-based practices. They are also required to identify a teaching practice as a "Do or Don't" after studying a list of "Do's and Don'ts." The prediction exercises help the students create their own schemas for good and bad teaching practices. When building schemas, structures for organizing information, students must create and refine categories for concepts (Woolfolk, 1998). After the students have created their own structures for predicting good and bad teaching practices, professors lead students in a discussion of their predictions, helping the students in a powerful scaffolding exercise which has been defined as a more knowledgeable person helping a less knowledgeable person master a problem beyond his or her current level of functioning (Arends, 2000). The constructivist experience of creating a schema combined with the scaffolding exercise through classroom discussion has proved to be effective in assisting students to create meaning for themselves.

Another exercise requiring students to create schemas then make predictions based on those schemas involves word associations. Key phrases such as *first step* usually found in the question stem are associated with key words or phrases such as *analyze*, *evaluate*, and *needs assessment* usually found in the correct answers. Students are encouraged to study the associations given as well as create their own. Professors encourage students to share these associations in class discussions.

RESULTS

Data collected with all students in the seminar course using the interactive materials indicated an average gain of over 10% and a maximum gain of over 40% between practice tests. Students participating in the pilot study demonstrated an average gain of 14% and a maximum gain of 32% between the pretest and practice test one (see Table 6.1). After practice

Table 6.1. Gains Between Pretest and Practice Tests

Subject #	Pretest	Practice 1	Gain 1	Practice 2	Gain 2
1	58	70	12	64	6
2	68	75	7	—	—
3	60	73	13	59	−1
4	68	84	16	80	12
5	66	80	14	—	—
6	56	76	20	69	13
7	65	70	5	78	13
8	60	73	13	76	16
9	61	61	0	84	23
10	56	88	32	85	29
11	64	83	19	77	13
12	54	76	22	73	19
13	65	65	0	65	0
14	50	56	6	78	28
15	53	68	15	71	18
16	65	78	13	83	18
17	39	63	24	63	24
18	63	81	18	78	15
19	53	73	20	66	13
20	63	73	10	83	20
21	66	81	15	74	8
22	64	84	20	85	21

Note: Dash indicates subject exempt from taking Practice 2 test.

test two, the average gain was 15% with a maximum gain of 29%, as shown in Table 6.1.

On the Woodcock Diagnostic Reading Battery (Woodcock, 1997), pilot study students' scores yielded a wide range of grade equivalent reading levels from 6.9 to 16.9 (see Table 6.2). Although 77% of these students were unable to comprehend reading material at their appropriate grade level, to date, 73% of the 15 who have taken their TExES certification exam have passed (see Table 6.2).

Observation of these students during test administration revealed the following qualitative results:

1. Most students read the selection out loud or sub-vocally.
2. Students reread the missed question several times in an attempt to comprehend.
3. The most frequent answer to an unknown response was, "Don't know."

Table 6.2. Grade Equivalent Reading Scores and TExES Results

Subject #	WDRB Score	TExES Exam
1	12	Fail
2	15.6	Pass
3	8.3	Fail
4	9.2	Pass
5	6.9	Pass
6	12	Pass
7	10	Fail
8	13	Not taken
9	9.2	Pass
10	16.9	Pass
11	10	Pass
12	14.2	Not taken
13	13	Not taken
14	11	Not taken
15	9.2	Not taken
16	16.9	Pass
17	16.9	Not taken
18	16.9	Pass
19	8.3	Not taken
20	14.2	Pass
21	16.9	Fail
22	14.2	Pass

Note: WDRB = Woodcock Diagnostic Reading Battery (Woodcock, 1997).

4. Students generally gave several words synonymous with the correct word.
5. Some students answered with a plural term, rather than one word as directed.
6. Students would not persist if the answer was not clear during their first attempt.
7. Complete silence was necessary for some students.
8. Finger pointing and lip movements were common.

Beginning readers often use many of these basic strategies in attempting to supplement their inability to read, however such behaviors are symptomatic for struggling readers at the college level. While students were employing various forms or methods to answer questions using the "cloze" technique, they were still unable to supply the correct missing term. These students indicated through their incorrect answers that their ability to comprehend short, one sentence passages was below expectation for the number of years of college completed. Many of their comments closely resembled the correct answer but were not correct as listed in the examiner's manual.

CONCLUSIONS

Despite the wide range of grade equivalent reading levels and behaviors indicative of beginning readers, gains between pretest and practice tests indicate the success of interactive materials provided in the seminar course. As reported in the literature, when students develop new learning strategies, success is realized (Porter, 1994; Song, 1998). Although a portion of these students scored lower on the second practice test, the average gain remained consistent.

There does not appear to be a direct connection between grade equivalent reading scores and passing the TExES exam. Even the students scoring at sixth and ninth grade reading levels passed the actual exam. Apparently, struggling readers were able to maneuver the intent of the questions by employing the strategies and tactics presented in the study guide (Hadley & Eisenwine, 2004). As stated by one preservice teacher, "You train us to lift a 100 pound weight, and it feels 20 pounds lighter when we finally take the real test."

Poor readers are not without strategies; they are simply not using effective ones. As many college students underline their text and read it over and over, they are expecting "something mystical that happen to them" (Friend, 2001, p. 320). However, information processing research and interventions with disabled readers provide concrete evidence that students can use more effective means to improve their reading skills when given direct instruction in this area (Friend, 2001; Porter, 1994; Song, 1998; Vogel & Adelman, 1993). According to Pressley (1998), the abundance of high-stakes testing requires a high degree of comprehension from students, but comprehension is seldom taught. With the interactive approach presented in this study, students learned a variety of comprehension strategies.

IMPLICATIONS

Preliminary findings suggest that an interactive, constructivist approach is successfully providing needed assistance for struggling preservice teachers to increase their comprehension skills and pass their certification exams. When commenting on national teacher candidate testing, Wakefield (2003) states, "Because of Praxis, some passionate and gifted teachers will fail to find places of service in public schools" (p. 386). Using strategies presented in this study, undergraduate students successfully increased their critical reading comprehension skills in order find their place in public schools. By learning to be "test-wise," students who are in need of remediation have successfully transitioned from failing the pretest to passing practice tests and the TExES exam. They are in turn successful completers of their university program and become certified teachers equipped with a heightened awareness of both comprehension and test-taking strategies they can eventually disseminate in their own classrooms. Because these teacher candidates have been struggling students themselves, they are more likely to empathize with students who have difficulty.

As a continuously evolving project, the authors will continue to implement new ideas for helping struggling preservice teachers to overcome the high-stakes barrier which can keep them from becoming teachers. According to Wakefield (2003), high-stakes tests often "guard the door to the teaching profession" (p. 380). The key to opening the door is learning to interpret the intent of test questions. More general reading comprehension strategies emphasized in this study include summarizing, inference, elaboration, and prediction, as well as study techniques such as condensing content, vocabulary development, and instructor modeling. Although the limited results from this study cannot be generalized to a larger audience, university instructors, as well as educators at any level, may employ these strategies and techniques as they seek to increase comprehension tactics for their students.

REFERENCES

Arends, R. I. (2000). *Learning to teach* (5th ed.). Boston, MA: McGraw Hill.

Barry, A. L. (2002). Reading strategies teachers say they use. *Journal of Adolescent & Adult Literacy, 46*(2), 132-141.

Callahan, J. F., Clark, L. H., & Kellough, R. D. (1995). *Teaching in the middle and secondary schools*. Englewood, NJ: Merrill/Prentice Hall.

Fielding, L. G., & Pearson, P. D. (1994). Synthesis of research: Reading comprehension: What works. *Educational Leadership, 51*(5), 62-67.

Francis, M. A., & Simpson, M. L. (2003). Using theory, our institutions, and a research study to enhance students' vocabulary knowledge. *Journal of Adolescent & Adult Literacy, 47*(1), 66-78.

Friend, R. (2001). Teaching summarization as a content area reading strategy. *Journal of Adolescent & Adult Literacy, 44*(4), 320-329.

Hadley, N., & Eisenwine, M. (2004). *TExES bold and bulleted: Study guide for the Texas Examinations of Educator Standards Pedagogy and Professional Responsibilities Test*. San Angelo, TX: Nancy J. Hadley, Publisher.

Porter, J. (1994). Disability in higher education. *Journal on Excellence in College Teaching, 5*(1), 69-75.

Pressley, M. (1998). *Reading instruction that works: The case for balanced teaching*. New York: Guilford Press.

Sattler, J. (2001). *Assessment of children* (4th ed.). San Diego, CA: Sattler.

Song, M. (1998). Teaching reading strategies in an ongoing EFL university reading classroom. *Asian Journal of English Language Teaching, 8*, 41-54.

Steffy, B. E., & English, F. W. (1997). *Curriculum and assessment for world-class schools*. Lancaster, PA: Technomic.

Vogel, S., & Adelman, P. B. (1993). *College students with learning disabilities: A handbook*. New York: Springer-Verlag.

Vygotsky, L. (1962). *Thought and language*. Cambridge, MA: MIT Press.

Wakefield, D. (2003, Summer). Screening teacher candidates: Problems with high-stakes testing. *The Education Forum, 67*(4), 380-388.

Woodcock, R. W. (1997). *Woodcock Diagnostic Reading Battery*. Itasca, IL: Riverside.

Woolfolk, A. E. (1998). *Educational psychology* (7th ed.). Boston: Allyn & Bacon.

CHAPTER 7

EDUCATORS' ACCEPTANCE OF AND RESISTANCE TO HANDHELD TECHNOLOGIES

Steven L. Purcell

Handheld technologies offer educators an affordable, convenient way to integrate technology into the classroom. Despite their near commonplace use in business, medicine and law, public education has not witnessed the wholesale adoption of these tools for classroom use. At issue are the number and types of devices to choose from; real and perceived obstacles to effective implementation; fewer opportunities for ongoing professional development and training; limited software; difficulties entering, displaying, and exporting text and data; and the perception of handheld devices as toys, not learning tools. While early reports suggest that handheld technologies can and do support student learning, teachers remain reluctant to use them.

INTRODUCTION

Proponents of handheld technologies proclaim these devices are on the cusp of revolutionizing mainstream education as we know it. For all their advantages, promise, and potential, public education has not witnessed the wholesale adoption of these tools for classroom use. At best are a number of mostly vendor-funded initiatives that consider limited specific uses of handhelds in single-subject content areas. Yet, early reports suggest that handhelds can and do support student learning. Why then, are teachers so reluctant to use them? This chapter examines the issues educators confront as they consider the use of handheld technologies in their own classrooms.

SO MANY DEVICES SO LITTLE TIME

One of the issues that makes handheld technology so perplexing to many would-be adopters is the sheer number and types of devices that can be classified as *handheld*. In this age of faster, smaller, cheaper, better technology, the consumer electronics industry has unleashed a plethora of products that, given suitable thought and consideration, could have genuine instructional value in the classroom when used appropriately. But which device will best help teachers teach and learners learn?

Many people think of handhelds as small, pocket-sized devices for keeping track of appointments, phone numbers, and to-do lists (although they are not limited to just these functions). Often referred to as personal digital assistants (PDAs), they come in a variety of models each with their own decided advantages and disadvantages. While it is beyond the scope of this chapter to define and discuss those differences, the number of choices and options quickly can become overwhelming given the myriad of models, features, sizes, operating systems, input devices, and communications protocols (to name a few). With so many models being introduced and then phased out, it may be difficult to decide if a particular brand and/or model represents the latest and greatest a manufacturer has to offer or whether it will quickly be replaced by its next generation sibling. Little wonder that teachers are reluctant to embrace handheld technologies when they have so few assurances that the device they purchase today won't be quickly replaced by another model tomorrow.

Handhelds are a subset of technologies generally referred to as mobile computing devices. Mobile computing devices also include laptops and tablet PCs but could be expanded to include other popular technologies like smart cellular phones, global positioning system (GPS) units, graphing calculators, MP3 players (e.g., Apple iPod), portable DVD players, and video-game consoles. Each of these technologies accomplishes one or more tasks exceedingly well, yet there is no all-in-one information appliance that does it all and still meets the end-user requirements of utility, portability, affordability, reliability, and usability. In the end, instructional objectives should drive technology selection and use, not the glimmer, hype, and glamour that accompanies so many of today's electronic products.

In a recent comparison between laptop computers, handhelds, and tablet PCs, *Education World* asked members of its Tech Team to share their thoughts about how each of these mobile computing devices might benefit teaching and learning. Tablet PCs were seen as an emerging tool whose primary strengths are drawn from their capacity for multiple inputs (e.g., handwriting, keyboarding, and free-form drawing), search capabilities, small profile, connectivity, and "closest-to-the-edge" status (Jackson, 2004b, para. 4). Handhelds were ranked highly for their "extreme portability, instant file sharing, ease of collaboration, differentiated price range, and optional word-processing functionality" (Jackson, 2004b, para. 7). The Tech Team noted that handhelds are particularly well-suited for use by students for collecting data in science classes and by teachers for managing planning tasks, e-mail, and maintaining student information systems. Laptops were seen as the clear "winner" among mobile computing devices given that they are "time tested" and have widely available applications, enjoy extensive community support and accessibility tools, and support a variety of media and probeware (Jackson, 2004b, para. 13). As one Tech Team member pointed out, since laptops more closely resemble desktop computers than do tablet PCs and handhelds, they require less end-user training, too.

TEACHERS' PERCEIVED OBSTACLES DON'T MATCH THE REALITIES OF CLASSROOM IMPLEMENTATION

Left unchecked, teachers' reasonable hesitations about computers and other devices can become deeply embedded sources of resistance to technology use and integration. These same hesitations become increasingly difficult to overcome given insufficient professional development opportunities to overcome teachers' lack of skills and the lack of sustained curriculum development support for effective and efficient technology use being afforded teachers today. When held up for closer examination, though, teachers' perceived obstacles to using handheld technologies do not always match the realities they encounter in their classrooms.

For the past 3 years, Dr. Bob Kolvoord—of James Madison University—and I have worked with 36 science and math teachers to integrate global positioning system (GPS) and geographic information system (GIS) technologies into their classrooms. Conducted as a series of intensive, 2-week-long summer institutes, the Great Outdoors, Digital Indoors (GODI) program permits participants to hone, refine, and extend their data visualization skills as they define and develop lessons for use in their

Table 7.1. Perceived Obstacles to Teachers' Use of Handheld Technologies in the Classroom

	1 Not an Obstacle	2	3	4	5 Serious Obstacle	Avg.	SD
Lack of space in an already crowded curriculum	1	2	3	3	3	3.42	1.31
Lack of well-designed curriculum-based materials using these tools	1	5	2	4	0	2.75	1.06
Relating the use of these kinds of tools to increasing student achievement scores	2	3	4	2	1	2.75	1.22
Lack of teacher knowledge of software tools	0	5	6	1	0	2.67	.65
Difficulty students have in learning to use these advanced tools	1	5	4	2	0	2.54	.89
Lack of hardware	4	4	2	2	0	2.17	1.11
Incompatibility of these tools with district's stated objectives	6	3	2	1	0	1.83	1.03

own classrooms. One of our early tasks was to ask participants to rate various factors that might explain why teachers, in general, might not use handheld technologies in the classroom (see Table 7.1). Our understanding of these initial perceptions shaped and informed subsequent implementations of GODI institutes as our participants became more effective and efficient integrators of GPS and GIS technologies.

As indicated in Table 7.1, lack of space in an already crowded curriculum was perceived by our participants to be the greatest obstacle to teachers' use of handheld technologies. However, when asked to reflect on their own experiences in implementing GPS and GIS activities, our participants recounted much different *actual* obstacles. Chief among these was time. All of the participants reported investing much more time and energy devising and implementing GPS and GIS activities when compared to other classroom assignments. GIS applications are sophisticated, high-end software, and it takes many hours of study to become proficient in their use. Our participants reported that few, if any, of their students had ever seen a handheld GPS unit, much less used one. Helping students acquire the fundamental skills to complete the class activities consumed more instructional time than the teachers had planned. Generally speaking, that posed quite a risk to our teacher participants given the pressure that is borne of this era of high-stakes standardized testing and academic accountability where each minute counts.

While our participants displayed a high degree of competency using GIS software at the conclusion of the program, they were challenged by the complexity of the program and struggled with it at some level when time came to implement it in the classroom. Competence in using GPS and GIS technologies at the end of the institute did not necessarily transfer to competence and confidence in applying the technologies as part of their own professional practice.

Nearly all our GODI participants reported having hardware-related issues, and these surfaced as the single greatest obstacle to our participants' effective and efficient implementation of GPS and GIS activities in their classrooms. These issues include not having enough GPS units for students' use, having only one PC download cable for multiple GPS units, incompatible computer hardware for data downloads, and inadequate access time to the school's computer lab for data analysis and mapping. Interestingly, hardware-related issues were not *perceived* as being a significant obstacle to GPS and GIS implementation (see Table 7.1), yet they proved to be the most frequently encountered impediment in our participants' own classrooms.

Despite their significant apprehensions about having space within their curriculums, GODI teachers recognized the potential that GPS and GIS technologies offer to promote collaborative problem solving, engage student's interests, and encourage higher-order cognitive skills such as data analysis and synthesis. All of our participants indicated they were planning to continue using GPS and GIS technologies in their classrooms, and although it took more time to learn and implement, the opportunities for engaging students at a much higher level was worth the additional effort.

The problems our GODI teachers encountered implementing GPS and GIS activities in their classrooms are not easily rectified with additional professional development but speak to the larger need to give teachers the ample time they need to *plan* for effective technology use. This seems to be particularly true for handheld technologies in general as their use may require significant training for both teachers and students (as in the case of GPS and GIS). At a time when teachers are being asked to do more with less, the increased demands on their time due to technology implementation may only heighten their anxiety and reluctance to apply these tools in their classrooms.

WHAT TEACHERS DON'T KNOW WON'T HURT THEM—OR WILL IT?

Trying to master technology is like shooting at a moving target. Moore's Law suggests that the information processing capacity of modern computers doubles about every 18 months (Moore, 1965). No longer is it possible for anyone to know all there is about technology since the hardware and software change so quickly. A set of skills learned one year may continue to serve teachers well for 1 or 2 years, but those skills could quickly become outdated in as few as 3 or 4 years. One need only look at Microsoft's product offerings to see why. Microsoft has released a new version of its operating system (Windows®) or its productivity software (Office®) nearly every year since 1997. On Virginia's higher education software pricelist, there are 36 separate line items and descriptions for Microsoft Office® alone! When the number of titles produced by other software developers is considered, it is no wonder that educators throw their hands up in frustration and surrender.

In keeping their technology skills well honed, teachers must not only keep up with software upgrades, but they must keep up with advances in hardware, too. As noted earlier, the consumer electronics industry is flooding the market with the latest generation of cellular phones, digital cameras and camcorders, computers, and more. As these products become more commonplace in America's homes, the current generation of students has mounting expectations that these devices will eventually make their debut in the classroom. Of course, the implication is that teachers will not only recognize these devices, but also they just might have a plan to use them effectively to promote inquiry, learner engagement, collaboration, and problem solving in their classrooms. Each semester, I teach a course for preservice education candidates that explores how various technologies can be used to enhance learning and teaching. I tell my students straight out: "Let this course be the beginning of *your* lifelong study of technology! It has to be, because the technology changes so quickly."

Given the unprecedented growth of the consumer electronics industry, it is not surprising that teachers are having a difficult time keeping up with the technology. However, the problem only becomes magnified as colleges of education struggle to adequately prepare preservice candidates with appropriate technology competencies. A recent American Association of Colleges for Teacher Education study surveyed 416 teacher education programs across the United States about the extent to which future teachers are being exposed to technology in their classes, practicum experiences, and curriculum. Not only are most teacher-education programs failing to show their students how to appropriately integrate technology into their professional practice, but student teachers did not routinely use computers during their internship or work with cooperating teachers who could show them how (Hasselbring, Barron, & Risko, 2000).

As the latest generation of handheld devices makes its way to the education marketplace, it is likely the problem will only get worse before it gets better. Recently, I e-mailed the technology representatives at Virginia's teacher preparation institutions about the extent to which they were providing *any* instruction about handheld technologies (either as part of a standard technology course and/or as part of their content area methods courses). Only two representatives responded with any positive indication that the topic was being broached to preservice candidates. In one of those replies, the faculty member wrote, "We gave a presentation to all the secondary preservice teachers and we had one group of social studies preservice teachers who we gave Palms to for a semester. Due to the amount of work they already were receiving from their classwork and reluctance of their graduate student mentor, most of the students did not use them. I am hoping next semester to try the project again with a more willing group" (J. Falls, personal communication, September 27, 2004).

In a cursory review of sessions either presented or planning to be presented at recent national-level teacher conferences, I found very few references to handheld integration. At the upcoming National Council of Teachers of English conference I could not find any sessions relating to handhelds, and I could find only one planned for the 2004 conference of the National Council for the Social Studies. Of the sessions listed on its Website, I found only one that related to handhelds at the 2004 conference of the National Council of Teachers of Mathematics (NCTM), although I suspect the Website may not have contained a comprehensive index of the sessions presented. Not surprisingly, I noted that 20 sessions were conducted at the 2003 conference of the National Science Teachers Association (NSTA), however, all but two of those were exhibitor workshops. By far, the greatest number of sessions about handheld technology was conducted at the 2004 National Education Computing Conference. That conference alone hosted over 55 events with many of them presented by classroom practitioners, not just vendors. Clearly, the successful use and integration of any technology is commensurate with the amount of professional development afforded practitioners, but this quick review suggests that instruction about handheld technology is still much critically needed.

LEARNING TOOL OR TOY?

Handheld PDAs represent advancements in computer technology that combine the capabilities of desktop computers with the portability of popular video games like those from Sony and Nintendo. Yet it is the very game-like nature of many handheld devices that cause some educators to remain skeptical of their potential and use in the classroom. When used as a tool to help convey content, clarify concepts, or promote collaboration, technology frees teachers to coach and facilitate students' learning. Current No Child Left Behind legislation with its emphasis standardized testing has created an environment where it is essential that educators expand students' learning opportunities by using technology in achieving instructional goals and preparing them for future success (Hudgins, 2001). Handheld computers are now being examined as effective tools that can empower learners and give teachers the resources they need to meet expectations. They offer a solution to integrating technology into the classroom by making computers portable, more accessible, affordable, and perhaps even easier to understand.

Handheld computers offer a number of advantages that make them particularly well suited as learning tools. Topp and Hanquist (n.d.) offer five reasons that handheld computers are a logical choice for schools and classrooms. First, they note, handhelds are becoming widely used in the "real world," especially in business and industry. If adults are using these devices at work, they reason, then we should be teaching about and modeling those uses in the classroom. Second, low cost affordable handheld computers provide each student with full-time access to technology. Citing his own work, Topp found that in 2001, 50% of the teachers who responded to his survey reported that their students used computers for 15 minutes or less per week. My own experience suggests that technology works best when it is placed at the point of instruction, and handhelds do appear to offer some advantages over traditional computer labs in connecting technology to learning. Third, handheld computers are versatile—students can write, create animations, develop concept maps, draw pictures, collect and analyze data, use spreadsheets, query databases, read documents, conduct research, take quizzes, and more. Fourth, the potential for sharing and collaborative inquiry and learning are enhanced through students' ability to wirelessly transmit documents to each other. Collaboration is an essential element of a student-centered, active learning classroom. Finally, professional associations like NCTM and NSTA are building technology experiences into their national standards. The NCTM standards include technology as one of its six principles, and the National Science Education Standards includes technology at each level in their standards.

Given their limited, but focused introduction into classrooms nationally, research into the efficacy of handheld computers is still in its beginning stages. While a simple Web search yields thousands of documents on handheld computers, research connecting their use to student learning is scant. Jackson (2004a) discusses the general characteristics that make handheld computers attractive as learning tools (e.g., cost, functionality, software and hardware, mobility, weight, etc.) while the K12 Handhelds website (http://www.k12handhelds.com/101list.php) lists "101 great educational uses for your handheld computer." While interesting, the list of

101 uses alone does not, in and of itself, address the deeper issues surrounding student learning, teacher training, or equitable technology access for all learners. Norris and Soloway (2003) note students' increased time on task, higher test scores, increased motivation, and handheld computers' lower costs as reasons for why the personal computer of choice in K-12 classrooms "ought to fit in a student's palm." However, they acknowledge other factors—access, teacher preparation, curriculum, assessment, and administrative and community support—that directly influence handhelds' potential for success in the classroom.

Perhaps the most comprehensive study to date about the use of handheld computers was conducted by SRI International in 2002. Seventy-nine Palm Education Pioneers (PEP) were given Palm-branded handheld computers to use in their classes for at least 1 hour each week for one or two semesters. Noting the similar advantages of portability, flexibility, and cost mentioned in other studies, Crawford and Vahey (2002) list more substantial learning benefits. In particular, teachers in their study reported the following benefits:

- Improved quality of instructional activities, especially in science;
- Enhanced student communication and collaboration;
- Improved student organizational skills;
- Enhanced student motivation;
- Promoted students' autonomous learning;
- More than 95% of teachers thought that handheld computers were effective instructional tools that could positively influence student learning;
- More than 90% of teachers thought that handheld computers positively influenced learning activities and teaching practices;
- Seventy-three percent reported that handheld computers were more consistent with the "flow of classroom activity" than were desktop computers; and
- Ninety-seven percent of the teachers intend to continue using handheld computers in instructional activities (para. 2).

Despite these early reports that suggest handheld computers do impact learning and teaching favorably, administrators in some states have banned their use completely saying students will use the handheld computers to cheat on tests, play noneducational games, or e-mail friends inside or outside of school. In West Virginia, students at one school downloaded software from the Internet that that enabled their handheld computers to turn on the school's television sets with their handheld's infrared communications port. Several days passed before teachers caught on (Trotter, 2001). A 1989 Maryland law banning "personal communication devices" (designed to keep pagers out of schools) also bars student-owned handheld computers in classrooms. While the legislature has since repealed the law, 9 of the state's 24 school systems received permission to keep the ban in place (Trotter, 2001). Jackson (2004c) observed some teachers complain that handhelds detract from learning, rather than enhance it. Instead of taking notes, they fear, students will be watching videos, surfing the Internet, or instant messaging friends and strangers. For other teachers, the resulting classroom management issues outweigh the benefits of handhelds in the classrooms, and a number of large scale initiatives, in which potentially thousands of students will be issued handheld computers, are under way in Texas, California, and Michigan.

DATA IN AND DATA OUT

In working with participants in the GODI program, we found that it was the small, but not inconsequential problems that impeded the efficient use of handhelds in their classrooms. We have been reminded since childhood that it is the little things that cause the biggest problems. When it comes to technology, that statement becomes particularly prophetic. Earlier it was noted that GODI participants reported hardware issues as the single greatest obstacle to using GPS and GIS tools in their classrooms. Indeed, just getting access to the handheld units posed a major challenge to many of our participants. Our solution to this problem was to purchase four class sets of GPS units and circulate them on a part-time basis among our participants' classes. Generally speaking, we were successful getting the technology to the teachers when they needed it, but ideally, full-time access to the tools would permit teachers to increase the level of use and enhance the overall quality of implementation. Presently, some of our participants continue to view GPS and GIS technologies as somewhat of an add-on to their curricula rather than the integral tool we envision for helping students solve problems and analyze data.

Getting the GPS units in students' hands was the first step in helping learners collect geospatial data that could be analyzed once they returned to the classroom or computer lab. That is, the *data in* process consisted of a straightforward series of steps in which students switched on their GPS receivers, waited for the handheld units to connect to three or more satellites (called a constellation), and then logged their longitude, latitude, and elevation as a series of waypoints. Once students returned to the classroom, the waypoints could then be downloaded to the GIS software for plotting, map construction, and analysis. At this point, another set of problems appeared. Teachers quickly discovered that having only one data transfer cable for 20+ handheld GPS units created an unworkable bottleneck to downloading data. At $20 a piece, we could not afford to purchase 80+ cables to distribute with the four class sets of GPS receivers, but we did purchase three or four additional cables for each class set. While not a perfect solution, this alleviated some of the problems getting the data out of the handheld units. Still another problem arose concerning the data transfer cables themselves—the cables were designed to be connected to the serial port of a PC and not to an Apple Macintosh computer. Since the GIS software used to plot the GPS data runs on both Macs and PCs, our participants assumed they would have little difficulty moving the data from the GPS units to Macs. Some of them were surprised (and disappointed) to find that despite having the cables, students still could not move the data from the GPS units into the GIS software running on an Apple Macintosh. The short-term solution required students to manually enter their data directly into the GIS software. As long as there were only a few waypoints to be entered, this proved to be an adequate, although not ideal, solution. Concerns about the accuracy of manual data entry eventually led us to purchase several serial-port-to-USB adapters that allowed the GPS units to be connected to an Apple Macintosh directly.

The final hardware-related issue that our participants faced was gaining adequate access to computers that ran the GIS software. The school's computer lab was the one area that permitted each student the opportunity to work with the GIS software, but frequently, it was unavailable at the desired time or the lab had to be scheduled weeks in advance. While not an insurmountable problem to overcome, it does underscore the need for focused planning and practice that must accompany many uses of technology in the classroom.

Recent advances in alternate input devices, peripheral connectivity, and wireless communication protocols may help address many of the hardware issues that all educators confront when using handheld technologies in their classrooms. Full-sized collapsible (or fold up) keyboards, which greatly facilitate text entry, have been available for use with PDAs for several years, though their use has not become commonplace. Most PDA users enter information into their handhelds using a stylus and a language called graffiti. While not difficult to learn, graffiti can be a bit awkward to use initially, particularly if special characters are required. VKB, Inc. (http://www.vkb-tech.com/) recently unveiled a virtual keyboard that uses beams of light to detect users' movements. The virtual keyboard can be integrated into handheld computers, mobile phones, laptops, tablet PCs or even sterile medical environments. Finally, natural language interfaces (supporting voice recognition) are gaining popularity in the consumer-driven personal computer and cellular telephone industries, and it will not be long before they begin appearing on handhelds as well.

COMPETING FEATURES

In some ways, the very features that make handheld technologies so popular in the consumer market also make them less than desirable as learning tools in the education arena. These highly portable, lightweight, incredibly hip, pocket-sized information appliances suffer from small screens, low-resolution and low contrast displays that are unreasonably fragile, teeny-tiny input buttons that make text entry possible but inefficient, and small, nearly unreadable text displays. While many handheld computers can be used for longer periods of time than laptops or tablet PCs, battery life still remains an issue (e.g., my handheld GPS unit consumes two AA batteries every 8 hours). As one technology facilitator noted, "We have concerns that with students each having their own handheld, we will have the same issues as with supplies. They [students] will forget them at home or in their locker, not charge them, lose the data, etc." (Roland, 2003, para. 16).

WHERE IS THE SOFTWARE?

Current PDA software offerings pale in comparison to the numbers and varieties available for desktop and laptop computers. The lack of software argument, while a legitimate concern, simply does not justify teachers' decision to outright reject handhelds in the classroom in light of the software that *is* available. Zwiers (n.d.), Pride (2003), and Norris and Soloway (2003) all list low-cost and no-cost applications for handheld computers, and the offerings continue to grow both in number and variety each year.

The protests teachers lodge about lack of software are symptomatic of much deeper pedagogical problems confronting education. Based on my work with teachers in Virginia and North Carolina in both middle and high schools, I have observed that many teachers are still stuck in the launch-the-program-and-get-out-of-the-way paradigm of computer use. Perhaps this is a throwback to the days when hardware and software vendors suggested we could do as much. "Purchase our software and students will learn," they claimed. The only problem is students did not learn, at least not in the predictable, replicable manner we anticipated back then and now demand today. New technologies that complement and nurture active learning, collaborative problem solving, and knowledge construction are not being embraced by teachers in lieu of more traditional, didactic instructional approaches to learning and teaching. If teachers remain unwilling to change their approach to instruction to reflect the promise and potential afforded by handheld technologies, then there may be little hope for the success of these devices regardless of how much or how little software is available.

CONCLUSION

Ubiquitous computing, or calm technology, is a paradigm shift where technology becomes virtually invisible in our lives. Instead of having a desktop, laptop, or handheld computer, the technology we use will be embedded in our environment (Riley, 1997). Of this, Weiser (1993) writes

> A good tool is an invisible tool. By invisible, I mean that the tool does not intrude on your consciousness; you focus on the task, not the tool. Eyeglasses are a good tool—you look at the world, not the eyeglasses. The blind man tapping the cane feels the street, not the cane. Of course, tools are not invisible in themselves, but as part of a context of use. With enough practice we can make many apparently difficult things disappear.... But good tools enhance invisibility. (para. 2)

This idea of ubiquitous computing perhaps best explains why handhelds, like so many of the technology tools that preceded them, have enjoyed only a lukewarm reception by teachers. Indeed, handhelds are not mainstream (at least in education), except in limited circles like law, medicine, and business (where they are nearing commonplace). Handhelds are still seen as add-on components that somehow must be positioned within all the other events of instruction and done so in a way that they compensate for the failures attributed to earlier technology-based interventions. Cuban (1996) writes "This persistent dream of technology driving school and classroom changes has continually foundered in transforming teaching practices. Although teachers have slowly added a few technologies to their repertoires, techno-reformers have seldom been pleased with either the pace of classroom change or the ways that teachers have used new machines" (para. 3). Buying machines, he reminds us, has always been an administrative decision, but using them has always been a teacher decision. In deciding to use any electronic tool, teachers' criteria for effective and efficient use are borne of their experiences.

> Teachers ask: Is the machine simple enough for me to learn quickly? Can it be used in more than one situation? Is it reliable or does it break down often? If it breaks down, do I have to fix it or will someone else repair it? How much time and energy do I have to invest in learning to use the

machine versus the return it will have for my students? When students use the machine, will there be disruption? Will it maintain or compromise my authority to maintain order and cultivate learning? (Cuban, 1996, para. 20)

As handhelds continue to make their way into the education mainstream, perhaps it is the answers to these questions that may ultimately predict handhelds' success or failure as genuine learning tools.

REFERENCES

Cuban, L. (1996). *Techno-reformers and classroom teachers.* Retrieved September 25, 2004, from http://www.edweek.org/ew/vol-16/06cuban.h16

Crawford, V., & Vahey, P. (2002). *Palm education pioneers program, March 2002 evaluation report.* Menlo Park, CA: SRI International. Retrieved September 2, 2004, from http://caret.iste.org/index.cfm?StudyID=399&fuseaction=studySummary

Hasselbring, T., Barron, L., & Risko, V. (2000). *Uses of technology in standards-based teacher education.* Retrieved September 10, 2004, from http://www.aacte.org/research/edtechprep.htm

Hudgins, B. (2001). Leveraging handheld technology in the classroom. *T.H.E. Journal, 29*(5). Retrieved September 14, 2004, from http://www.thejournal.com/magazine/vault/A3809.cfm?kw=805

Jackson, L. (2004a). *The 411 on one-to-one computing.* Retrieved August 28, 2004, from http://www.educationworld.com/a_tech/tech/tech194.shtml

Jackson, L. (2004b). *Laptops, handhelds, or tablet PCs?* Retrieved August 28, 2004, from http://www.educationworld.com/a_tech/tech/tech198.shtml

Jackson, L. (2004c). *One-to-one computing: Lessons learned and pitfalls to avoid.* Retrieved September 6, 2004 from http://www.educationworld.com/a_tech/tech/tech197.shtml

Moore, G. E. (1965). Cramming more components onto integrated circuits. *Electronics, 38*(8), 1-4.

Norris, C., & Soloway, E. (2003). *The viable alternative: Handhelds; Why the personal computer of choice in K-12 ought to fit in a student's palm.* Retrieved September 2, 2004, from http://www.findarticles.com/p/articles/mi_m0JSD/is_4_60/ai_99555575

Pride, C. (2003). *Handhelds in the classroom—tools for teachers.* Retrieved October 1, 2004, from http://www.techlearning.com/story/showArticle.jhtml?articleID=12803444

Riley, M. (1997). *Ubiquitous computing: An interesting new paradigm.* Retrieved September 15, 2004, from http://www.cc.gatech.edu/classes/cs6751_97_fall/projects/say-cheese/marcia/mfinal.html

Roland, J. (2003). *Getting a handle on handhelds.* Retrieved September 2, 2004 from http://www.iste.org/inhouse/publications/11/31/4/06r/index.cfm?Section=LL314

Topp, N. W., & Hanquist, S. (n.d.). Handhelds in schools 2002. Retrieved September 10, 2004, from http://www.unocoe.unomaha.edu/handhelds/chapter1.htm

Trotter, A. (2001). *Learning tool or toy?* Retrieved August 1, 2004, from http://www.edweek.org/ew/newstory.cfm?slug=04palm.h21

Weiser, M. (1993). *The world is not a desktop.* Retrieved September 18, 2004, from http://www.ubiq.com/hypertext/weiser/ACMInteractions2.html

Zwiers, J. (n.d.). *Teaching.* Retrieved October 1, 2004 from http://www.palmsource.com/interests/education_teacher

PART II

IMPROVING K-12 LEARNING EXPERIENCES

CHAPTER 8

DIDN'T YOU SEE WHAT I MEANT?

Informing Gestures in Teaching and Learning

Edie S. Gaythwaite

Gesture, the way the hands are used with the spoken word or as a substitute for a word in conversation, is a process of communicating multiple meanings from speaker to listener. The relationship of gesture and thinking to teaching and learning is the focus of this chapter. The review will center on iconic, metaphoric, and deictic gesture that are spontaneously produced by a speaker in a given situation. A teacher witnessing the speech-gesture act is in a better position to assess student understanding of the concept at hand.

INTRODUCTION

You are a teacher in a classroom engaged in verbally expressing course material to your students. Your students listen, watch, and then participate in the conversation. You listen and watch your students solve a problem or explain an idea that is tied into the course material. As you listen, do you look for meaning in the student hand gestures? As you speak, do you reveal meaning in your hand gestures? There are many nonverbal behaviors that occur within the learning environment including facial expressions, whole body movements, posture, and vocal variation or paralanguage. While these nonverbal behaviors are telling, the hand gesture complements the verbal exchange in conversation, reveals the speaker's thoughts, and may serve as an informant in teaching and learning. The relationship of gesture and thinking to teaching and learning is the focus of this chapter.

The study of gesture has evolved from simply coding facial expression during the Renaissance period to examining the social and cultural differences of gesture production (Bremmer & Roodenberg, 1991). What constitutes a gesture is widely defined among scholars today. The term *gesture*, as a classification of nonverbal communication, has been applied to everything from comparing animal and human behavior to exploring the inner and outward displays of emotion and attitude of speakers. Language researchers became increasingly interested in gesture following the publication of David McNeill's 1992 innovative book *Hand and Mind*. McNeill's 1992 work amplifies the study of the hand gesture as a means of revealing thought. Following McNeill, the way hands are used with the spoken word or as a substitute for a word in conversation is how gesture is defined in this paper and leads the investigation into how gesture can inform teaching and learning.

Defining Gesture

In the classroom, conversation is seen and heard by teacher and student. What is heard is language or speech, and what is seen is gesture. Where language has the effect of sectioning and extending meaning in a linear perspective to form a hierarchal structure, the meaning gestures produce are multidimensional and in no way hierarchal (McNeill, 1992). According to McNeill (1992), the speech-gesture act should be viewed as a single, unified process where one gesture can have many meanings as it informs the complete meaning of its components. For example, the fingers wiggle in a downward motion to represent falling rain. The hand is used to represent not the hand but as a symbol to represent something else, in this case rain. Hand movements explicitly joined to speech co-express meaning as gestures "beat the tempo of speech, point out referents of speech, or exploit imagery to elaborate the contents of speech" (Goldin-Meadow, 2003, p. 4). The integration of gesture with speech conveys meaning to both the speaker and the listener. If listeners modify their actions correspondingly to gestures produced, then gestures can be utilized as a means to create understanding and develop cognition (Goldin-Meadow, 2003).

To understand teaching and learning, consider the role gesture plays in the learning environment. To illustrate, student gestures may signal knowing or not knowing while teacher gestures may help or hinder student learning. Teachers may see how a student's gesture has the ability to indicate that an actual concept is in a student's inventory, but the student can not easily reach and articulate the concept verbally. In an effort to examine the role gesture can play in teaching and learning it is useful to elaborate on the types of gestures that accompany the definition of gesture and the methods of research.

Types of Gesture and Research Methods

Gesture is defined as the way hands are used with the spoken word or as a substitute for a word in conversation. Gestures are simultaneously, instantaneously, and individually produced by a speaker. They are produced in effort to bring symbolic meaning to the spoken word, as well as bring meaning to a situation when no word can be produced by the speaker. A gesture is a symbol, and a symbol has one meaning, yet gesture can transmit numerous meanings as it imitates and creates a complete meaning (McNeill, 1992).

McNeill (1992) asserts the purpose in studying gestures is "to bring out semiotic values ... to classify the gesture by means of asking (a) is the movement a symbol? and (b) what type of symbol is it?" (p. 77). Iconic, metaphoric, deictic, and beats are the common types of gesture researchers use in classifying and coding gesture in an effort to gain understanding.

Iconic gesture "in its execution and manner of performance, refers to a concrete event, object, or action that is also referred to in speech at the same time" (McNeill, 1992, p. 77). For example, a person is describing pulling the flag down from the flag pole while simultaneously using the arms and hands to demonstrate the pulling down of the flag.

McNeill (1992) defines metaphoric gesture as "similar to iconics in that they present imagery, but present an image of an abstract concept, such as knowledge, language itself, the genre of the narrative, etc." (p. 80). Metaphoric gestures are dualistic in that the concrete image informs the abstract meaning presented in the imagery (McNeill, 1992). For example, a speaker announces that he just viewed a cartoon holds up his hands as if holding an object and announces the type of cartoon viewed (McNeill, 1992).

Pointing with a finger, another body part, or by way of an object constitutes a deictic gesture (McNeill, 1992). Deictic gestures usually occur within a specific region of the gesture space (the distance between speaker and listener), can be used to point to a real or imagined object, and they may accompany or be used as a substitution for speech (Krauss, Chen, & Gottesman, 2000; McNeill, 1992).

The beat (also known as baton) gesture is a quick movement made by the speaker that represents the beginning of the dialogue or to stress the importance of a word within the dialogue (Goldin-Meadow, 2003; McNeill, 1992). Beat gesture does not represent the semantic content of the corresponding speech (Krauss et al., 2000).

Researchers studying gesture attempt to associate the gesture with talk, describe the type of gesture, and assign meaning from the contextual framework through a coding system (see McNeill, 1992). Studies characteristically rely "on video recordings of people talking—conversing naturally, narrating a story, explaining how they solve a problem and so on" (Goldin-Meadow, 2003, p. 10). One of the main objectives in studying gesture is to understand the thoughts of the speaker and how gesture may structure thinking (Goldin-Meadow, 2003). Gesture research can lead us to better understand the multiple meanings of gesturing and how this impacts teaching and learning.

Having identified the major types of gestures and the common methods used in research, it is relevant to note the primary focus herein will be on iconic, metaphoric, and deictic gestures, and how these gestures and the gesture space (which varies in dimension with adults and children and from culture to culture) are informing teaching and learning today.

THE RELATIONSHIP OF GESTURE TO TEACHING AND LEARNING

Learning is enhanced when various modes of communicating with students are used and gestures can be classified as a learning mode. Gestures may be fleeting but when built-in with speech, may provide a "more naturally unified picture to the student than a diagram used in conjunction with speech" (Goldin-Meadow, 2003, p. 112). In their study on learner articulation, Koschmann and LeBaron (2002) found participants respond straightforwardly to meaningful gestures that develop in discourse. They conclude not only do gestures influence and contribute to the interaction but also gestures exemplify knowledge being expressed by the speaker (Koschmann & LeBaron, 2002). For these reasons, it is important for teachers to be able to draw meaning from gestures produced by the learner, to modify their own behavior in response to the gesture created, and to structure the modification in a way that is most beneficial to the learner (Goldin-Meadow, 2003). This is particularly salient when teaching and learning a second language.

Second Language Learning

Gestures do not carry universal meaning and the meaning given to a gesture is rooted in the culture of the producer (Archer, 1997). For example, there are universally recognized facial expressions across all cultures; however, societies differ on when these expressions can be shown (Beall, 2004). The structure of the culture, from collectivistic to individualistic, and the language bear significantly on gesture. McNeill (2000) shows the significance of cultural to gesture by studying the different ways gesture is displayed by English and Spanish speakers. The study reveals Spanish speakers gesture in a *curvilinear* motion where English speaker's segment the gesture. The conclusion drawn from this research is the inseparable relationship between imagery and language, and the influence of gesture in penetrating language and the mind (McNeill, 2000).

Church, Ayman-Nolley, and Mahootian (2004) examined the role of gesture among 51 Spanish-speaking and English-speaking first grade students attending an English-speaking classroom. Half of the members from each group were shown either a mathematic instructional videotape where the instructor used gesture or did not use gesture. The study found learning doubled with both Spanish-speaking and English-speaking students when instruction included gesture versus instruction without gesture.

McCafferty (2002) studied the role of gesture in coconstructing meaning when learning and teaching a second language using Vygotsky's zone of proximal development. The author concluded that gestures play an important role in (a) adjusting one's thought development and expression, (b) gestures act as a replacement for missing words, (c) gestures help develop vocabulary, and (d) gestures help create an understanding of personal interests (McCafferty, 2002). McNeill and Duncan (2000) studied speakers of different languages in the context of thinking-for-speaking which is how speakers organize their thinking to meet the demands of linguistic encoding. McNeill and Duncan (2000) state speakers display knowing by producing gestures with words and when loss of context is great, more gestures are produced.

Language acquisition is improved when there is a gesture system in place (Acredolo & Goodwyn, 1988). Church et al. (2004) argue that second language learners may acquire English speaking skills quicker and gain more satisfaction if a gesture system is taught while learning English. Moreover, the research is beginning to exemplify how learning can be understood when student and teacher gesture are recognized as an integral part of communicating understanding in the classroom.

The Gesture Mismatch

When a student produces gestures in a classroom situation, teachers may treat those gestures as a means to evaluate student knowledge. Mismatched gestures occur when the verbal message and gesture conflict (Goldin-Meadow, 2003). When mismatched gestures are produced unknowingly by the speaker, the meaning of the speaker may be misunderstood. For example, the student may become confused about the lesson because of the mismatch gesture produced by the teacher. A teacher may see through gesture a student correctly identify a solution but may hear through language that the student is unable to articulate the knowledge. Students who produce numerous mismatches tend to be in a "state of cognitive uncertainty, possessing the knowledge about the task that they cannot quite organize into a coherent whole" (Goldin-Meadow, 2003, p. 129). The mismatch can actually help bring the student who is on the edge of learning a new concept over to the side of understanding as it provides the teacher with an opportunity to present different strategies to the learner (Goldin-Meadow, 2003). The key is the teacher's ability to recognize and react to the gesture mismatch.

Because it is up to the teacher to recognize and then search for a way to integrate the verbal-gesture conflict of a student, it would serve well to have teachers gain knowledge in interpreting gestures. Kelly, Singer, Hicks, and Goldin-Meadow (2002) investigated the plausibility of teaching untrained adults how to read children's hand gestures. The researchers found that, following gesture training, adults could accurately decipher 92% of the conversation gestures compared to 36% in the pretest, and 60% of the math gestures compared to 3% on the pretest (Kelly et al., 2002). The supposition here indicates teachers trained in decoding gestures may positively impact a teacher's ability to recognize and react appropriately to student thinking.

Teacher Gesture

What students take from their lessons is influenced by teacher gestures too (Goldin-Meadow, 2003). Teachers not only need to decipher gestures produced but need to be cognizant of the gestures they produce and its effect on learning. For example, 80% of students will believe the teacher's gesture over the verbal message when there is verbal-gesture conflict or mismatch (White, 2000). Furthermore, a teacher's gesture can either disclose a lack of confidence or accent a point when skillfully delivered (White, 2000).

Furuyama (2000) investigated iconic and deictic gestures in origami instruction and how learners respond to and incorporate instructor gestures into their own speech and gestures. The results from this study concluded that when instructors center their gestures in the direction of the learner collaborative speech-gesturing occurred. When the instructor's gesture did not face the focal side of the learner, the learner's gesture occurred without speech and without collaboration. The inference toward teaching is teachers who engage in producing visible gestures may create a more collaborative classroom environment.

The hand choice used by a teacher to explain a concept may be relevant to student understanding as well. Research conducted by Lausberg and Kita (2002) found among subjects who narrate the content of animation, hand choice matches the object location as viewed in the animation. For example, the speaker is explaining how the bird flew and the speaker uses the left hand as an iconic gesture that accompanies the speech because the bird appeared on the left side of the screen when viewed. Teachers who give consideration to the spatial position of the object of reference may help students build a stronger mental image that may assist in recall of information.

Teachers interested in receiving positive student evaluations may want to employ more gesture in lecture courses. Babad, Avni-Babad, and Rosenthal (2004) examined 67 college lecturers to determine if higher, end of term student ratings would be awarded to professors engaged in more nonverbal communication. The researchers found a positive correlation between teacher rating and gesture production when professors used gestures to engage their learners in the classroom.

Students may understand content better and enjoy the learning environment more when the teacher is aware of and utilizes gesturing in the classroom. For example, when a teacher uses gesture in lecturing it may satisfy the visual learner as well as the aural learner. To emphasize, brain research has added to our understanding of the difference between procedural and declarative memory and its building on educational practice. If the teacher consciously chooses to produce a verbal-gesture match repetitively, it may serve as a rehearsal strategy that may be stored in memory and assist in the reconstruction of information which is necessary for recall.

Gesture and Thought

The human brain is divided into two cerebral hemispheres: right and left. Simply put, the left side controls speech, the right side controls image, and both sides generally work together (McNeill, 1992). Feyereisen (1999) gives evidence from neuropsychological research that the right hemisphere processes significant gestures and the left hemisphere processes insignificant gestures. Goldin-Meadow's (2003) review of research focusing on gesture use in relation to thinking asserts (a) difficult tasks produce more gesturing, (b) gesturing helps to release the strains of cognition whereby a freeing up of cognitive resources occurs, and (c) explanations are processed more easily by the speaker when gestures are utilized versus when gestures are not utilized. The implication for instruction is in the possibility that gesturing may help ease the cognitive strains on the individual student and allow additional information to be processed and learned.

Incidental research implies, not only does gesture ease cognition and let new information enter, gesture permits speakers to produce suitable images (concrete and metaphoric) that represent ideas that may be difficult to produce verbally. This process may assist the learner in creating and advancing ideas that allows for cognitive transformation (Goldin-Meadow, 2003). There is still a great deal researchers have yet to learn about the human brain and how it processes information, specifically, the manner in which gestures are apprehended, stored, reproduced, organized, and learned.

GESTURE RESEARCH IN THE CLASSROOM

A majority of the scant gesture research in teaching and learning environments has taken place in the fields of mathematic and science. Roth and Lawless (2002) engaged in researching how metaphorical gestures can help students gain conceptual and abstract knowledge in the presence of material objects. The researchers gathered 10 years worth of videotaped science classroom sessions with subjects ranging from Grade 4 through 8, Grade 10 and 12. Their investigation supported their hypothesis and revealed "the perceptual ground and gestures have an important scaffolding function in students' development of scientific language because they take on a representative function" (Roth & Lawless, 2002, p. 302). Additionally, the research found that students should be given ample time to transform from gesture, to verbal, to written states when concepts are abstract. In another study, Roth (2002) examined 30 German students engaged in a 10th-grade physics classroom. Roth (2002) found when students work with and gain knowledge of objects, iconic gestures are developed which helps pave the way for scientific language acquisition. Roth and Welzel (2001) studied the role of gestures and scientific discourse in a scientific laboratory setting and found "gestures have a bridging function between hands-on activity and language" (p. 126).

Research conducted by LeBaron and Streeck (2000) found "practical settings where gestures share the situation with the experiences that they formulate, we can begin to see the important indexical underpinnings of the pairings of form and meaning, of signifier and signified" (p. 136). The researchers state "hands learn how to handle things before they learn how to gesticulate," and because of this, gestures are constructed from interacting with material objects, performing and participating in a physical, culture and social world (LeBaron & Streeck, 2000, p. 137). The role material objects play in the orientation toward gesture, speech, thought, and meaning has practical application for classroom teaching.

In moving from material objects to gesture space, Crowder (1996) studied how students in a sixth-grade science class use gesture and gesture space when engaging in explanation and description of scientific discourse. The observations reveal (a) rote-learning is employed when a student remains outside the gesture space, (b) more sophisticated gestures are utilized when a student is inside the gesture space, and (c) when these events are viewed collectively it provides insight into the level of student understanding (Crowder, 1996). The study also illustrates when students are earnestly partaking and have integrated the descriptive and explanatory knowledge, the student inside the gesture space begins to function as a problem solver.

Ozyurek (2000) studied addressee location in relation to "spatial language and gesturing orientation to express direction" (p. 69). The research consisted of an experimental condition where there was either one addressee to the side of the narrator or two addressees on each side of the narrator, and a controlled condition where two addresses were in a fixed position on each side of the narrator. Sixteen undergraduate students participated as either narrator or addressee in a storytelling situation. The study shows how narrator's "gesture orientation changes in different contexts to keep the meaning conveyed by speech and gesture the same" (Ozyurek, 2000, p. 80). The research on gesture space expands the conventional concept that gesture and speech serve different but complementary roles in the creation and expression of meaning. The research conducted by Ozyurek (2000) implies that meaning creation is enhanced when audience members can visually process gesture production with speech.

DISCUSSION

Gesture can never be described as a simple body movement because research has begun to show the value gesture has on teaching and learning. Knowing that gesture creates multiple meanings and the structuring of meaning may link knowing and not knowing, educators may be inclined to complement the way instruction is designed and delivered in a multimodal classroom setting.

Teachers who understand that gestures are produced with speech or in absence of speech are better prepared to assess the meaning of the gesturer. Teachers who understand that gesture production may reduce cognitive strain or indicate knowledge integration may pay heed to student gestures. Teachers who understand how the manipulation of material objects help in developing the scientific language of students, and how gesture production may signal the status of learning will be better equipped to judge students understanding of abstract and concrete concepts. Teachers who understand gesture and its socio-cultural heritage have an opportunity to enhance learning in a diverse classroom.

The process of teachers understanding the role gesture plays in teaching and learning can begin by designing a gesture training model for student-teachers. For example, student-teachers can learn how to improve their own gestures, how to interpret gestures and learn the role culture plays in gesture. Incorporating classroom exercises throughout a semester to build skills in producing and understanding gesture meaning can include students examining their own gesture behavior and comparing their sociocultural perspective with those of cultures different from their own. Videotaping instruction and then analyzing gesture behavior of teacher and student interaction is another way to approach understanding. For example, have the teacher take note of where he or she positions himself or herself in the classroom, how they use gesture and respond to gesture, and how they can use gesture to help with their verbal message. Designing a study around a gesture training model in a student-teacher course may also prove valuable to gesture research and the relationship of gesture and thinking to teaching and learning.

This chapter set out to review gesture literature and its implication in teaching and learning. This chapter did not discuss gesture production in people who use sign language, who are hearing or sight impaired, or give consideration to people who have other communication difficulties. This in no way diminishes the importance of the research conducted in these areas and its relationship to teaching and learning. Certainly, today's classrooms are populated with students who are diverse in knowledge and ability. The overarching difficulty with gesture research, as Roth (2001) has indicated, "there exists virtually no educational research that focuses on the role of gestures in knowing and learning and the implications they have for designing and evaluating learning environments" (p. 365). This deficiency provides many opportunities for further research and possible instruction. As McNeill (1992) states, iconic gestures enable us to "observe thoughts as they occur" (p. 132). What better way to impact teaching and learning than to have the skills to react to student thoughts?

ACKNOWLEDGMENT

The author would like to thank David N. Boote, Assistant Professor, College of Education at the University of Central Florida for his editing assistance.

REFERENCES

Acredolo, L., & Goodwyn, S. (1988). Symbolic gesturing in normal infants. *Child Development, 59*, 450-466.

Archer, D. (1997). Unspoken diversity: Cultural differences in gestures. *Qualitative Sociology, 20*(1), 79-105.

Babad, E., Avni-Babad, D., & Rosenthal, R. (2004). Prediction of students' evaluations from brief instances of professors' nonverbal behavior in defined instructional situations. *Social Psychology of Education, 7*, 3-33.

Beall, A. E. (2004). Body language speaks. *Communication World, 21*(2), 18-20.

Bremmer, J., & Roodenburg, H. (Eds.). (1991). *A cultural history of gesture*. Ithaca, NY: Cornell University Press.

Church, B. R., Ayman-Nolley, S., & Mahootain, S. (2004). The role of gesture in bilingual learning: Does gesture enhance learning? *Bilingual Education & Bilingualism, 7*(4), 303-319.

Crowder, E. M. (1996). Gestures at work in sense-making science talk. *Journal of the Learning Sciences, 5*(3), 173-209.

Feyereisen, P. (1999). Neuropsychological of communicative movements. In L. S. Messing & R. Campbell (Eds.), *Gesture, speech, and sign* (pp. 3-25). New York: Oxford University Press.

Furuyama, N. (2000). Gestural interaction between the instructor and the learner in origami instruction. In D. McNeill (Ed.), *Language and gesture* (pp. 99-117). Chicago: Cambridge University Press.

Goldin-Meadow, S. (2003). *Hearing gesture: How our hands help us think*. Cambridge, MA: The Belknap Press of Harvard University Press.

Kelly, S. D., Singer, M., Hicks, J., & Goldin-Meadow, S. (2002). A helping hand in assessing children's knowledge: Instructing adults to attend to gesture. *Cognition and Instruction, 20*(1), 1-26.

Koschmann, T., & LeBaron, C. (2002). Learner articulation as interactional achievement: Studying the conversation of gesture. *Cognition and Instruction 20*(2), 249-282.

Krauss, R. M., Chen, Y., & Gottesman, R. F. (2000). Lexical gestures and lexical access: A process model. In D. McNeill (Ed.), *Language and gesture* (pp. 261-283). Chicago: Cambridge University Press.

Lausberg, H., & Kita, S. (2002). The content of the message influences the hand choice in co-speech gestures and in gesturing without speaking. *Brain and Language, 86,* 57-69.

LeBaron, C., & Streeck, J. (2000). Gestures, knowledge and the world. In D. McNeill (Ed.), *Language and gesture* (pp. 118-138). Chicago: Cambridge University Press.

McCafferty, S. G. (2002). Gesture and creating zones of proximal development for second language learning. *The Modern Language Journal, 86*(2), 192-203.

McNeill, D. (1992). *Hand and mind: What gestures reveal about thought.* Chicago: The University of Chicago Press.

McNeill, D. (2000). Analogic/analytic representations and cross-linguistic differences in thinking for speaking. *Language and Culture, 11*(1/2), 43-60.

McNeill, D., & Duncan, S. D. (2000). Growth points in thinking-for-speaking. In D. McNeill (Ed.), *Language and gesture* (pp. 141-161). Chicago: Cambridge University Press.

Ozyurek, A. (2000). The influence of addressee location on spatial language and representational gestures of direction. In D. McNeill (Ed.), *Language and gesture* (pp. 64-83). New York: Oxford University Press.

Roth, W. -M. (2001). Gestures: Their role in teaching and learning. *Review of Educational Research, 71*(3), 365-392.

Roth, W. -M. (2002). From action to discourse: The bridging function of gestures. *Cognitive Systems Research, 3,* 535-554.

Roth, W. -M., & Lawless, D. (2002). Scientific investigations, metaphorical gestures, and the emergence of abstract scientific concepts. *Learning and Instruction, 12*(3), 285-304.

Roth, W. -M., & Welzel, M. (2001). From activity to gestures and scientific language. *Journal of Research in Science Teaching, 38*(1), 103-136.

White, G. W. (2000). Non-verbal communications: Key to improved teacher effectiveness. *The Delta Kappa Gamma Bulletin, 66*(4), 12-16.

CHAPTER 9

THE NATURE OF STUDENT AND TEACHER DISCOURSE IN AN ELEMENTARY CLASSROOM

Violet Dickson

This study examined the various types of student and teacher discourse that occurred in a regular fourth grade elementary classroom during a 6-week period. The study categorized and defined the different types of discourse and found that the majority of student talk was productive and on task. The study also examined the kinds of teacher talk that encouraged or inhibited productive student talk in the classroom and found that asking open-ended questions and providing students more time to process their responses led to greater levels of productive student talk.

INTRODUCTION

"To raise new questions, new problems, to regard old problems from a new angle requires creative imagination and makes real advances."

—Albert Einstein

In a decade-long study of effective teaching, Allington, Johnson, and Day (2002) identified student talk as the "single most striking feature in effective classrooms" (p. 463). Classroom activities that include discussion, collaboration, and negotiation of information allow students the opportunity to become active participants in the learning process. In Cazden's (1995) evaluation of research on classroom discourse, she found that classroom teachers themselves were doing more of the research, with the focus on the content of talk and how it related to curriculum goals.

This study of student and teacher discourse was a qualitative study that served as the beginning of an ongoing teacher-action research on the types of discourse that take place in elementary classrooms. The teacher-researcher, who conducted this initial study in her fourth grade classroom over a 6-week period of time, wanted to know what kinds of discourse occur in a regular classroom, how much of the student discourse is productive talk, and how teacher discourse can encourage productive talk. Currently, the author is continuing the study of student and teacher discourse with plans to replicate the study in kindergarten, second grade, and additional fourth grade classrooms. Therefore, a future study could include comparisons or contrasts to student and teacher discourse occurring at different grade levels.

PURPOSE

The purpose of this study was to answer three questions:

1. What types of student and teacher discourse go on in an elementary classroom every day?
2. Is the majority of student talk in the classroom productive or off-task talk?
3. How does teacher talk encourage or inhibit productive student talk?

The first part of the study involved collecting samples of various types of student and teacher discourse that take place in a regular fourth grade classroom of 22 students during a 6-week period of time. The second part of the study involved examining student talk and teacher talk to determine the nature of student talk (productive versus off-task) and to identify ways teachers either encourage or inhibit productive student talk in the classroom.

THEORETICAL FRAMEWORK

Providing opportunities and support for student discourse in the classroom can lead to questioning, reflection, engagement, and response, causing students to actively seek information (Allington, 2002; Allington, et al., 2002; Hamm & Adams, 2002). Thoughtful questioning and strategic classroom discussion may also play a critical role in student learning, leading to higher levels of thinking and improved comprehension (Allington, 2002; Applegate, Quinn, & Applegate, 2002). For years, typical questions in the traditional classroom were concrete questions that involved single-answer responses (Harvey, 2002). In contrast, Applegate et al. (2002) found curricular discussions that lead to higher comprehension levels involve processing skills, such as analyzing, synthesizing, hypothesizing, and forming generalizations related to the subject matter. Comprehending on a higher level involves making deep connections that move the student beyond the concrete to the abstract to deal with more complex issues (Harvey, 2002; Taylor, Peterson, Pearson, & Rodriguez, 2002). When students are faced with authentic questions that reflect real life situations, they often become personally involved as they work through the process of inquiry to search for answers.

What is inquiry? It is more than simply asking questions. Hamm and Adams (2002) describe inquiry as a process of learning through questioning, examination, and explanation. Real life involves a continual process of asking questions and finding solutions or answers. Life in the classroom can and should involve questioning and problem solving. According to Joyce, Weil, and Calhoun (2000), problem solving involves reasoning, good thinking, and the ability to learn in puzzling situations. Problem solving also becomes a social process as students question, share information, compare ideas, and discuss solutions with peers.

Group inquiry, a collaborative process for finding answers and building knowledge, involves questioning, investigating, evaluating, and sharing ideas with others in a group setting (Hamm & Adams, 2002). Group inquiry builds on students' strengths instead of focusing on their weaknesses, allowing all students an opportunity to participate in learning. Not only do students learn by working with others but also, they learn to ask questions, search for answers, contribute ideas, pool resources, and collaborate to solve problems. These are valuable skills that students will need in order to participate productively in the future workplace (Hamm & Adams, 2002).

Since inquiry involves not only questioning but also explanations, then student dialogue and discussion must play a key role in the process. Allington et al. (2002) found productive student dialogue at the inquiry level differed greatly from idle classroom chatter. Allington (2002) defined productive dialogue as student talk that is directly related to the curriculum as well as conversational talk that may be personal but relevant to the learning situation.

Teachers can support this type of student dialogue by creating an environment that "surrounds the curriculum with thoughtful conversation"

(Allington, 2002, p. 475). Teachers also must capitalize on students' curiosity by providing the time and opportunities to explore questions and problems (Allington, 2002; Harvey, 2002; Jewell & Pratt, 1999). Einstein once remarked, "I have no special talents, I'm just passionately curious" (Calaprice, 1996, p. 12). Creating a classroom filled with rich student dialogue opens the door to curiosity and can provide a rewarding experience for both teacher and students. However, opening the door to inquiry and dialogue also requires teacher planning, organization, and modeling.

Teachers must understand the social nature of inquiry and establish guidelines and boundaries for appropriate classroom discussions. Teachers also should model inquiry and dialogue by asking open-ended questions that stimulate discussion and encourage purposeful, problem solving talk (Allington, 2002; Applegate et al., 2002; Jewell & Pratt, 1999). In Allington's study, he found that exemplary teachers provided models and gave explicit demonstrations of skills and strategies for learning (Allington, 2002). Moller (2002) found that simply telling students to read, write, and talk was not sufficient. A foundation first had to be laid in which the teacher modeled inquiry, discussion, and interpersonal skills.

There are various roles a teacher may assume when moving a class from a traditional structure to one that utilizes inquiry and dialogue. A teacher may operate in the role of a facilitator, participant, mediator, or listener (Short, Kaufman, Kaser, Kahn, & Crawford, 1999). Teachers in inquiry-based classrooms move from the traditional roles of lecturer, interrogator, and evaluator to more supportive roles that motivate, clarify, organize, and give directions (Moller, 2002). Teachers also must be willing for their classrooms to be rather noisy with productive chatter. Classrooms utilizing inquiry and dialogue have a constant hum of voices and activity as students talk and work together on projects or problems (Hamm & Adams, 2002).

Students must also make the shift from being receivers of knowledge to becoming active participants in the search for knowledge (Hamm & Adams, 2002). Students must learn to develop skills and attitudes that will enable them to become self-regulated learners, which Perry and Drummond (2002) define as students who are not only motivated to learn, but who have a repertoire of problem-solving strategies they can use effectively. As student responsibilities are defined, modeled, and practiced, students will learn to shift from teacher dependence to learner independence (Hamm & Adams, 2002; Noonan, 2001). Like teachers, students also can operate in a variety of roles, such as facilitator, motivator, encourager, listener, researcher, or reporter (Daniels, 1994; Short et al., 1999). As students take greater responsibility for their learning, they will be able to articulate their thoughts more clearly and provide support for their ideas as well as incorporate the thoughts, ideas, questions, and opinions of others (Allington et al., 2002; Jewell & Pratt, 1999; Moller, 2002; Noonan, 2001).

Which students can benefit from classrooms that utilize inquiry and student discourse? Research indicates that *all* students benefit from classroom environments that provide opportunities for student discourse. In one study of at-risk learners (students identified as being at risk of failing or dropping out of school), struggling, resistant readers improved their reading levels and became more motivated to learn after participating in reading clubs that encouraged discussions and social interactions revolving around literacy (Worthy, Patterson, Salas, Prater, & Turner, 2002). Mansukhani (2002) and Palincsar (1998) also found that second language learners and special education students were more successful when they were provided opportunities to learn in inquiry-based environments where student discourse was encouraged.

The use of inquiry and dialogue in the classroom opens the door to multiple possibilities. Teachers can create classroom settings in which students build knowledge, further their learning, and move from a state of dependence to one of independence as they use reading, writing, listening, thinking, and speaking skills (in collaboration with other students) to ask questions, examine issues, and solve complex problems.

METHOD

In this action research, a fourth grade classroom was videotaped and observed by outside observers at different times of day during a 6-week time period in order to collect samples of student and teacher discourse. The teacher-researcher also kept a journal of classroom occurrences, student comments, and personal reflections during the same time period. For the videotaping, eight dates and times were randomly drawn to determine which 30-minute segments would be taped. The videotaped segments included science lessons, math lessons, reading groups, class discussions, and independent work.

For the classroom observations, four student interns from the local university observed and recorded classroom discourse. The elementary school where this study took place is a PDS (Professional Development School) setting in which student interns are assigned for a school year to be trained as observers and serve as data collectors while completing their assignments on the school campus. The teacher-researcher arranged with the university professor to have the student interns schedule eight visits to her fourth grade class during the 6-week time period to conduct the classroom observations. Each observation lasted 30 minutes and occurred at different times of day, based on the availability of the intern.

To keep a record of the video observations and classroom observations, the teacher-researcher designed an observation sheet (Tables 9.1 and 9.2), which was used to identify various types of student and teacher discourse in the classroom. The observation sheet was based on a compilation of different types of discourse collected by the teacher-researcher from several teachers in the school prior to the study. The teacher-researcher took the compiled list and grouped various kinds of student and teacher discourse into categories. For example, the "exploratory" category in student discourse included student brainstorming, exploring possible answers, and investigating phenomena. The "encouraging" category in teacher discourse included teacher praise, compliments, and words of encouragement to students. The "responsive" category in teacher discourse also could include praise, but only as a *response* to a student's question or statement. The final product was an observation sheet that served as a checklist for many categories of teacher talk and student talk that occur in a classroom every day.

Interns used the observation sheets to record and tally the various kinds of discourse occurring in the classroom as well as the frequency of each occurrence. During each 30-minute observation period, the intern would note the different kinds of talk going on every 3 minutes. Therefore, the interns recorded their observations 10 different times during each 30-minute observation period.

The teacher-researcher observed the classroom videotapes in the same manner, using the observation sheet. A total of eight 30-minute segments were viewed, and tallies were made every 3 minutes, for a total of 10 observations per segment.

After the classroom observations and videotaped observations were completed, the author totaled and averaged the tallies to find the mean number of occurrences for each discourse category. The author then triangulated the results of the classroom observations, videotapes, and excerpts from the teacher's journal to see if a picture emerged regarding the types of student and teacher discourse that occurred in the classroom.

DATA COLLECTION

The literature on action research indicates that by using a systematic approach to addressing classroom questions, teacher-researchers can use results from their own studies to assess, develop, or improve their classroom practices (Gilbert & Smith, 2003; Hashey & Connors, 2003). Research also indicates that triangulation is one way to check out the same data from three different angles to get a new perspective (MacLean & Mohr, 1999). The three methods of data collection in this action

Table 9.1. Student Discourse

Types of Student Discourse	Average Tallies during 30-Minute Period
Exploratory (using language to discuss, explore, or investigate)	3.38
Informative (providing information to others)	4.44
Reasoning (using language to persuade or reason with others)	1.12
Evaluative (evaluating work or actions)	0.50
Interrogative (posing questions)	3.50
Responsive (replying to questions)	3.13
Organizational (using language to organize, including self talk)	1.56
Collaborative (working with other students in a group)	4.93
Peer tutoring (assisting other students)	1.81
Creative (creating stories, text, etc.)	0.56
Reading aloud (reading text out loud)	3.06
Connecting (making connections between topics)	1.69
Affective (expressing feelings)	1.81
Sharing personal experiences	1.75
Disagreeing or justifying opinions or actions	1.50
Casual talk but on task (joking, laughing, teasing)	2.13
Off task language (language not related to the task)	1.68
Other	0.68

Table 9.2. Teacher Discourse

Types of Teacher Discourse	Average Tallies during 30-Minute Period
Encourages (gives praise/compliments)	4.18
Interrogative (asks questions)	4.75
Responsive (answers questions)	4.43
Tutors or conferences with students	2.06
Repeats information (to clarify or reteach)	2.94
Summarizes (text or student statements)	1.06
Reminds (reminds students of rules/procedures/tasks)	3.25
Invites student to participate/share/make connections	3.13
Conferences with students	2.13
Shares personal experiences/anecdotes	0.44
Casual conversation with students (laughing/joking with students)	0.44
Lectures	0.25
Provides direct instruction	4.75
Reads aloud	0.20
Addresses off-task behavior	1.06
Other	0.93

research included videotaping, observation checklists, and teacher journal entries. A total of 16 observation sheets were completed during a 6-week time period. Eight observation sheets were based on interns' independent observations in the classroom and eight were based on the author's observations of videos of the classroom. The tallies from the interns' and the author's observation sheets were totaled and averaged to find the average number of occurrences for each type of student or teacher discourse. Tables 9.1 and 9.2 show the average number of occurrences for each category, based on 10 observations during each 30-minute time period (one observation every 3 minutes).

FINDINGS

The analysis and comparisons of student and teacher discourse yielded interesting findings. Since tallies were given a maximum of ten times during each thirty-minute observation period, student and teacher talk that yielded an average occurrence of three or more times were noted. While there was considerable variety in the different types of student talk occurring, it is interesting to note that the majority of student talk was productive and on-task.

The greatest occurrence of student talk was collaborative talk, which is the type of talk students use when they work together on an activity, collaborate on a project, or problem solve. An example of collaborative talk follows:

> (Students collaborating on a science project for animal habitats)
> S1: A crowtel! What the heck is that?
> S2: Well ... you know ... like people would stay in a hotel. Well, this is a place for birds.
> S3: Yeah, get it? Hotel – Crowtel!
> S1: Oh, I get it. Cool! What about a zootel?
> S3: No, no ... how about an "Aquatel"?
> S2: Yeah, that would be for aquatic animals. You know; animals that live in the sea.
> S3: Or any kind of water.
> S1: Yeah, agua means water in Spanish, so they have to live in water.

Another type of student talk that occurred frequently was informative talk, which is the type of talk students use when they share information they have found with other students, either as a whole class or in small groups.

(Students using informative talk to share information)

- S1: Look, if you can't find the picture you want, just go back where you found your stuff on Indians ... remember ... you had some cool pictures.
- S2: Oh yeah, the tomahawk and weapons ...
- S3: Yeah, and the drums.
- S2: Oh yeah ... lots of drums!
- S1: Yeah ... go back there. No, that's not it. Where's that place?
- S3: Yeah, find it. I wanna use it too for my brochure.
- S2: Look. I found it. How do I put it in the thing ... in the brochure?
- S1: It's easy. Look (student demonstrates how to copy and paste a picture into a document).

Other types of student talk that averaged more than three times per observation included interrogative talk, exploratory talk, responsive talk, and reading aloud. Interrogative talk involved students who posed questions for others or asked for information from the teacher or from other students. Exploratory talk included language that students used to explore topics, discuss options, or investigate phenomena. Responsive talk included answering questions asked by the teacher or other students, as well as responding to comments made by others. Reading aloud not only included reading aloud text, but also reading and sharing information from other sources with fellow students.

The type of teacher talk that occurred most frequently in the classroom was interrogative, or questioning. The questions came in many forms and from all levels of Bloom's taxonomy, which includes questions from concrete levels as well as questions that involve higher levels of thinking.

(Example of Teacher questioning)

- T: So what's the next step in the scientific method?
- S: The hypothesis.
- T: And what's a hypothesis?
- S: A good guess.
- T: So, what do you think will happen? What's your "good guess"?
- S: Oh ... the red color will stay ... mix with the water, and the oil and syrup will float. The sand will go to the bottom 'cause it's heavier.

T: Well, why do you think the red food coloring will mix with the water?
S: Cause its like water. It'll just mix in and turn the water red.
T: And what about the oil and syrup?
S: They're gonna float 'cause I saw it once.
T: You saw oil and syrup float on water?
S: Yeah, when my mom was cooking something ... the oil floated on top.
T: Did you see the syrup float too?
S: No, but it's just like oil 'cause it's sticky.
T: So, what are you planning ... to see if your hypothesis is correct?

Another type of teacher talk that was used frequently was responsive talk, which included answering questions as well as responding to student comments. An example of the teacher's response to a student follows:

Teacher response to student (math)

S: I worked it out another way. Instead of multiplying, I thought about money. See, I know that eight quarters is $2.00, and I remember what you said about multiplying zeros ... that you just bring down the zero at the end. So, I thought ... if 8 x 25 is 200, then 80 x 25 has gotta be 2,000 because you just put a zero on the end of 200 and you get 2,000. Get it?

T: Yeah, I get it! Remember when I told you that in math, there's usually more than one way to look at a problem? Well, you just found another way to look at it, and I like that. I also liked the way you thought through each step and explained it to me rather than just giving an answer.

The third most frequent type of teacher talk was encouragement. This type of talk included praising students for completing a task or making progress as well as encouraging students to try another approach. It also included thanking students for helping the teacher or for assisting another student.

The other types of teacher talk that averaged more than three occurrences were direct instruction, reminding students of things, and inviting students to participate. Teacher talk that involved direct instruction included providing background information on a subject, teaching major concepts, and directing activities for a variety of topics in science, social studies, language arts, and math. Teacher talk that involved reminding included reminding students of rules and procedures for classroom organization or reminding students about expected behavior. Finally, teacher talk that invited students to participate included talk that invited students to share with the class, a group of students or another student. This type of talk also invited students to think for themselves, make connections, and respond to a variety of situations.

An interesting observation from the data was that several kinds of student and teacher talk seemed to compliment each other well. For example, interrogative teacher talk often led to responsive and exploratory student talk. In the same manner, informative student talk led to encouraging and responsive comments from the teacher. Collaborative and exploratory student talk also occurred most frequently when the teacher talk was inviting, encouraging, and responsive. It was also interesting to note that although there was a higher occurrence of casual (on-task) conversation between students than between students and teacher, the classroom atmosphere was comfortable, allowing for some casual conversation with very little off-task student talk and very little need for teacher talk that addressed off-task behavior. Also the low occurrence of teacher lecturing in preference to questioning and encouraging could possibly lead to higher occurrences of exploratory, informative, and collaborative student talk, thereby leading to more productive talk in the classroom.

CONCLUSION

The first purpose of this study was to examine the different types of student and teacher discourse that occur in an elementary classroom. It is difficult to form a comprehensive list of student and teacher talk because there are many different kinds of talk going on in an elementary classroom during the course of the day and over the course of many weeks. The "Other" category that was added to Table 9.1 included occurrences of student encouragement, students correcting others, making suggestions, agreeing, and thinking out loud. Teacher talk that fell under the "Other" category of Table 9.2 included occurrences of teacher redirection, clarification, giving permission, making suggestions, and making qualifying statements. Due to the fact that discourse is very fluid and ever changing, it is likely that in another study of this type, there could be additional categories that would need to be added to the types of student and teacher discourse that were discovered in this study. Based on the observations of this study, the types of student talk that were most evident included talk that was informing, questioning, exploratory, and responsive. The types of teacher talk that were most evident included questioning, responding, encouraging, reminding, and inviting students to share, make connections, and think out loud.

Based on this study, the majority of student talk that occurred in the classroom was productive and on-task. There was very little idle chatter, " off-task talk, or silliness. Much of the productive student talk also seemed to be directly related and in response to the type of teacher talk that was occurring in the classroom. In other words, teacher talk appeared to affect directly the type of student talk that occurred in the classroom.

The classroom atmosphere also helped create an environment in which students were allowed to talk and problem solve. In this study, the kinds of teacher talk and student talk that were evident seemed to establish a classroom environment that had an emphasis on learning, student choice, independence, and cooperation between teacher and students.

IMPLICATION FOR EDUCATIONAL PRACTICE

In this study the teacher learned, from viewing the videos of her own classroom, that there were things she did both to encourage and inhibit student talk. When the teacher observed herself asking and answering some of her own questions in the video, she realized she was not allowing students time to process and work through the problems for themselves. As a result, the teacher changed this aspect of her teaching style. It was interesting to note in the teacher's journal, there were times when the teacher was concerned that the talk might be too loud or seem chaotic to an outside observer. However, when the videotape was viewed, it was evident that all of the students were productive and busy. Teachers who desire to provide students opportunities to talk and process out loud must be willing to have classrooms that are sometimes rather noisy with productive chatter. To encourage productive student talk, teachers must also be willing to give up some control of their classrooms in order to allow student choice and to encourage students to take an active role in the learning process.

According to Cazden (1995), educators need to analyze the social and cognitive functions of classroom talk to consider the reasoning behind students' comments and students' thinking. More than ever before in our society, young adults are expected to be able to explain their reasoning for understanding, and students need the opportunity to practice doing so in the classroom (Cazden, 1995). A greater emphasis on inquiry and dialogue in the classroom, which leads to exploratory, informative, and problem solving talk, may also lead to noticeable gains in student achievement. In an article in the *Chicago Sun-Times* (Rossi, 2000), a study by the Consortium on Chicago School Research found that students who were exposed to interactive teaching and participated in extensive student discussions, open-ended questions, and group or individual projects, produced higher Chicago test gains than students in more traditional classrooms that stressed memorization and multiple-choice tests.

LIMITATIONS

The present study was phase one of an ongoing study of student and teacher discourse in an elementary classroom. This study was limited in the fact that it took place in one fourth grade classroom over a period of 6 weeks. The author hopes to gain additional information and insights into student and teacher discourse by replicating this study in additional fourth grade classes as well as in other grade levels.

REFERENCES

Allington, R. L. (2002). What I've learned about effective reading instruction. *Phi Delta Kappan, 79*(6), 740-747.

Allington, R. L., Johnston, P. H., & Day, J. P. (2002). Exemplary fourth-grade teachers. *Language Arts, 79*, 462-466.

Applegate, M. D., Quinn, K. B., & Applegate, A. J. (2002). Levels of thinking required by comprehension questions in informal reading inventories. *The Reading Teacher, 56*, 174-180.

Calaprice, A. (1996). *The quotable Einstein.* Princeton, NJ: Princeton University Press.

Cazden, C. B. (1995). New ideas for research on classroom discourse. *TESOL Quarterly, 29*, 384-387.

Daniels, H. (1994). *Literature circles: Voice and choice in the student-centered classroom.* Portland, ME: Stenhouse.

Gilbert, S. L., & Smith, L. C. (2003). A bumpy road to action research. *Kappa Delta Pi Record, 39*, 80-83.

Hamm, M., & Adams, D. (2002). Collaborative inquiry: Working toward shared goals. *Kappa Delta Pi Record, 38*(3), 115-118.

Harvey, S. (2002). Nonfiction inquiry: Using read reading and writing to explore the world. *Language Arts, 80*, 12-22.

Hashey, J. M., & Connors, D. J. (2003). Learn from our journey: Reciprocal teaching action research. *The Reading Teacher, 57*, 224-232.

Jewell, T. A., & Pratt, D. (1999). Literature discussions in the primary grades: Children's thoughtful discourse about books and what teachers can do to make it happen. *The Reading Teacher, 52*, 842-850.

Joyce, R., Weil, M., & Calhoun, E. (2000). *Models of teaching* (6th ed.). Needham Heights, MA: Allyn & Bacon.

MacLean, M. S., & Mohr, M. M (1999). *Teacher-researchers at work.* Berkeley, CA: National Writing Project.

Mansukhani, P. (2002). The explorers' club: The sky is no limit for learning. *Language Arts, 80*, 31-39.

Moller, K. J. (2002). Providing support for dialogue in literature discussions about social justice. *Language Arts, 79*, 467-477.

Noonan, S. (2001). Literature circles in a fifth-grade classroom. *The State of Reading, 6*(2), 16-19.

Palincsar, A. (1998). Keeping the metaphor of scaffolding fresh: A response to C. Addison Stone's The metaphor of scaffolding: Its utility for the field of learning disabilities. *Journal of Learning Disabilities, 31*, 370-373.

Perry, N. & Drummond, L. (2002). Helping young students become self-regulated researchers and writers. *The Reading Teacher, 56*, 298-310.

Rossi, R. (2000, November 1). Old-style teaching gets lower scores. *Chicago Sun-Times.* Retrieved September 20, 2004, from http://suntimes.com/output/news/educ01.html

Short, K., Kaufman, G., Kaser, S., Kahn, L. H., & Crawford, K. M. (1999). Teacher-watching: Examining teacher talk in literature circles. *Language Arts, 76*, 377-385.

Taylor, B. M., Peterson, D. S., Pearson, P. D., & Rodriguez, M. C. (2002). Looking inside classrooms: Reflecting on the "how" as well as the "what" in effective reading instruction. *The Reading Teacher, 56*, 270-279.

Worthy, J., Patterson, E., Salas, R., Prater, S., & Turner, M. (2002). More than just reading: The human factor in reaching resistant readers. *Reading Research and Instruction, 41*, 177-202.

CHAPTER 10

COMMON GROUND

An Ecological Perspective on Teaching and Learning

Christy M. Moroye

This chapter outlines a study of 2 public school classrooms researched through eco-educational criticism and connoisseurship. The purpose of the study is to use ecological metaphors to shed light on sound educational practice.

INTRODUCTION AND RATIONALE FOR THE STUDY

By failing to include ecological perspectives in any number of subjects, students are taught that ecology is unimportant for history, politics, economics, society, and so forth. And through television they learn that the earth is theirs for the taking. The result is a generation of ecological yahoos without a clue why the color of the water in their rivers is related to their food supply, or why storms are becoming more severe as the planet warms. (Orr, 1992, p. 85).

As the world faces an unprecedented environmental crisis, many people look to schools and education for a solution. Global conferences, national think tanks, and grassroots organizations call on education, both formal and informal, to create a citizenry capable of critical thinking, problem solving, and global collaboration. But addressing this problem is a tall order for our nation's schools, particularly in a climate of high stakes testing and standardization. Before we make more blanket mandates, we should consider environmental education, which is an appropriate focus for school reform. Environmental education not only benefits the environment, but it also helps students to develop intellectually and developmentally (Hutchison, 1998). We must look carefully at what schools are already doing. What environmental education programs exist? What national and state standards align with environmental education? And, perhaps most importantly, what messages, both implicit and explicit, are students receiving about environmental ethics and values? Before we can make recommendations about how to proceed with this delicate and important task of awakening students to environmental concerns, we must, I believe, meet schools, teachers, and students where they are.

David Orr (1992), professor at Oberlin College and a leading advocate for environmental education, says that "All education is environmental education" (p. 90). If this is true, then everything that happens in a school speaks. The way a school deals with trash, buys food, mediates the natural environment, organizes outdoor activities, and uses and reuses paper and materials all communicate implicit and explicit values about the environment. The learning environment and its members collectively make statements about personal beliefs, community values, and ultimately our intentions for the environment and our global neighbors. In order to see and understand these trends, and in order to know where schools, teachers, and students are, we can look to individual classrooms and teachers to explore the rich environments they create. To focus on these actions by individual teachers and students in classrooms was the purpose of this study. Furthermore, through this study, I explored ecological metaphors as ways to understand and evaluate classroom practice.

THE STUDY DESIGN

Methodology: Educational Connoisseurship and Criticism through an Ecological Lens

Three questions guided this study: What appears when we look at classroom practice through an ecological lens? How can we organize the implicit and explicit themes that emerge from that lens? What do these themes help us to understand about educational practice? In order to investigate these questions, I used Educational Criticism and Connoisseurship, a qualitative method devised by Elliot Eisner.

"Connoisseurship is the art of appreciation, criticism is the art of disclosure," Eisner explains (2002, p. 215). Through connoisseurship, the researcher utilizes his sensibilities to appreciate the intricacies of a particular artifact, practice, or environment. Connoisseurship requires expertise in order to discern the qualities of that which is being observed or experienced. Connoisseurship is a private act of appreciation. Criticism, then, is the act of making private knowledge public. In order to make private knowledge and appreciation public, the researcher engages in four steps: description (an account *of*), interpretation (an account *for*), evaluation, and thematics. This systematic inquiry guides the informed researcher through the process of disclosure and evaluation of educational practice.

With this study, I wanted to explore classrooms through an ecological lens using Educational Connoisseurship and Criticism. In a research setting, that means first attending to, in the private art of connoisseurship, ecological practices, themes, and ideas evident in classroom. Therefore, by *ecological lens* I mean a perspective that attends to the relationships and interconnectedness, both literal and figurative, present between and among humans and their environments.

Educational criticism from an ecological lens, or *eco-educational criticism*, is the process by which I attempt to describe the intricacies of the classroom environment and practices that can be related to ecological themes. My working definition of eco-educational connoisseurship and criticism is seeing and reseeing concepts and constructs in education as they relate to ecological and environmental issues. By *ecological* I mean situations, ideas, and issues that address the inescapable embeddedness of humans and the environment. By *environmental* I mean issues and problems related to the sustainability of life on our planet, which could include recycling, pollution, and other generally accepted environmental issues or problems. Eco-educational criticism, then, allows me to focus on the ways in which teachers negotiate the materials, physical environment, curricular decisions, and student learning in relation to a broad ecological/environmental perspective while uncovering both the implicit and explicit messages inherent in those decisions. These themes may include environmental issues or scientific concepts; metaphorical understandings, such as connectedness and interdependence; and/or understanding the systems at work that promote balance, stability, and individual and collective growth in a classroom environment. The ecological themes may be present in content, instruction, student-teacher relations, the physical space, materials, or other aspects of a teacher's practice. Through description, interpretation, evaluation, and thematics, the ecological workings of a classroom can be brought to light for the purpose of evaluating the implicit and explicit messages inherent in teachers' intentions and practices.

During my initial observations, I was unsure if the ecological lens would yield anything of interest. I often questioned whether or not it was appropriate to impose an ecological lens on practice that was not explicitly intended to be ecological. However, as the study developed, many ecological themes emerged, many in places that surprised me. As you read the descriptions and interpretations, keep the following themes in mind: *connectedness*, *contexts*, and *learning cycles*. These themes are ecological metaphors that emerged from my observations and were supported by interviews with the teachers. The themes provide a way to think about what is happening in these two classrooms—a way to use ecological metaphors to describe strong teaching practice. I will return to the themes later in the discussion.

Setting and Participants

Because educational connoisseurship and criticism require some expertise in the area of study, I stayed focused on the arena with which I am most knowledgeable—public high school classrooms. I was able to choose two excellent teachers at one large, diverse, suburban high school in the Denver area. I observed each classroom several times over a period of 3 weeks each, and I completed lengthy interviews with each teacher. One classroom was a freshman reading class composed of students reading much below grade level (two to five grade levels below). The topic of study was the novel *Don't Look Behind You*, by Lois Duncan. The second class was an accelerated freshmen geography class studying the effects of rainforest destruction. Although only one of the lessons was devoted to explicit environmental curriculum, I found ecological themes throughout both of these educational environments.

During and after my observations and interviews, I analyzed the data for ecological themes paying particular attention to those themes that seemed essential to the teachers' practices. Using common definitions and understandings of ecology, I found that three ideas inherent in ecological studies could shed light on the activities in these teachers' classrooms. Those themes were connectedness, contexts, and cycles. Certainly there were others, but I observed practices in both classrooms that relied on these ideas. In other words, neither teacher's practice would look the same if any one of these principles was missing.

To illustrate this point, I first describe each teacher's practice in detail. I include details and dialogue that specifically relate the emergent themes. Next, I explain the emergent themes—connectedness, contexts, and cycles—as they are in nature and what they mean for classroom practice. Then I elaborate on how the themes play out in each teacher's practice before offering implications of the study. It is important to note that the major findings of this study are the emergent ecological themes that can be used to describe strong educational practice. Along the way, I provide charts as a way of organizing and summarizing each section.

SCANNING THE LANDSCAPE

Ms. Riley's Reading Class

I mix with a trickle of students as we enter Ms. Riley's freshmen reading class. I move to a seemingly inconspicuous corner back by the picture window and a mostly empty book shelf, adorned only with five empty, metal baskets. Along the back wall, next to the huge window covered by closed gray mini blinds, stretches a clean blackboard. The chalk tray is lined with books instead of chalk, and the board is covered with student work, rather than teacher's notes. "Books we suggest" reads the poster identifying the parade of texts. The south wall, painted eggshell white, is flanked by two large beige cabinets. The cabinet doors dangle languidly open revealing piles of thick three-ring binders on the inside shelves. Students dig through the piles and pull out their own notebooks as Ms. Riley brightly greets them.

"Hi! How are you?" Ms. Riley smiles and makes eye contact with each member of the class. "I want to reiterate how important it is to be here daily and on time. We will be reading a novel, so you will want to be here for all of it. What questions do you have about that?" Students continue to shuffle about organizing themselves for the day. One student tries to push the cabinet doors closed, but they stubbornly swing open again. On top of one cabinet is a butcher-paper covered box labeled "BOX" in large black letters. Behind it are three Denzel Washington "READ" posters alongside a student-made superhero poster. The posters almost run in to a teacher-made sign on the wall composed of black lettering on brown butcher paper. It reads "Reading Strategies—Background Knowledge, Purpose, Marking the Text" with each strategy written in a different color. Underneath the sign, stacks of papers and books precariously cover a trapezoidal table toward the front of the room. The stacks cover part of the front bulletin board, which is saturated with typed strips of suffixes, prefixes, and root words.

Ms. Riley turns on the overhead projector, which is placed at the center of the front of the room. She explains the importance of owning words as students read, and she shows them a list of words they will *own*, including *contentment, respective, retaliate, and oration*. The directions are on a colorful flip chart. "You will choose a word and then follow the directions for your respective word," Ms. Riley explains as she points to the directions.

Behind the overhead projector and flip chart stand hangs a second large blackboard, mostly clean. A student-made poster is taped on the far left side. It shows a girl looking in a broken mirror underneath the title, *You Can't Sniff Away your Scorpions*. Hanging from clips above the blackboard are plastic key-shaped posters with motivational words and phrases like *commitment*, *speak with good purpose*, *this is it*, and *flexibility*. To the right of the blackboard is another bulletin board entitled "Things We Read." Included are bumper stickers, *Parade* magazine, *Sports Illustrated*, cartoons, and a word search. The classroom door is just to the right of this bulletin board, which seems to bridge the outside world and the inside classroom experience.

The north wall is largely open, but a huge bulletin board covered in light blue paper reads boldly "Text to Self, Text to World, Text to Text." A yellow smiley face, a round picture of the earth, and a book punctuate each phrase. This bulletin board is accompanied by a "Four Step Poetry Read" poster, which urges students first to read for enjoyment, second read for meaning, third read for language and structure, and fourth read for how the poem makes them feel. The last wall companion is a map of the earth with every country's flag lining the borders, and that poster hangs above the bookshelf with the empty metal baskets behind where I sit.

Ms. Riley springs around the classroom in a sleeveless sweater, black dress pants, and Merrill flip-flops, the only sign of her rheumatoid arthritis. Ms. Riley's blonde curly hair and wafer-thin frame exude energy, optimism, and care for her students. "I treat them like I want them to become, versus who some of them are—troublemakers. Some of them just came out of the foot, which would be juvie. I treat them like I want them to become—adults, responsible, and really successful." Ms. Riley uses the power of language, positive reinforcement, and kindness to create pathways for students in to the world of school, which for some of her students is their only safe place.

Ms. Riley always assumes the best intentions in her students. One class period before she arrived, I watched as students were searching the room for something, and their intentions seemed less than honorable. Ms. Riley walked in and said, "Hi Jerrod. Are you looking for a good book to read?" Jerrod smiled and slunk back to his seat. He later left the room rapping with a word he had learned that day—*barrage*. In another instance, a student sauntered in to class several minutes late. Ms. Riley said, "Good morning, Ms. Mason. Do you have a pass?" Ms. Mason shook her head and paused next to Ms. Riley. "Well then, you are going to have to get some orthopedic shoes like me so you can get here faster." Ms. Mason smiled and sat at her desk. She led her group in reading aloud that day.

Reading is important here. Text wraps around the room like vines in a swamp; it grows from books, posters, cabinets, bulletin boards, and flipcharts while seeping in to students' lives in *Sports Illustrated*, bumper stickers, and even cartoons. Text lives here. Ms. Riley uses words in her instructions that she wants them to know. "Yesterday you worked on *episodic* notes." "Run up here—*maneuver* yourself so you can be a part of this activity." Her inclusive language provides the context for students' connections between new words and their meanings.

Mr. Lambic's Geography Class

I walk in as Mr. Lambic and his students scurry around just before the first hour bell. Mr. Lambic then moves to the front of the room, his booming voice signaling that class is about to begin. "Are you guys ready to get started?" he invites. "We are going to start the rainforest activity that I talked about." Behind Mr. Lambic is a neatly decorated wall displaying a long chalkboard with the day's lesson outline.

Rainforest
   I. What is it?
  II. Statistics
 III. Reasons for destruction
  IV. Long-term effects

Above the blackboard are 12 laminated posters, calendar size, perfectly spaced and straight, sporting baseball heroes. To the right of the blackboard is Mr. Lambic's desk covered with short, neat stacks of student papers. The floor-to-ceiling window on the adjacent wall is covered with brown metal mini-blinds masking the morning sunlight. The soft white paint on the south wall is broken up by two huge world maps, an embossed leather Aztec calendar, and a Pearl Harbor poster, again straight as a pin. Ten other world maps, a Colorado Avalanche flag, and another 12-poster series displaying various golf swings, complete the wall hangings. Each is perfectly spaced, perfectly straight, and perfectly trimmed. The north wall is softened by a well kept but ancient sofa upholstered with rust-colored farm-scene velvet. The center of the room is occupied by six straight rows of five desks, all with matching wooden tops and blue plastic chairs. Order reigns.

"Go ahead and brainstorm two examples of what would happen if we had no rainforest." As students bend their heads over their notebooks, Mr. Lambic offers three leftover donuts to the class. Several hands sprout up, so he asks, "Who was the last to hit more than 70 homeruns in a season?" "Barry Bonds!" shouts a girl from the center of class, pleased to earn a donut. Two more sports trivia questions determine the donuts' destiny and quell the eager chatter. Students quickly return to jotting ideas down about the destruction of the rainforest as Mr. Lambic throws away the large cardboard donut box.

"I had you write two specific ideas," Mr. Lambic reviews before he asks for their lists. Together the class generates a list of effects of rainforest destruction, including reduction in oxygen, climate change, loss of species (which also included a negative effect on pet stores for one student), and the general disruption of the ecosystem. "Do we all have a basic understanding that all species survive because of others?" Students affirm their understanding, and Mr. Lambic proceeds with a brief and inclusive lecture on the rainforest addressing each of the four points listed on the board.

Students learn that temperature and rainfall determine the location of rainforests, which they place between the tropic of cancer and Capricorn. Next, Mr. Lambic recites shocking statistics about the rate of rainforest destruction—30,000 square miles are destroyed every year. "What are the reasons for the destruction?" he asks. Mr. Lambic walks to the front board, and with a white piece of chalk, he sketches the rainforest. He includes trees of varying heights and writes three words on next to the drawing: 1. Above; 2. Ground; 3. Below.

He walks to the back of the classroom and sits in a vacant desk. He explains that above ground, the trees are harvested for their lumber, such as mahogany and teak. This answer I expected, and I was prepared for the familiar, requisite guilt for being a greedy westerner harvesting the raw materials of the exotic tropics. The second category, ground, does not elicit my own guilt, but instead sympathy. "People in developing countries need the land to farm. But rainforest soil is no good without the replenishing nutrients of the plants, so the land quickly becomes fallow. Then, the farmers slash and burn more ground." The final category, below, includes coal mining, which is an international commodity. Again, a small pang of guilt.

"Ultimately, the goal of the lesson is for students to figure out what the effects of destruction of the rainforest are." Mr. Lambic's intentions are fairly straightforward; he wants them to be knowledgeable. He states:

I don't know if it is my role as a teacher to ask them to change their lifestyles—to be more sustainable—that would make me uncomfortable—to push my own agenda. But I want them to have the knowledge, and then they will know what to do with it. It is clear to them that the destruction of the rainforest is partially their responsibility as consumers. Are they still going to be apathetic? Probably. But they are 14 years old. They will start to see the big picture. This is one building block.

Mr. Lambic's intentions for his students to become knowledgeable are supported by his lesson plan structure. Students chose from a list of rainforest products like tuba root, ylang-ylang, or teak, and they were each responsible for researching the product and creating a well-organized poster from which the class would learn. On the third day of the lesson, students hung their posters and then walked around the room taking notes from each other's work. Each student learned from others' expertise.

In this way, the students' voices, and in a sense the rainforest's voice, spoke the loudest. This was not simply a lecture on environmental degradation. Mr. Lambic is cautious about letting his own politics taint the classroom. "Destruction of the rainforest is an outcome of capitalism. That sounds kind of liberal, and I would never say I am liberal, but that is the truth." When I asked him, however, if he considered himself an environmentalist, after a long pause he said':

Yeah ... in a way. I think there are different types of environmentalists. There are ones who burn down ski lodges, and there are ones who understand that (living sustainably) is just the best thing to do. There are different ways to participate in an interest that you have. If you are an environmentalist, you have compassion for the environment in one way or another. And you can have compassion for the environment no matter what your political ideologies are. Being an environmentalist means more than being outside. It means keeping Mother Nature in balance. That is the way it was intended.

ZOOMING IN ON THE NICHE: VALUE AND EVALUATION

The two distinct accounts of Ms. Riley and Mr. Lambic may seem to have little in common. However, an ecological perspective illuminates several underlying systems at work, all of which contribute to their effective teaching practices.

We can evaluate educational practice using three ecological concepts or themes that emerged during the study: connectedness, context, and learning cycles (see Table 10.1).

Table 10.1. Ecological Framework for Evaluation

	Connectedness	Contexts	Learning Cycles
Content and Pedagogy	Interdisciplinary; related to school and nonschool world; Eco-pedagogy	Technology, materials; Relevant to student needs	Knowledge sources: Blend of teacher, student, and expert; Pacing, fluctuating activities

Connectedness

Connectedness as an ecological concept shows the interrelatedness of all things. Connectedness, as an educational concept, shows the degree to which content is related to other disciplines, previously studied ideas, student lives, and the nonschool world (see Orr, 1992, pp. 85-95; Orr, 1994, pp. 89-98). From an instructional stand point, we can also describe the ways in which teachers employ "eco-pedagogy," which is the tension and relation between seemingly opposite philosophies (see Jardine, 2000, pp. 47-68).

Contexts

Ecological contexts help us to see the necessity and type of environment required for growth. In nature, ecological niches, or ecosystems, support growth of all organisms within it. All life within an ecosystem is interdependent, and the health of the system relies on diversity. A healthy ecosystem relies on its members having access to nourishment for growth so that they in turn can fulfill their places in the niche. An educational context, when viewed through this metaphor, includes the physical environment, the types of materials used (or not used), and the degree to which the environment (place) supports growth of students, their learning, and the interdependence within the community. Contexts help us to understand the degree to which teachers create meaningful learning experiences that are relevant to student needs.

Cycles

In nature, cycles promote the regeneration of life and provide sources of nourishment through cyclical change and phases of action and dormancy. Seasons, the food chain, tides, and phases of the moon are just a few examples of observable natural cycles. In an educational setting, cycles of learning include instructional strategies and ways of knowing. John Dewey's (1938/1997) criteria for experience, which requires continuity and interaction, is one example of a learning cycle. Experiences must be connected to previous and future experiences, and the combination of various modes and processes of learning regenerate the educational environment and intellectual processes.

We also can view learning cycles as those which connect learning and action as promoted by stages of action and reflection during an educational experience. As Dewey (1916/1944) explains, "reflection is the acceptance of (the) responsibility for the future consequences which flow from present action" (p. 146). In this way, consequences of knowledge and action are explored. *Knowledge* is not an end in itself, but a part of a larger cycle or way of being.

Cycles of learning also may include the sources of knowledge, including that of the teacher, the student, and the expert. These cycles of knowledge work together to form a *knowledge ecosystem*, or interconnected and overlapping set of ideas that is greater than the sum of its parts. Learning cycles, like cycles in nature, allow time for learning, reflection, action, and creation.

Ecological Content and Pedagogy in Ms. Riley's Class

Clearly the intent of Ms. Riley's unit on *Don't Look Behind You* has little to do with the environment. However, her methods are strikingly ecological. Ms. Riley uses reading strategies that connect school and life. From the bulletin board that holds bumper stickers and comic strips to her attention to reading strategies for all disciplines, Ms. Riley's class radiates relationships to other courses and to the students' lives. The context is congruous with the content in Ms. Riley's class, and it supports growth and learning.

Table 10.2. Ecological Evaluation of Ms. Riley's Classroom

	Connectedness	*Contexts*	*Learning Cycles*
Content and Pedagogy	Reading strategies connect school and life; Combines phonics and whole language approaches	Integrated with lessons; manipulatives; student generated work adorns walls; context reinforces concepts; Reading-level appropriate materials; high interest	Text to self-text to text-text to world; accessing background knowledge; questioning the text; Varied individual and group activities; time for sharing and reflecting

The context also fosters interdependence among students. The walls speak the lessons students are learning, and the physical environment celebrates students' successes, as well as values their opinions. An extremely diverse population of students works together to learn and practice reading is supported by a full expression of culture and individuality. The classroom is healthy because, as in a natural ecosystem, diversity thrives.

Finally, Ms. Riley's class is a conglomeration of knowledge, ideas, and questions that come from a variety of sources, including genuine questions from the teacher about what she is reading. By using words students are expected to know in her instructions, Ms. Riley blurs the lines between student and expert, teacher and students, class and real world. The giant bulletin board boasts a clear learning cycle: text to self, text to world, text to text. By teaching students that knowledge is bound up in connections, the learning cycle allows students' knowledge and ideas to enter the world of experts. For Ms. Riley's low-performing students, this is a gift.

Ecological Content and Pedagogy in Mr. Lambic's Class

Mr. Lambic's lesson on the destruction of the rainforest clearly has environmental content. But his lesson also includes ecological concepts that go beyond what we might consider traditional environmental education. In terms of content, Mr. Lambic relied on contributions from other areas of study besides geography including economics, politics, and science. From the first moment students began this lesson, he asked them to brainstorm what would happen if the rainforest disappeared. In order for students to analyze this effect, they would have to have some knowledge of the causes, which accesses their background knowledge and scaffolds new information. Mr. Lambic's actions, with the exception of throwing away a recyclable donut box, matched the message he was trying to con-

Table 10.3. Ecological Evaluation of Mr. Lambic's Classroom

	Connectedness	*Contexts*	*Learning Cycles*
Content and Pedagogy	Combines geography, economics, politics, and science; Utilizes Hunter structure with constructivist components	Efficient use of materials; Age appropriate topic; connected to student life styles	Students as experts; teacher as knowledgeable resource but not only resource; Sharing student knowledge is integral part of lesson; time for reflection and synthesis of personal knowledge

vey. The context as measured by the materials he used supported the concepts of the lesson. The physical environment reinforced the expectation of order and sequence as evidenced by the perfectly aligned posters and meticulous organization of materials and lesson (4 steps).

Very few materials were used. Students took about one page of notes. They had one double-sided handout, and each student created one small poster. Most of the research was done through the Internet rather than in printed materials. This research and poster process allowed students to be experts and the teacher to be a knowledgeable resource, but not the only source of information.

Mr. Lambic's teaching style is a bit more traditional than Ms. Riley's. Clearly he is the authority in the classroom as evidenced by his deep, confident voice and clear, precise directions about what students are to do minute to minute. However, Mr. Lambic draws on a variety of learning theories such as constructivism. Furthermore, the pedagogical choices he makes—to have students research a product that is in their medicine cabinets and that contributes to the destruction of the rainforest—connect student life styles and choices to school life. The pedagogical context breaks down the walls between school knowledge and *useful* knowledge.

Finally, learning cycles in Mr. Lambic's class, while largely seated in the absorption of knowledge, also thrive on highlighting student knowledge both through questioning during lectures and during information sharing. Students are also given time to work independently as they reflect and synthesize the information they have absorbed.

SEEING WITH NEW EYES: SYNTHESIS AND FINDINGS

Both Ms. Riley and Mr. Lambic have similar intentions for their students: to learn content in their classes that is relevant to students' lives outside of school, and for students to grow and change because of lessons and activities in their classrooms. We can see through the ecological lens that each teacher achieves this goal in a variety of ways that are brought into focus by connectedness, contexts, and learning cycles. Furthermore, we see that the ecological lens has zeroed in on the ways in which teachers employ these techniques to contribute to their students' learning. The study suggests that perhaps ecological practices are inherent in good teaching.

Turning again to the three emergent themes, each one shows a powerful tool or approach to teaching and learning. Connectedness in both classrooms helps students to explore life beyond the classroom walls and see relevance in their education. Moreover, the learning contexts support the teachers' intentions and strategies. Learning cycles allow students' to explore ideas in a variety of ways. The use of the ecological lens brought these ideas to light, and it shows a way to bridge environmental education with traditional schools.

This finding warrants further investigation, and it might help us to answer the question of whether ecological perspectives in education benefit students and humans as well as the earth. In future studies, I also might apply the ecological framework to new environments, such as supplemental environmental education curriculum, private schools, or rural schools. I also believe there is room to expand the ecological framework, which might include themes of community and creativity, as well as more emphasis on interdependence.

DISCUSSION AND CONCLUSION

I believe that as long as we continue to argue that environmental education primarily benefits the environment, it will have a limited place in the schools. We must make environmental education about human beings and about children, not just about the environment. Are there ecological practices that enhance all learning, not just that of earth-centered/environmental learning?

The intention of this study was to use an ecological framework for understanding, interpreting, and evaluating a classroom setting. What appears when we look at classroom practice through an ecological lens? How can we organize the implicit and explicit themes that emerge from that lens? What do these themes help us to understand about education and ecology? In exploring these questions, I have found that there is substantial common ground between sound educational practices and sustaining ecological concepts.

As the ecological framework emerged, I saw that ecological concepts lurk wherever we turn. Perhaps this is because we are ecological beings, even if we do not always recognize this situation. The framework suggests categories (connectedness, contexts, and learning cycles) that indicate the degree to which we are in touch with the power of an ecological metaphor for education. By bringing these ideas to the forefront, we may begin to see teaching and learning as sources for ecological and human renewal.

REFERENCES

Dewey, J. (1944). *Democracy and education*. New York: Simon and Schuster. (Original work published 1916)

Dewey, J. (1997). *Experience and education*. New York: Simon and Schuster. (Original work published 1938)

Eisner, E. (2002). *The educational imagination* (3rd ed.) Upper Saddle River, NJ: Merrill Prentice Hall.

Hutchison, D. (1998). *Growing up green: Education for ecological renewal*. New York: Teachers College Press.

Jardine, D. (2000). *Under the tough old stars: Ecopedagogical essays*. Brandon, VT: Solomon.

Orr, D. (1992). *Ecological literacy: Education and the transition to a postmodern world*. Albany: State University of New York.

Orr, D. (1994). *Earth in mind: On education, environment, and the human prospect*. Wahington , DC: Island.

CHAPTER 11

THE CONNECTION BETWEEN MEDIA VIEWING AND LITERACY SKILLS

An Action Research Study

Teresa Russell and David W. Nicholson

> This action research study, conducted by a high school English teacher, examines student transfer of literacy skills between a critical media viewing elective course and a traditional English literature course. The findings suggest that critical viewing of media aids in the acquisition of literacy skills.

INTRODUCTION

TV or not TV; that is the question. Educators differ on the value of using film and television as teaching tools in the classroom. Many opponents feel that video instruction hinders the development of literacy skills, while others remain undecided about the effects. Another view suggests that media viewing can be a powerful instructional tool, being an extremely relevant medium to today's electronically immersed students. Responses compiled from seniors enrolled in a critical viewing course tend to support using film and television as academic tools. In addition, assessment activities conducted in a traditional English literature course and a critical viewing course support the contention that critical viewing of media aids in the acquisition of literacy skills.

As a secondary English teacher, my responsibilities entail teaching students the art of language acquisition. One particular aspect of my duties, teaching a course on critical viewing of media, has caused me to revisit my philosophy on film and television use in the classroom. This elective course, open to seniors, develops literacy, critical thinking, and writing skills using film and television as instructional tools. The Mid-continent Research for Education and Learning Website (McREL, 2005) has developed standards for viewing skills instruction that emphasize interpreting and critiquing the visual, auditory, language, format, technical, and stylistic choices of the various media. For the purposes of the course, critical viewing is defined as analysis and interpretation of the interaction of form and content in media productions (i.e., television, film, and video). Students in the critical viewing course explore the various ways different media convey information, express ideas, portray characters, and examine themes. Objectives for the course include gaining an understanding of film and television history, developing an awareness of different genres in film and television, recognizing and analyzing audio and visual elements in media, and examining the effects of media on culture.

In my experience, students in the critical viewing course appear to develop improved literacy skills and, during the course, begin to better comprehend literary elements in comparison to students enrolled in traditional English courses. I have often wondered if the use of tools such as videotapes aid in the development of these skills. To address this question, I administered two surveys and two assessment activities in these classes to collect information on student acquisition, retention, and application of specific literary terminology shared within the context of the respective courses.

The literature on the instructional effectiveness of media such as film, video, and television offers inconclusive findings. Researchers and theorists disagree about the value of incorporating critical viewing skills in the curriculum. Certain educators maintain that use of media in the classroom may actually deter literacy development. The findings of this study suggest otherwise. The students in the critical viewing classes scored higher overall on the assessments than the students in the literature classes, and the literature students showed a marked improvement in recall and use of literary terms when content was presented in both written and videotaped forms. On the surveys, critical viewing students reported an increased understanding of literary elements. These findings support my initial observation that incorporating critical viewing of media into instruction aids in the acquisition of literacy skills.

LITERATURE REVIEW

Research on the effectiveness of media to achieve instructional objectives has often focused on the learner's ability to comprehend and recall factual information. In a seminal review of media research, Clark (1983) argues that studies on the instructional effectiveness of media "clearly suggest that media do not influence learning under any conditions" (p. 445). He contends that the content of a presentation, not the form, remains the critical factor in learning, concluding that media "are mere vehicles that deliver instruction but do not influence student achievement any more than the truck that delivers our groceries causes changes in our nutrition" (p. 445). Most reviews of research conclude that little difference can be detected in a direct comparison between media presentation and conventional classroom instruction when the same information is conveyed (Wetzel, Radtke, & Stern, 1994).

David Walsh (2002), president of the National Institute on Media and Family, believes that television viewing habits deter children from reading, adversely affecting their literacy development. Walsh supports this assertion with data obtained from the 2000 National Assessment of Educational Progress (NAEP), which reports that students who watch television more than 6 hours per day scored lower than students who watch television fewer than 3 hours per day. Freeman (1997) cites research supporting her claim that television's effects on students include decreased reading, writing, and thinking skills.

Others argue that teaching critical viewing of media in the classroom has benefits. Educators interested in media literacy have begun to shift the emphasis from media as a delivery system to media as a means of developing literacy among different forms. Gardner (1997) observes that contemporary society expects individuals to master and purposively use various media, each entailing different forms of literacy. Hobbs (1997) contends that an expanded concept of literacy, to include media literacy, develops higher-order thinking skills.

Kozma (1991) offers a review of research that suggests viewers may demonstrate greater recall and more actively process content when presented with a combination of verbal, auditory, and visual information. The Association for Educational Communications and Technology (AECT, 2001), in a review of formative and summative evaluations and experimental studies, offers evidence of positive results from integrating critical viewing into classroom instruction. Critical viewing can increase knowledge of television's symbols and codes and awareness of the social aspects of the medium.

Critical viewing may serve as a means to transfer literacy from one form to another. Singer and Singer (1998) report on research that demonstrates media literacy instruction can increase comprehension of story content and other specific cognitive skills. In a study by Hobbs and Frost (2003), students in a media literacy treatment group achieved higher reading comprehension scores than a control group. The authors suggest that the students who received media literacy instruction were better able to identify specific techniques used to create messages. The purpose of this action research study focuses on indications that critical viewing of media can assist students in acquiring and applying literacy skills.

METHODS

This action research study collected data at a rural high school (student population approximately 1,000, predominantly White, equal ratio of males to females) using (a) two survey instruments and a (b) quasi-experimental design. The surveys were administered in the spring of 2003 to senior students enrolled in a critical viewing course and an English 12 literature course. The quasi-experiment compared the two intact groups using two assessments. A quasi-experiment was conducted in the spring of 2003 and subsequently replicated in the fall of 2003 (assisted by a student teacher). A second replication was conducted in the spring of 2004; however, records and data were lost during a classroom relocation. Currently, the study is being replicated for a third time, comparing students in the critical viewing course with students in an Advanced Placement English course.

The open-ended surveys were used to determine the reading and television viewing habits of students and their response to critical viewing instruction. Survey One (Appendix A) was administered at the beginning of the 2003 spring semester to 64 twelfth-grade students in the English and critical viewing classes. Adapted from Owen, Silet, and Brown (1998), the survey asked students to respond to seven questions related to reading preferences and television viewing habits. Additionally, students were asked which medium they felt was most beneficial in helping them to remember specific facts or details. Likewise, the survey questioned students whether they felt it was easier to comprehend a book or video and which medium (book or television) they felt was easier to write about. Finally, students responded to specific questions relating to reading and viewing genres. For each question, students were asked to explain why they answered the way they did.

Survey Two (Appendix B) was administered near the end of the semester to 23 critical viewing students to determine if students perceived that the course had helped them to better understand the basic elements of literature, such as plot, character, and genre. It also questioned students' beliefs as to whether or not the skills taught in the course had assisted them in writing about the elements discussed. Students were asked to elaborate specifically as to what and why they felt critical viewing had helped them in attaining literacy acquisition skills. They also were asked if they believed teachers should use videos to enhance instruction. Finally, students responded to questions regarding personal benefits from video instruction.

Two classroom activities, in the form of assessments, compare the acquisition and application of literary terms between the critical viewing and traditional English classes. Activity One, a reading/viewing comparison, was administered to 24 students in the spring 2003 critical viewing class and to 19 students in the fall 2003 critical viewing class. Students read aloud the short story, "The Tell-Tale Heart" by Edgar Alan Poe (1843/2004). Upon completion of the reading activity, students wrote down as many facts about the story as they could recall in 10 minutes. Next, students were shown a video version of *The Tell-Tale Heart* (Carver, 1991). This particular video selection, running about 30 minutes, adheres to the story line nearly verbatim. After the viewing, the papers listing facts recalled from reading the story were returned to each student. Students were asked to read the facts they had listed for the story and to write down any additional facts observed in the video but not noticed from reading.

Activity Two was administered in spring 2003 to 24 seniors in the English class and 23 seniors in the critical viewing class and in fall 2003 to 18 seniors in the English class and 22 seniors in the critical viewing class. The activity was comprised of literary terminology application questions, based on the selection read or viewed. The students applied the following terms: genre, theme, plot, suspense, setting, atmosphere, character, protagonist, antagonist, dynamic character, static character, stereotypical character, motif, epiphany, predictable, formula, montage, and comic relief. Students in the English class were asked to apply the terms to the literary epic, *Beowulf* (Raffel, 2000). Literary terminology was taught prior to, during, and after reading the selection. A comparable video of *Beowulf* was not available for viewing. Therefore, students in the critical viewing class were asked to apply the same terminology to the film, *On the Waterfront* (Spiegel & Kazan, 1954). The term *montage* was included in this class's activity because it is a critical viewing term.

FINDINGS

Surveys

To analyze Survey One (Appendix A), spring 2003 respondents were divided into two categories based on individual perception of self: readers (54.7%) and nonreaders (45.3%). These two categories enabled comparison of preferences and learning styles between readers and nonreaders. Both readers and nonreaders replied similarly as to reasons why they embodied certain preferences. For example, when questioning students as to why they read on their own, or read outside assignments required for school, most replied that they read because they found reading enjoyable and interesting. By comparison, students who watch television and film outside the classroom stated that they did so because viewing was entertaining and enjoyable. Additionally, both readers and viewers stated they participated in their preferred activity for educational purposes, for reasons of escape, for stress relief or relaxation, and for keeping their minds occupied. Trivial reasons such as boredom, easy activity, and medium to help induce sleep were also supplied for viewing. All 64 students surveyed affirmed that they were viewers. However, only 35 students identified themselves as readers. The 29 students who identified themselves as non-readers stated they did not have enough time to read due to school, work, and/or other activities. On the other hand, these students did find time to watch television. Other reasons students stated for not reading included lack of interest and laziness. Some students felt reading was too much like work, that it was pointless, and that they simply had better things to do.

The overwhelmingly favorite genre within television and film for readers and nonreaders alike was comedy. The students appeared to choose this genre because they enjoy being entertained. When students were questioned as to memory of details, an overwhelming majority of readers (57%) and nonreaders (79%) felt they remembered more facts, for a longer period of time, from viewing. The students who held this view reported that viewing afforded them a medium where facts and details were easier to visualize, which aided comprehension. Students also were asked to identify which medium was easier for them to understand--a book or a video. Again, the majority of readers (77%) and nonreaders (84%) stated that videos were easier to understand than books. The most common reasons provided were seeing helps understanding, videos show more (vivid) details, words are harder to understand, and details are explained. The last question on the survey asked students which was easier from them to write about—a book or a video. A majority of readers (51%) and nonreaders (69%) alike stated they felt it was easier to write from a literary perspective about videos. Various responses, which were inclusive for both groups, stated that visualization made it easier to write as well as to comprehend, made recall easier, and made the plot easier to follow, which in turn made it easier to know exactly what happens.

On Survey Two (Appendix B), a vast majority (91%) responded that the critical viewing class had helped them better understand the elements of literature. The same majority (91%) believed that the class had been beneficial in helping them write about the basic elements of literature. When asked to comment on which elements of the class had helped the most, students chose discussions (28.5%), visuals (28.5%), discussions plus visuals (9.5%), and writing assignments based on literary elements (33.3%) as being the most beneficial components of literary acquisition. Additionally, students stated that discussions helped them to see things they missed and allowed them to see different points of view. Visuals helped them to see emotions, which aided understanding. Discussions in conjunction with visuals helped students to see and understand vocabulary and identify technical aspects of filmmaking. Writing exercises allowed students to visualize the plot, to comprehend the story, to more fully analyze the elements of the story, and to practice writing in different formats and styles. Due to these reasons, students (95%) felt teachers should incorporate video instruction into lessons when possible. Specific literary elements students reported they now understood better, after only one semester (8.5 weeks) of critical viewing class, included genre (23.8%), theme (23.8), characterization (23.8%), and plot (23.8%).

Activity One: "The Tell-Tale Heart"

Activity One used both reading and viewing to assess comprehension and recall of factual information. Students were categorized into three groups (strong, average, and weak) based on reading ability. An instrument adapted by Marshall University from Pinnell (2002), which coded student reading behaviors, determined the reading levels. In spring 2003, 24 students recalled 272 facts from reading "The Tell-Tale Heart." However, when allowed to view the video as well, these same students observed an additional 162 facts, an increase of 60%. The strong readers retained 169 facts from reading and observed an additional 90 facts from viewing the video (a 53% increase.) The average readers appeared to fare even better when aided with the medium of video. Reading the story garnered this group of students a total of 99 facts, and a total of 64 facts was added to their list of observances when aided with video, resulting in a 65% increase. The most dramatic observance occurred with the weak reader. For this category, only four facts were recalled from reading the short

Table 11.1. Activity One: Reading/Video Comprehension (*The Tell-Tale Heart*)

Reading Ability	Facts from Reading	Additional Facts from Video Viewing	% Increase
Critical Viewing Class Summary (Spring 2003)			
Strong (n = 13, 5*)	169	90	53
Average (n = 10, 6*)	99	64	65
Weak (n = 1, 1*)	4	8	200
All students (n = 24)	272	162	60
Critical Viewing Class Summary (Fall 2003)			
Strong (n = 9, 2**)	70	103	147
Average (n = 9, 3**)	38	77	203
Weak (n = 1, 1**)	4	4	100
All students (n = 19)	112	188	168

*Denotes 12 students also concurrently enrolled in English literature course.
**Denotes 6 students also concurrently enrolled in English literature course.

story selection. When allowed to view the story, this student observed eight additional facts, a dramatic increase of 200%.

The fall 2003 replication produced higher results. Nineteen critical viewing students recalled 112 facts from reading "The Tell-Tale Heart" and an additional 188 facts from viewing the video, an increase of 168%. The strong readers recalled 70 facts from reading and an additional 103 facts from viewing (a 147% increase); the average readers 38 facts from reading and 77 facts from viewing (203% increase); the weak reader 4 facts from reading and 4 facts from viewing (100% increase).

Activity Two: *Beowulf*

Activity Two took two forms. Students in the English class were assessed on the application of literary terms based on reading *Beowulf*; students in the critical viewing class were assessed on the application of literary terms based on viewing *On the Waterfront*.

In the spring 2003 English class, 17 items multiplied by 24 students yielded a total of 408 responses in applying literary terms to *Beowulf*. Of these responses, 276 were correct, which translates into 67.6% of the students being able to apply the literary terminology correctly. Students were classified as strong, average, or weak based on a combination of reading ability, classroom performance (i.e., grades), and overall grade point average. Strong students ($n = 6$) answered 73.5% items correctly, average students ($n = 13$) 69%, and weak students ($n = 5$) 57.6%. Overall, only two students missed the basic terms of setting, protagonist, and antagonist (92% correct) while fourteen students each missed epiphany, formula, stereotype, and static character (42% correct). Eleven students were unable to identify a specific character from the epic (54% correct).

The fall 2003 replication produced similar results. Nineteen students recalled 195 items out of 289 (67% correct). Strong students ($n = 3$) answered 88% items correctly, average students ($n = 10$) 70.5%, and weak students ($n = 4$) 44%. The highest scores were recorded for atmosphere (94% correct) and character, protagonist, and antagonist (89% correct). The lowest scores were for stereotypical character (44% correct), epiphany (33% correct), and motif (28% correct). The high results are similar for protagonist and antagonist, the low results for epiphany. The biggest differences were character (54% in spring, 89% in fall) and motif (71% in spring, 28% in fall).

Activity Two: *On the Waterfront*

Activity Two for the spring 2003 Critical Viewing class resulted in 414 responses (18 items multiplied by 23 students) for *On the Waterfront*. Of these responses, 356 were correct (86%). Strong students ($n = 10$) answered 93% items correctly, average students ($n = 11$) 82%, and weak students ($n = 2$) 72%. As was the case in the English class, the most missed term overall was formula (13 students, or 56.5%, responded incorrectly). Only one student in this class missed the term plot, and one student was unable to identify a specific character. The most amazing result was that no students missed genre, dynamic character, antagonist, comic relief, or predictable (100% correct responses). Although it only had been introduced on two previous occasions and was not taught specifically for the film viewing, the term montage was correctly applied by 56.5% of the students.

In the fall of 2003, 22 students supplied 396 responses, with 340 (86%) correct, the same percentage as the spring. The results were nearly identical for each category of student: strong students ($n = 6$) answered 94% items correctly, average students ($n = 15$) 83%, and the weak student ($n = 1$) 72%. Students scored 100% on genre, plot, setting, and comic relief (genre and comic relief score shared with spring class, plot was nearly identical). Montage was emphasized more in instruction, producing a higher score of 77%. The lowest score was a 50% on motif, which was also the lowest score in the English class (28%).

The most striking findings occur from comparing the Activity Two results. First, results from both the spring study and the fall replication remain highly consistent. The overall scores of the two English classes on *Beowulf* match extremely closely (67.6% and 67% respectively), and the *On the Waterfront* results are identical (both 86%). In the subcategories from the critical viewing classes, the strong students scored 93% in the spring and 94% in the fall, the average students 82% in the spring and 83% in the fall, and the weak students scored 72% in both fall and spring. The results from the critical viewing classes are also consistently higher than those from the English classes. Overall, and in each subcategory, the students in the critical viewing classes conspicuously outperformed the students in the English classes in applying literary terminology.

One might speculate that students found viewing the film an easier and more accessible task than reading the epic poem. However, I selected *Beowulf* because it is a reading assignment that most students have enjoyed and related to in past classes, partly due to its heroic themes and action. In contrast, *On the Waterfront* has been a difficult lesson for most students because it derives from an era with which they do not associate themselves. Additionally, students today are accustomed to viewing color films, not black and white. Consequently, the storyline and characterizations need to be strong to hold students' attention and overcome their resistance. These factors dissuade me from attributing the differences in the results solely to the argument that film is an *easier* medium to comprehend than print.

LIMITATIONS

Due to the nature of this study (action research conducted by a classroom teacher), not all questions regarding the research design can be fully satisfied. The survey data was intended to inform my instruction by providing background knowledge about my students and to serve as a means to ascertain student perceptions of the value and effectiveness of the critical viewing course. That information does not claim to verify the premise that critical viewing instruction can increase students' ability to acquire and apply literacy skills. However, those responses provide descriptive findings valuable in revising and refining the course curriculum, instruction, and objectives.

The use of the two assessment activities did not adhere to the rigor of a true quasi-experiment. This action research study emerged from reflection about my own practice and the comparisons between classes developed out of actual instruction. One error detected during analysis was the lack of control between the two groups. One may note that in Table 11.1,

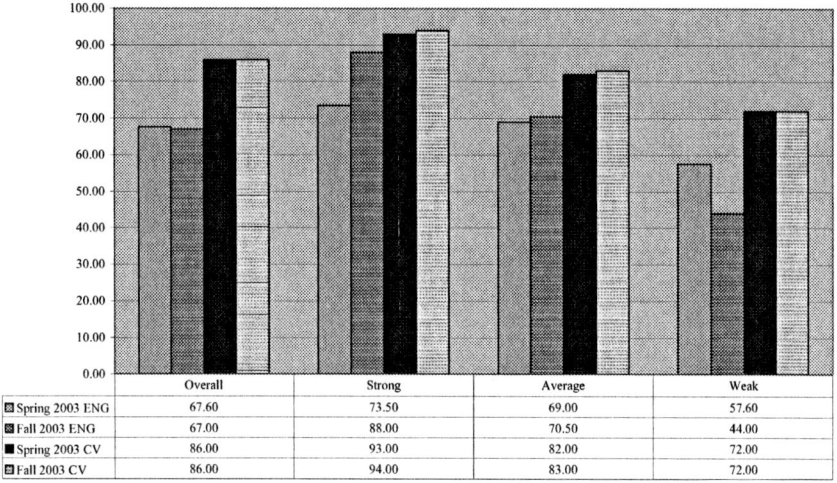

Figure 11.1. Activity two: Literary terminology activity.

a number of students were concurrently enrolled in both the critical viewing and the English classes (marked by an asterisk). From the outset, the coding process should have distinguished between students enrolled in either one class or the other, or concurrently in both, to better report differences on the assessments.

Another weakness is that the results only report scores on posttests; no pretests were administered prior to instruction. In response, Activity One, on "The Tell-Tale Heart," measured additional facts recalled after first reading the story and then viewing the video. The intention was to show an initial score from reading and a subsequent score from viewing, and as such functioned as my version of a pretest/posttest design. Feedback received from colleagues on this activity further recommends that I conduct more than one version of the comparison. One group could read the story first and view the video second, while another group could reverse this order, viewing the video first and reading the story second. This could help determine if viewing increased the scores or if the combination of reading and viewing accounts for the increased recall of information. More variations are possible. A group could read the story, take the assessment, and then reread the story; a group could view the video only, take the assessment, and then review the video. Practical time considerations may prevent exploring all these possible avenues.

Activity Two used two different texts as source material. Students read *Beowulf* in one class but viewed *On the Waterfront* in the other. One might conclude that I assumed the two were equivalent. As explained above, I was unable to locate a video or film version of *Beowulf* through available sources. My choice of *On the Waterfront* may appear arbitrary, and that could confuse the reader when comparing the findings between the two classes. However, in my experience, acquiring literary terminology from viewing the film *On the Waterfront* is more difficult for the high school students I teach than acquiring the same terminology from reading *Beowulf*. I agree that a better choice for a future comparison would be to select a film adaptation of a novel, and have student experience both versions. In this case, *Beowulf* was required reading for the course and could not be substituted.

Finally, I initiated this research in my own classroom to use the results to affect changes in my own practice. Because of that, and due to the above limitations, generalizability to other classrooms and other students was not an objective of this particular study. Therefore, the analysis does not report tests for external validity or statistical significance. However, the findings suggest that further study using more controlled methods may be of great interest and relevance.

IMPLICATIONS

In an era of standards-driven instruction and high stakes assessment, teachers who offer electives often find themselves in the position of defending and justifying the existence of these courses in the secondary curriculum. The development of literacy skills remains a cornerstone for reform efforts in schools. In the context of this study, critical viewing appears to reinforce and strengthen these essential skills. The students were better able to apply literary terminology in examples of both written text and media productions. Students demonstrated the ability to analyze and interpret media techniques and relate them to literary techniques.

From Activity One, I infer that students can observe additional facts from viewing a video version of a reading selection. The findings from Activity Two suggest that students who take the critical viewing class acquire and apply literary terminology better than students who take English 12. Students enrolled concurrently in both the critical viewing and English classes receive even more reinforcement of literary terms, as well as guided practice in both reading and viewing, and therefore may be able produce higher results compared to students only in one of the classes.

The findings have impacted my teaching. I have incorporated increased use of video presentations in my English classes. One example is my use of video in teaching *The Tragedy of Macbeth*. For many years, I showed the entire video immediately following the teaching of the play.

Now, I show a video segment for each act of the play. I pause the video frequently and ask for discussion when techniques are displayed (e.g., foreshadowing, flashback, setting, imagery, etc.). I facilitate students in using literary terminology when discussing the video. I intend to use both the Franco Zeffirelli and the Kenneth Branagh film versions of *Hamlet* when teaching the play in the AP literature classes. The students will be expected to analyze (orally and written) both versions of key scenes using appropriate literary terminology. Previously, I thought that I needed to show a video in its entirety for it to be beneficial to student learning, but I have come to realize that sometimes only one or two scenes are necessary.

TV or not TV is no longer an issue in my mind. The real issue is how to use TV most persuasively as a teacher. Consequently, based on the data collected from this action research study, I believe teaching critical viewing holds educational value. By using student-centered viewing activities and requiring students to apply literary terminology, students have shown growth in the area of literacy acquisition. Additionally, students have been afforded opportunities to see literature come to life, so to speak, in critical viewing class. As students reported on the second survey, when they can *visualize the story,* they *understand it better.* When students understand the story and the literary points, they can better analyze and write about the content. As one student stated, "You made us write about these terms so much that you forced us to learn them." By doing so, I have tried to empower students with skills necessary to connect the world of literacy to their world of images. Since connection is the goal of literacy development, the medium used to acquire results should not be such a controversial issue. As Owen et al. (1998) recommend, if educators want students to cultivate literacy, then educators need to teach students *how* to cultivate literacy. For me, this includes teaching students appropriate media viewing skills.

APPENDIX A: SURVEY ONE

Administered to students in spring 2003 critical viewing and English literature courses ($n = 64$)

1. Do you read outside the assignments required for school? Why or why not?
2. If yes, what genre of books do you enjoy reading the most? Why?
3. Do you watch films or television outside the school environment? Why or why not?

4. If yes, what genre of film/television do you enjoy watching most? Why?
5. As a student, do you feel you remember more (details for a longer period of time) from reading a story or viewing a story? Why (please be specific)?
6. Which is easier for you to understand—a book or a video? Why (be specific)?
7. Which is easier for you to write about—a book or a video? Why (be specific)?

APPENDIX B: SURVEY TWO

Administered to students in spring 2003 critical viewing course ($n = 23$)

1. Do you feel this class has been/is beneficial in helping you to understand the basic elements of literature—plot, character, genre, and so forth? Why or why not?
2. Do you feel this class has been/is beneficial in helping you to write about the basic elements of literature? Why or why not?

    - If you answered "no" to questions one and two, please *stop* here.
    - If you answered "yes," please *continue* with the survey.

3. What element of the class has helped you the most? For example, has it been the fact that you could see the story played out on the screen or has it been the discussions, writing assignments, etc? Please tell what has helped you the most and why you feel it has helped you?
4. Do you think that teachers of literature should incorporate video selections into their lesson plans when possible? Why?
5. What literary element(s) do you feel you now understand better because of this class? (May list more than one)

REFERENCES

Association for Educational Communications and Technology. (2001). *The handbook of research for educational communications and tech*nology. Retrieved February 8, 2003, from http://www.aect.org/Intranet/Publications/edtech/11/11-08.html

Carver, S. (Director). (1991). *The tell-tale heart* [Motion Picture]. Malibu, CA: Monterey Home Video.

Clark, R. E. (1983). Reconsidering research on learning from media. *Review of Educational Research, 53*(4), 445-459.

Freeman, M. (1997). Electronic media and how kids (don't) think. *The Education Digest, 63*, 22-27.

Gardner, H. (1997). Extraordinary cognitive achievements (ECA): A symbol systems approach. In W. Damon & R. M. Lerner (Eds.), *Handbook of child psychology*, (5th ed., Vol. 1, pp. 415-466). New York: John Wiley and Sons.

Hobbs, R. (1997). Literacy for the information age. In J. Flood, S. B. Heath, & D. Lapp (Eds.), *Handbook of research on teaching literacy through the communicative and visual arts* (pp. 7-14). New York: Macmillan.

Hobbs, R., & Frost, R. (2003). Measuring the acquisition of media-literacy skills. *Reading Research Quarterly, 38*(3), 330(26). Retrieved February 7, 2005, from InfoTrac database.

Kozma, R. B. (1991). Learning with media. *Review of Educational Research, 61*(2), 179-211.

McREL. (2005). Retrieved February 7, 2005, from http://www.mcrel.org/

Owen, D. B., Silet, C. L. P., & Brown, S. E. (1998). Empowering students by teaching television. *The Education Digest 63*, 10-17.

Pinnell, G. S. (2002). *Guided reading program: Blue edition* [Teacher's guide]. New York: Scholastic.

Poe, E. A. (1843/2004). The tell-tale heart. *The Poe Decoder.* Retrieved September 7, 2004, from http://www.poedecoder.com/Qrisse/works/tth.html

Raffel, B. (Trans.). (2000). *Beowulf.* In K. Daniel (Ed.), *Elements of literature: Literature of Britain with world classics* (pp. 21-46). New York: Holt, Rinehart, and Winston.

Singer, D. G., & Singer, J. L. (1998). Developing critical viewing skills and media literacy in children. In A. B. Jordan & K. H. Jamieson (Eds.), *The annals of the American Academy of Political and Social Science, 557: Children and Television* (pp. 164-179). Thousand Oaks, CA: Sage.

Spiegel, S. (Producer), & Kazan, E. (Director). (1954). *On the waterfront* [Motion Picture]. Culver City, CA: Columbia TriStar.

Walsh, D. (2002). Kids don't read because they can't read. *The Education Digest, 67*, 20-30.

Wetzel, C. D., Radtke, P. H., & Stern, H. W. (1994). *Instructional effectiveness of video media.* Hillsdale, NJ: Erlbaum.

CHAPTER 12

THE ROLE OF ISLAM AND MUSLIMS IN AMERICAN EDUCATION

Critical Issues in Teaching and Curriculum

James R. Moore

This chapter will explore the rationale for teaching about religion in public schools and examine critical teaching and curriculum issues regarding Islam, a religion that is often characterized by myths, distortions, and stereotypes. Teaching about Islam will allow students to obtain a knowledge base, engage in critical thinking, develop a sense of the complexities and contradictions common to all religious and political worldviews, and make informed and rational decisions that, hopefully, will lead to greater intercultural understanding and social justice—2 primary goals in American education today.

INTRODUCTION

One of the most important issues confronting American educational institutions concerns the role of Islam in society and its relationship to American national security and foreign policy (Lewis, 2003; Wheeler, 2003).

Islam, one of the fastest growing religions in the world including the United States, is a dynamic faith that is characterized by tremendous cultural, political, geographical, ethnic, and ideological diversity (Esposito, 1999; Findley, 2001; Hasan, 2000). And, it is in the realm of ideological diversity—where there are sharp divisions over worldviews, methods, and goals—where many Americans are uncertain about Islam and its relationship to a democratic America. Questions pertaining to the nature of Islam, its basic values, goals, and practices, the divisions within Islam, the compatibility of Islam with the modern world, teaching about Islam and the treatment of Muslims in America, are now central issues in a national conversation that is occurring throughout America's major educational and political institutions.

Considering the importance of Islam in American and world affairs and the myths, distortions, and stereotypes associated with Islam (Findley, 2001), it is critically important that secondary school students be taught about the religion of Islam. However, sharp disagreements among scholars over the nature of Islam, the profound differences and divisions within Islam, and the failure of American educational systems to provide students with a comprehensive education about world religions, exacerbate the challenges now facing our educational institutions (Wheeler, 2003). American democracy and national security depends, to a large extent, on the ability of citizens to make rational and informed decisions on relevant political, economic, social, *and* religious issues; therefore, this chapter will discuss the rationale for teaching about world religions in public schools and examine the salient teaching and curricular issues related to the teaching of Islam and American Muslims in secondary schools.

THE RATIONALE FOR TEACHING ABOUT WORLD RELIGIONS IN PUBLIC SCHOOLS

Since the founding of the United States of America in the late eighteenth century, religion, particularly Christianity, has played a central role in our political, economic, social, and educational institutions (Carter, 1993; Gollnick & Chinn, 2002; Huntington, 2004; Nord, 1995). Religion remains very important to the vast majority of Americans with 90% of Americans identify themselves as belonging to a major faith (Christianity, 86%; Judaism, 1%; Islam, 2%; Orthodox, 1%) and educators must understand the importance so many Americans place on religion in their daily lives (Gollnick & Chinn, 2002, p. 203). In fact, America, as a nation formed by immigration and dedicated to the ideals of religious and political freedoms, is one of the most religiously diverse countries in the world (Huntington, 2004, p. 91).

Moreover, the world's major religions—Christianity, Islam, Judaism, Hinduism, and Buddhism—continue to play a central role in domestic and world politics; the violence in the Middle East, the India and Pakistan conflict over Kashmir, the ethnic cleansing in Bosnia, and many of America's culture wars are grounded, in large part, by religious differences (Nord & Haynes, 1998). Knowing about these religions, their core beliefs, values, practices and interactions over time, is critical to understanding history and current affairs. Religious worldviews, like secular worldviews, should be treated seriously by educational institutions interested in producing well-rounded students capable of understanding multiple perspectives.

Nonetheless, the proper role of religion in public education has been the subject of numerous debates throughout American history. Various religious groups, characterized by great diversity in terms of core beliefs and practices, historical experiences, ethnicity, socioeconomic status, geography and political ideology, have competing perspectives on the role religion should play in determining the school curriculum, teaching methods, and the educational environment (Gollnick & Chinn, 2002). The American founders, well aware of the historical consequences of fusing religion with politics, established a constitutional principle of separation of church from state; however, the first 16 words of the First Amendment: "Congress shall make no law respecting the establishment of religion, or prohibiting the free exercise thereof" have been the subject of widely contrasting interpretations, conflicts, and violence (Gollnick & Chinn, 2002; Nord, 1995; Nord & Haynes, 1998). These battles have been centered over issues such as sex education, prayer in schools, evolution, moral issues, the choice of books in social studies, science, and literature, school vouchers, and a host of other issues (Gollnick & Chinn, 2002; Nord, 1995).

Unfortunately, extreme positions tend to dominate the debate over the proper role of religion in public schools and the courts have had to make difficult decisions balancing the establishment and free exercise clauses of the First Amendment (Nord & Haynes, 1998). While schools cannot favor religion or indoctrinate students into a particular religion, they must teach *about* religion and respect the religious liberties of students, including making reasonable accommodations so students may engage in the free exercise of their religion (Nord & Haynes, 1998).

The appropriate role for religious education in public schools should conform to constitutional law, advocate respect and toleration for religious diversity and practices, protect the religious liberty of all students, and engage students in critical thinking about the pivotal role of religion in history and contemporary world affairs (Nord & Haynes, 1998). Educational institutions are obligated to provide a liberal education to all students; this entails a thorough and fair examination of the impact of religion on the humanities, history, and the social sciences. Indeed, religious thought has dominated all aspects of human existence until the seventeenth century scientific revolution and eighteenth century Enlightenment helped to create the modern and secular world (Nord, 1995). If students are to acquire a liberal education, including the ability to evaluate religious and secular perspectives on human history and critically discuss life's fundamental questions, they must learn about comparative religions, religion in world and American history, and the continued salience of religion in world affairs today.

This challenge is exacerbated by the fact that religious education, not indoctrinating students into any religion, but teaching them *about* major religions and their critical roles in world and American history, constitutes a very small part of the curriculum in American public schools and universities (Nord, 1995). Thus, the vast majority of secondary school and university students can earn diplomas and college degrees without ever taking any courses in religion. Public educational institutions, including colleges and schools of education reflecting the secularization of America's dominant political, economic, and social institutions and the remarkable success of science in explaining human existence, have removed religion from the curriculum (Kassam, 2003; Nord, 1995; Wheeler, 2003).

Indeed, some scholars assert that America's political, legal, and educational institutions are hostile to religion, which is often viewed, particularly by cultural elites, as an anachronism devoid of relevance in the modern world (Bruce, 2003; Carter, 1993; Nord, 1995). Many educators assume "that religion is irrelevant to virtually everything that is taken to be true and important" (Nord, 1995, p.1) and the vast majority of students are exposed to only secular ways of viewing history and reality (Nord & Haynes, 1998). Therefore, the scarcity of knowledge about Islam is symptomatic of a greater problem; the failure of American educational institutions to take religion seriously as a viable worldview to understand human existence (Kassam, 2003; Nord, 1995).

Thus, most Americans are woefully ignorant of the importance of religion in American and world history and have great difficulty in understanding political affairs in regions where religion is central to daily life (Findley, 2001; Nord, 1995; Reinhart, 2003). Indeed, if students do not know "how Islam traditionally fuses the sacred with the secular, how are they going to understand the politics of the Middle East?" (Nord, 1995, p. 207). Moreover, students must possess a basic knowledge of Judaism, Christianity, Hinduism, and Buddhism, as well as Islam, if they are to comprehend world events. Of course, without understanding Islam, students cannot comprehend the Indian (predominantly Hindu) and Pakistani (predominantly Muslim) conflict over Kashmir, recent political events in Asia, or some of the religious and political tensions in Western Europe or the United States. Religion is at the heart of many domestic and international events with important implications for all American citizens; therefore, improving religious education serves important national interests.

Furthermore, there are intense disagreements among scholars over the true nature of Islam that may leave teachers confused over the facts and deter them from teaching this important, albeit controversial, topic in their social studies classes. Islam, like all major religions, has competing schools of thought regarding theology, rituals, and practices that hinder understanding. Many different interpretations of Islamic history, beliefs, and traditions exacerbate the quest to fully comprehend this dynamic religion (Feldman, 2003; Findley, 2001; Hotaling, 2003; Nasr, 2004). This is unfortunate, because teaching about Islam, like all religions, presents students with opportunities to expand their knowledge and understanding of the world, develop tolerance for religious and cultural diversity, take an active and informed role in American politics, and develop critical thinking skills that could generate viable solutions to religious, political, and cultural conflicts (Nord & Haynes, 1998).

Thus, the complex nature of Islam should not deter educators from teaching about the vital role of Islam in world history and contemporary international affairs. It is important that all citizens become informed to the best of their ability about Islam in order to make rational decisions about a religion that has been the subject of numerous and profound myths, distortions, and stereotypes (Findley, 2001). Clearly, it is in America's national interests to produce competent citizens who can make informed decisions regarding Islam and its relationship to the United States; therefore, America's educational institutions must make a concerted effort to improve religious education across the curriculum (Nord & Haynes, 1998).

ISLAM AND AMERICAN EDUCATION: CHALLENGES, POLITICS AND CURRICULUM ISSUES

What should students be taught about Islam and why? What are the most appropriate methods and activities? Can American public schools accommodate Muslim students? What role does politics play in influencing the curriculum? Should Muslim students be assimilated into the dominant American culture? These questions pose a serious challenge to scholars, policymakers, curriculum specialists, educators and the American public.

The answers to these questions are fraught with significant educational, political, and religious concerns and consequences for American society. The task of developing an educationally appropriate curriculum is exacerbated by the profound disagreements among scholars over the true nature of Islam and its role in world history, the widespread perception that Islam is intricately linked with terrorism and violence, the marginalization of religious education by American universities, the lack of accurate teaching materials, and the dearth of Islamic scholars in the United States (Kassam, 2003; Reinhart, 2003; Wheeler, 2003). Various interests groups—characterized by ideological differences and opposing goals—attempt to influence the teaching of Islam by controlling the curriculum and the treatment of Muslims in public schools (Haddad, 1999).

Teaching about religion presents educators with numerous decisions regarding curriculum, resources, and instructional methods and strategies. Islam has a long and complex history, an intricate theological foundation, highly developed legal systems, sharp divisions among Muslims over theology, law, and practices, and a comprehensive list of achievements in philosophy, medicine, art, architecture, geography, mathematics, literature, and science (Esposito, 1999). Scholars and educators have a responsibility to develop an historically accurate curriculum and instructional program that complies with constitutional law and is pedagogically sound. This task is exacerbated because there is widespread disagreement among scholars, educators, and policymakers over curriculum philosophy and content. For example, teachers could focus on the theological tenets of Islam, the contributions of Muslims to human civilization, the divisions within Islam, the treatment of Muslims in contemporary America, the interactions between Islam and other religions/civilizations, the expansion of Islam, and a host of other topics.

The teaching of Islam to American students is a relatively recent phenomenon and is heavily influenced by the Arab-Israeli conflict, the legacy of colonialism, and American policies throughout the Islamic world (Douglass & Dunn, 2003, p. 52). Generally, the teaching of Islam in the United States has been characterized by numerous stereotypes, distortions, omissions, textbook inaccuracies, and within the boundaries of Western civilization's politically motivated narrative (Brockopp, 2003; Douglass & Dunn, 2003; Esposito, 1998; Findley, 2001; Hasan, 2000; Hermansen, 2003; Kassam, 2003; Reinhart, 2003; Wheeler, 2003). Many Americans are profoundly ignorant regarding Islam and often conflate Islam—a complex religion characterized by specific theologies, laws, and practices—with national identity, terrorism, and political regimes that unjustly conscript Islam to justify their oppressive policies and practices (Brockopp, 2003; Douglass & Dunn, 2003; Findley, 2001; Haddad, 1999; Hasan, 2000; Kassam, 2003; Reinhart, 2003).

Nevertheless, despite the difficult choices over designing an appropriate curriculum, scholars generally agree there are some core values, beliefs, historical events, and practices that characterize Islam and should be part of the secondary school curriculum (Wheeler, 2003). Most scholars agree students should know the theological meaning of Islam, the transcendence and indivisibility of Allah, the role of Muhammad and his deeds and sayings (*hadith*), the importance of the Quran to Islam, Shariah (law), the Five Pillars of Islam, the Six Pillars of Faith, the contributions of Muslims to world civilization, the reasons behind the rapid expansion of Islam and the divisions within Islam (Nord & Haynes, 1998; Wheeler, 2003). Of course, students, if they are to understand major historical events and current international affairs, must understand the conflicts and competition between Islam and Christianity spawned by different theological and political worldviews (Haddad, 1999; Lewis, 2003; Pipes, 2003).

Moreover, teachers should help students understand the Islamic worldview from the inside and not merely American interpretations of this highly complex religion (Nord & Haynes, 1998). This goal could be accomplished by using primary sources, such as the Quran, to allow Muslims to articulate the essentials of their religion. There are numerous Websites, scholarly books, and organizations that could assist teachers in accumulating knowledge, primary sources, teaching aids, and lesson plans. Naturally, teachers must exercise sound judgment when choosing resources and formulating lesson plans. Educators could verify the accuracy of their resources by engaging in research and considering a wide variety of sources for information.

Many organizations, for example, the American Muslim Council, the Council for American-Islamic Affairs, the United Muslims of America and the American-Arab Anti-Discrimination Committee, have been formed in order to increase the political power of Muslims in the United States, to fight racism and discrimination against Muslims, ensure constitutional rights, provide economic opportunities, provide accurate information and teaching resources regarding Islam to educators and the American public (Haddad, 1999). The Muslim population in the United States, currently estimated to be about 8 million, is growing rapidly due to immigration and relatively high birth rates. Simultaneously, this important demographic trend is being accompanied by the Muslim community's increasing political and economic power and contributions to American science, engineering, medicine, and business (Esposito, 1998; Findley, 2001; Hasan, 2000; Khan, 2002).

Furthermore, the Muslim population, far from being a monolithic entity, is characterized by enormous diversity in terms of national origin, language, socioeconomic status, historical experiences, ideology and theology. For example, there are profound differences between Sunni Muslims and Shiite Muslims, the two major divisions within Islam. Shiites believe that only direct descendants of Ali, Muhammad's son-in-law, can be the true leaders of Islam. Sunni Muslims, however, claim that only descendants from the Umayyad dynasty are the legitimate leaders of Islam. Over the centuries, Shiites developed their own legal code, created special rituals, and developed their own interpretations of the Quran (Donner, 1999; Spielvogel, 1999). This split continues today and is a major source of conflict within the Islamic world, especially in Iraq and Iran. These divisions within the Islamic world exacerbate America's attempts to formulate viable foreign policies in Muslim countries that are vital to American national interests. American Muslims are also divided over a wide variety of religious, cultural, and political issues. Thus, Muslims hold many competing views regarding Islam, American culture, politics, education and the desirability of assimilation into American society. The divisions and conflicts within Islam can offer students a vital lesson applicable to history and the social sciences; not only are there major differences among world religions and political ideologies, there are profound differences *within* religions and political ideologies.

The increased presence and political power of American Muslims, in conjunction with increased efforts by American institutions to accommodate the Muslim community, has presented special challenges to public schools. Most Muslim students in the United States attend public schools and these institutions have taken reasonable steps to protect students from discrimination and accommodate their religious needs, although Muslim students are occasionally victims of discrimination and violence (Haynes, 2004). The requirements of Islam, prayer at specific times, dietary needs, dress codes and many others are complex and accommodations can be very difficult and possibly requiring judicial decisions regarding the legality of the accommodations (Nord &Haynes, 1998). This is true for other religious groups as well; the courts and public schools face a challenge in balancing students' religious liberties with school policies and a required curriculum. The increasing religious diversity in the United States will accentuate the centuries-long struggle to balance pluralism with assimilation as America continues to redefine its national identity (Huntington, 2004).

Historically one of the primary functions of public schools has been to assimilate immigrant and minority populations into American society. This task, never easy and often controversial, could be more complicated now because of rapidly increasing immigration and public education's current emphasis on diversity as opposed to cultural unity (Huntington, 2004; Schlesinger, 1998). However, despite the emphasis on diversity and accommodation, many Muslims perceive public schools inculcate values and practices that are antithetical to the Islamic faith and traditions (Haddad, 1999; Hermansen, 2003). The mixing of males and females in the classroom, coed physical education (including swimming), and sex education are viewed unfavorably by many Muslims. Therefore, there has been a dramatic increase in the number of private Islamic schools, mosques, and Islamic centers that provide education to Muslims (Haddad, 1999; Hermansen, 2003; Khan, 2002). In some cases, these institutions have come under scrutiny from the federal government because of ties to terrorism and activities that may be a threat to American national security (Pipes, 2003).

Furthermore, many Muslims view Islam as a superior alternative to the morally bankrupt culture of American and Western civilization; materialistic, hedonistic, dysfunctional families, pervasive violence, rampant sexual promiscuity and drug abuse, psychological disorders and meaningless lives; and believe an Islamic education can provide a meaningful life grounded in morality, responsibility, social justice, and membership in a religious community (Haddad, 1999). Of course, at this time it remains uncertain to what extent American Muslims will assimilate into the mainstream. The desire of some Muslims to resist assimilation, which they view as a betrayal of Islam and a loss of identity, may result in conflicts with non-Muslims in America (Huntington, 2004). Thus, the issues of assimilation, pluralism, accommodation, and identity will continue to characterize the Muslim experience in the United States. Educational institutions responding to demographic changes, legal challenges, security issues, shifting political needs and attempts to increase tolerance will continue to redesign religious education in order to produce better-educated students and competent American citizens.

CONCLUSION

While Islam, like all major religions, is a highly complex religion that generates a significant amount of disagreement among scholars over the interpretation of Islamic values, history, beliefs, laws and practices, secondary students should be taught about all major religions in order to understand world history, current international affairs, foster cultural understanding, ameliorate religious conflicts and develop the analytical skills necessary to evaluate the contradictions and complexities inherent in any highly complex religion, political ideology or philosophy. Furthermore, the proper teaching of all major religions will help students discard stereotypes, reduce prejudice and discrimination against Muslims and other religious minorities in American schools. Teaching about Islam requires that teachers adopt multiple perspectives and a wide variety of activities that foster understanding; it also requires important choices regarding curriculum and teaching

The increase in religious diversity in the United States, especially the rapid expansion of Islam owing to conversion, high birth rates among Muslim populations, and current immigration trends, demands that educational institutions, the primary social institution charged with forging a common national identity and producing competent citizens, improve the teaching about all religions in history. Religious differences and conflicts continue to play a major role in American and international politics; citizens must possess a basic knowledge of these world religions if they are to make informed choices. Teaching about world religions is just as important as teaching about race, ethnicity, gender, and other areas of diversity. Often, there is a symbiotic relationship between religion, nationality, and ethnicity. By improving education about world religions, schools can help improve student knowledge and attitudes regarding Islam and Muslims in American society and throughout the world.

REFERENCES

Brockopp, J. E. (2003). The essential Shari'ah: Teaching Islamic law in the religious studies classroom. In B. M. Wheeler (Ed.), *Teaching Islam* (pp. 77-93). New York: Oxford University Press.

Bruce, T. (2003). *The death of right and wrong.* New York: Random House.

Carter, S. (1993). *The culture of disbelief: How American law and politics trivialize religious devotion.* New York: Basic Books.

Donner, F. M. (1999). Muhammad and the caliphate: Political history of the Islamic empire up to the Mongol conquest. In J. L. Esposito (Ed.), *The Oxford history of Islam* (pp. 1-61). New York: Oxford University Press.

Douglass, S. L. & Dunn, R. E. (2003). Interpreting Islam in American schools. *The Annals of the American Academy of Political and Social Sciences, 588*(1), 52-72.

Esposito, J. L. (1998). *Islam: The straight path.* New York: Oxford University Press.

Esposito, J. L. (Ed.). (1999). Contemporary Islam: Reformation or revolution. In *The Oxford history of Islam* (pp. 643-690). New York: Oxford University Press.

Feldman, N. (2003). *After jihad: America and the struggle for Islamic democracy.* New York: Farrar, Straus, and Giroux.

Findley, P. (2001). *Silent no more: Confronting America's false images of Islam.* Beltville, MD: Amana Press.

Gollnick, D. M., & Chinn, P. (2002). *Multicultural education in a pluralistic society.* Columbus, OH: Merrill/Prentice Hall.

Haddad, Y. Y. (1999). The globalization of Islam: The return of Muslims to the West. In J. L. Esposito (Ed.), *The Oxford history of Islam* (pp. 601-641). New York: Oxford University Press.

Hasan, A. G. (2000). *American Muslims: The new generation.* New York: Continuum.

Haynes, C. (2004). *Accommodating Muslims in public schools: Where to draw the line.* Retrieved September 24, 2004, from http://www.firstamendmentcenter.org/commentaryaaspx?id=13311

Hermansen, M. K. (2003). Teaching about Muslims in America. In B. M. Wheeler (Ed.), *Teaching Islam* (pp. 168-180). New York: Oxford University Press.

Hotaling, E. (2003). *Islam without illusions.* Syracuse, NY: Syracuse University Press.

Huntington, S. P. (2004). *Who are we?: The challenges to America's national identity.* New York: Simon & Schuster.

Kassam, T. R. (2003). Teaching religion in the 21st century. In B. M. Wheeler (Ed.), *Teaching Islam* (pp. 191-215). New York: Oxford University Press.

Khan, M. A. (2002). *American Muslims: Bridging faith and freedom.* Beltsville, MD: Amana Press.

Lewis, B. (2003). *The crisis of Islam.* New York: Random House.

Nasr, V. (2004). Regional implications of Shi'a revival in Iraq. *The Washington Quarterly, 27*(3), 7-24.

Nord, W. A. (1995). *Religion and American education: Rethinking a national dilemma.* Chapel Hill: University of North Carolina Press.

Nord, W. A., & Hayes, C. G. (1998). *Taking religion seriously across the curriculum.* Alexandra, VA: Association for Supervision and Curriculum Development.

Pipes, D. (2003). *Militant Islam reaches America.* New York: Norton.

Reinhart, A. K. (2003). On the "Introduction to Islam." In B. M. Wheeler (Ed.), *Teaching Islam* (pp. 22-45). New York: Oxford University Press.

Schlesinger, A. M. (1998). *The disuniting of America.* New York: Norton.

Spielvogel, J.J. (1999). *World history: The human odyssey.* New York: West Educational.

Wheeler, B. M. (Ed.). (2003). What can't be left out: The essentials of teaching Islam as a religion. In *Teaching Islam* (pp. 3-21). New York: Oxford University Press.

CHAPTER 13

FISHBOWL REFLECTIONS

A High School Teacher's Enlightenment During a Faculty Desegregation Experience

Judith D. Luckett

> In January 1970, Orange County Florida Public Schools began the desegregation of all K-12 schools in response to a federal court order. Short on funding to provide the necessary massive busing operation, the school board proposed immediate faculty transfers in order to delay student desegregation until the start of the new school year in August. A high school French teacher from Illinois became involved in the hastily planned, televised lottery drawing that changed the lives and careers of many teachers.

A televised lottery in January 1970 was Orange County, Florida Public Schools' response to a federal court order for immediate public school desegregation. Massive busing would have required the use of nearly half of the county school budget for the academic year, so a plan for desegregating school faculties in January and desegregating students at the start of the new school year in August was submitted to the Fifth Circuit Court of Appeals. The plan was accepted and, with little time to effect the faculty transfers, a lottery drawing was proposed by the Classroom Teachers' Association.

After the names of hundreds of Black and White teachers were paired for transfer purposes during the live broadcast of the lottery, the names of two high school French teachers were called. The White teacher called the television station to resign rather than be transferred to the all Black high school. A replacement teacher had to be found immediately, since the transferred teachers had been given one school day to move their books, supplies, and equipment to the new school. Students were given no warning. The whole process soon became known as the Fishbowl Transfers.

Having recently moved to Orlando from the Chicago area, I was substitute teaching that January for the Foreign Language Department of an Orlando high school in hopes of meeting other language teachers. My story is of a sudden, unexpected, and edifying semester as the fishbowl replacement French teacher at Jones, Orlando's only all Black high school. My fishbowl transfer experiences altered my purposes for teaching and changed the path of my teaching career.

I was willing to contribute whatever I could in this difficult teaching situation. At the time, I thought of myself as a tolerant northerner, understanding and knowledgeable about the effects of racial prejudice. I *was* tolerant and I *did* contribute; I found out, however, that I understood little and knew even less about the Black experience. Everything was the same as it was in my previous high school teaching position in a suburb of Chicago, yet everything was different. In retrospect, I was more a learner than I was a teacher at Jones High School. The Black principal, my Black students, my colleagues, and my classroom experiences began to lead me to deeper, although still incomplete, understandings about a people whose life experiences were very different from my own.

The Jones High Principal, Wilbur Gary, helped me to understand what the students expected and needed from my teaching—in addition to learning French. In his view, a teacher did so much more than teach a subject. Teachers were to be role models, counselors, and even "daytime parents" to students in his school. He knew who the good teachers were; he not only walked the halls and visited the classrooms regularly, he also sat down with students and with teachers and listened, really listened, to what they had to say. In faculty meetings and lunchroom conversations with the new White teachers, this principal also purposefully shared insights on Black etiquette and culture.

The new Spanish teacher and I were invited to one of these lunchroom visits with Mr. Gary in a cafeteria that was a delightful olfactory and culinary experience. He told us about the school's proud history, and he gently teased us about our ultraformal White table manners, encouraging us to be a little more relaxed, especially in one-on-one conversations with our students. He knew all the students by name, and he knew which ones were in our classes. He made us feel welcome and vitally important to

Jones and its students. By the time we finished that wonderful soul food meal, complete with Mr. Gary's explanations of what everything was and how the students in the commercial cooking class prepared it, I felt personally responsible for the future graduation of each one of my French students. I also knew that I could count on my principal to assist me in any way he could.

My Black students did not understand how or why their teachers could be taken away from them in the middle of the school year, and they were angry with the White people involved. I was replacing a young male French teacher whom they adored, and they made sure I understood that. They had lost almost all their beloved teachers; their resilience and their grace in such an unfair turn of events was a constant source of wonder for me.

They also shared other disappointments with me—stories of a few White teachers who weren't teaching them, didn't respect them, wouldn't bother to learn their names. I learned that the people in the Black community knew each other, *stuck together*, and had many local traditions that White Orlandoans knew little or nothing about. My students' daily lives were also different from my own life as a high school student. A few students told me that they would sometimes skip school to do day labor in the orange groves if their family needed money. A junior told me he worked in the groves every spring to earn money to take his girlfriend to the county fair. Other students talked about church activities and Jones events, especially sports and the senior prom. Their willingness to share their feelings about the fishbowl and their gradually more frequent revelations about their life outside of school helped me to understand the sorrow and the anger my students felt.

A small number of my White fishbowl colleagues at Jones exhibited attitudes and behaviors toward Blacks that showed me my students' anger was well founded. A few White teachers spent a great deal of time and energy trying to return to their pre-fishbowl positions, and they made sure everyone, including the students, knew how unhappy they were at the Black high school. Fear talk and gossip sometimes darkened the teachers' lounge—worries about cars getting keyed in the parking lot, about teachers being assaulted, and about the rumors of student violence or on-campus sexual escapades. Some of these teachers warned others not to eat "that food" in the cafeteria. No teacher that I knew or heard about was ever a victim or an eyewitness to the rumored events; all the talk was just talk, just rumor, just fear.

A much larger number of the White transfer teachers made me proud. Most of the new White faculty tried valiantly, under such difficult circumstances, to pick up where the previous teachers left off, learned their students' names, prepared well for their classes, and learned as much as they could about the Black community. Other teachers humbled me because their dedication was greater than mine. One White teacher who had been at the high school for 2 years introduced himself to all the new teachers and shared his positive experiences while offering to help in any way he could. A White history teacher observed that the students did not know much about Black history. She decided to return to school, get a master's degree in ethnic studies, and start a Black history club. She also proposed an ethnic studies program. A few White teachers went out of their way to attend team sport events and other extracurricular activities. Some of these exemplary educators remained at the Black high school until retirement.

My students also made me proud. Many demonstrated to me daily their remarkable language abilities. My predecessor must have had very good French pronunciation; I could hear it in their chorused and individual answers to my questions. By my third week at Jones, though, I began to hear a suggestion of a midwestern accent in their French—so many of my students could faithfully reproduce any sound they heard. I spoke English to them as little as possible, only, in fact, when a complicated explanation was required. Instead of asking me to speak English more, they seemed proud that I simply expected them to understand in French. How could the teachers' lounge gossips think these students were not good learners? My best students at the advanced levels were, for all practical purposes, trilingual. I remember going into a student restroom and hearing a group of my female students excitedly conversing in southern Black dialect. As soon as they saw me, they all changed to Standard English mid-sentence, greeted me, and talked to me about what we were doing in class that day. This code switching happened whenever a White teacher would appear suddenly in the hallway.

I used the same interactive foreign language teaching strategies I had used in the Illinois high school, with the same good results, but I found myself adapting the textbook content, sometimes uncomfortably, to suit the new learning context. Foreign language textbooks contain topical vocabulary lists. When the vocabulary dealt with family, home, furniture, clothing, and other possessions, the accompanying drawings and photos did not look like my students' families, the homes in their neighborhood, or their possessions. I was acutely aware that they could not see themselves in the textbook. I remembered that when I was learning to read in a "Dick, Jane, and Sally" book, I had always secretly wondered, "Who ARE these people?" My father did not wear a suit to work, and he carried a lunchbox instead of a briefcase. My mother did not wear pretty dresses, high heels, and jewelry to do housework. If I, a blond, green-eyed, English/Swedish child was made uncomfortable when my family wasn't like the family in the reader, then what must it be like for these students?

I added vocabulary to the textbook lists as often I could, vocabulary that was meaningful to my Jones students, and I invited them to bring in drawings, photos, or stories to match both the added vocabulary and the textbook vocabulary. I usually skipped textbook questions I thought might elicit negative feelings or highlight background differences—questions about travel, shopping, and family members, for example. I did that for my students and for myself; I was not sure I could handle the potential student discomfort (or my own) in the continuing classroom conversations in French.

Sometimes that discomfort could not be avoided, or it cropped up unexpectedly in classroom activities with students. For one of these activities, I had assigned each row of students a day of the week to regularly tell the class some news in French. We always started the class with five or six students answering my question, "Qu'est-ce qu'il y a de nouveau?" (What's New?). One day a 15-year-old boy's answer was, "Mon fils est né hier soir," (My son was born last night). He was one of my best students, a very quick language learner. The expression on his face was amused and watchful from the back of the classroom; he was waiting for my reaction. Since one of the rules for this activity was that students could be creative with their responses and were not bound by the truth, the situation was a bit complicated. The other students had understood him completely and looked at him, surprised and, perhaps, a little anxious. The conversation continued, completely in French. I asked the child's name and he responded. When I asked him to describe the baby, he said he hadn't seen him and didn't know when he would. By this time, the excited reactions of the other students led me to believe that this was not a made-up story, but a real occurrence in the boy's life. They were sitting up very straight and looking from the boy to me and back again, as if they were watching a fast-paced tennis match. The heightened interest and the tension in the air were almost palpable.

I probably went too far by asking him if he would play with the child and take him places when he was older. He said in perfect French, "It's not my responsibility, it's the mother's." I responded that that was sad for the child and for him. Then I said to the student behind him, "Qu'est-ce qu'il y a de nouveau?" praying for a more typical response like what movie the student had seen the weekend before.

There had probably never been another moment of more completely communicated, interesting information understood by everyone in any of my language classes anywhere *ever*. That the communication vehicle was French did not matter and was even below conscious awareness for all of us in those salient moments. It was an opportunity every language teacher dreams of—except that I *blew* it. I was too flustered to step out of the frame and talk to the class later about how and why that conscious awareness of French as the communication vehicle had evaporated. I could have taught a profound lesson in human communication and metalinguistic awareness that day. My teaching effectiveness suffered because I suddenly realized I had no business being judgmental, because I felt like an outsider in my own classroom, and because I was afraid to take this conversation about fatherhood any further.

I learned more every day by talking and working with students in groups and individually, in the classroom, in the hallways, and in the school neighborhood. One of my strongest memories is of being the faculty sponsor for the senior prom refreshment committee. I met with four female students several times. We made a shopping list, and I drove them to the supermarket where their families shopped. I was appalled to discover that the prices for just about everything were significantly higher than those in the supermarket in my own neighborhood. I told them about the difference in prices, and we decided to drive to the other supermarket. We were able to get much more for the money that had been allotted for refreshments. They were surprised by the prices and talked about having their mothers change supermarkets. Transportation would have been a problem, though, for some of the families.

Something else happened during that neighborhood outing that I have never been able to forget. As I dropped the girls off at their homes, I was winding back and forth through their almost completely Black neighborhoods. We passed a number of daycare centers where children were outside on playgrounds. In all the playgrounds there were so many children everywhere that they seemed to be swarming all over the ground and whatever play equipment was there, but the structures themselves were barely visible—they were defined only by the small, moving bodies of children playing on them. There must have been some adults supervising them, but I did not see them in any of the playgrounds. My memory flashed immediately to my daily classes and the constant, barely audible, low hum of movement that constituted about the only difference besides skin color that I could discern when I compared my Chicago students and my Orlando students. I wondered if day after day, year after year of such crowding and such poor supervision could affect a student's ability to remain still in the quieter, much slower daily routine of a classroom. I was distressed to see the overcrowded conditions that working mothers were probably forced to expose their children to.

Another group of girls taught me to look at Black faces in a new way. My experience with Black people had before been mostly one-on-one at different times and places. Now I was seeing the same students day after day in the same context, and I was beginning to see more, to remember the faces better. After school one day, a few female students mentioned a good friend of theirs and asked if I knew her. I said I did. They were a bit surprised and asked if I was sure. Then they challenged me to describe the girl. I froze for a few seconds because I instantly understood for the first time that I had no idea how Black people describe themselves. I was so used to starting with eye and hair color and *White* hairstyle names. They could see my problem. We ended up laughing about my being so "clutched," and they taught me to look for shape of face and shape of eyes; they taught me words to describe a lovely spectrum of skin colors and words for hairstyles. Height and weight I could do already. I could see my students even more clearly the next day. It was almost like correcting my vision with glasses. I loved that lesson. It has helped me to be more comfortable in meeting and remembering Black people. It also reminded me how much I can learn from my students.

I was, in retrospect, *much* more a learner than I was a teacher at Jones High School. My fishbowl transfer experiences changed my understandings about teaching. It is one thing to read about and understand intellectually the racial prejudice, the inequities in the schools, and the learning problems correlated with poverty; it is another thing to teach five classes a day of minority students you come to know and care about. It is also another thing to witness the problems they bring to class with them, to spend time in their neighborhoods, to hear their stories, and to know their longings.

Remembering how my relationships with the students at Jones High School taught me more about social justice than any scholarly reading I had previously done, I encourage my current preservice teachers to do internships in very diverse classrooms, and I tell parts of my fishbowl story to illustrate concepts covered in their reading assignments. I carefully structure seating arrangements and group activities to encourage students to meet as many classmates as possible. I look for one-on-one conversation opportunities with my students, provide copious written feedback on papers, and communicate regularly with students by e-mail. I am more willing to discuss sensitive social issues in the classroom. In my teaching, I also regularly make reference to novels, short stories, and films about prejudice that many of my preservice teachers are familiar with; when they have identified with a fictional character who experiences prejudice, readings and classroom discussion about social justice become more personally meaningful. I provide frequent opportunities for students to share personal experiences related to prejudice and attitudes about prejudice. Attitude and value changes are more likely to accompany conceptual understanding when connections to personal experience are perceived.

Since my Jones High teaching experience and my conversations with its wise and caring principal, I have also felt responsible for facilitating my students' learning well beyond the content of whatever course I am teaching. I integrate discussion of study skills with each course I teach. I gained advising skills in a 4-year position as an academic adviser; and I now consider myself an unofficial adviser to all my students. I have incorporated study skills information into all courses I teach, contextualizing it in ways that do not diminish course content; for example, review of an exam is an opportunity to teach test-taking strategies. I have done standalone presentations on study skills at several of my university's campuses. Many minority students come to the university lacking a broad repertoire of study skills; offering study skills information in all my classes is one way I can address that need. Another way is through a series of study skills presentations I have done for a minority student program in the College of Education. The lessons of the fishbowl have also led me to teaching a course for freshmen called "Strategies for Success in College," in which I can focus on academic skills and life skills that are vital for obtaining a college degree.

The pivotal fishbowl experience has deeply affected my career, my teaching, and, lately, my research directions. Many positive changes in my teaching and in my career happened because I was a transfer teacher in Orange County's dramatic desegregation effort. Someone else's name was pulled from the lottery fishbowl that long ago night in January, but serendipity made me the real winner.

CHAPTER 14

URBAN CHILDREN'S EXPERIENCES AND TEACHER PEDAGOGICAL PRACTICES

When It's About Race, Do Adults Care?

Amy L. Masko

The author conducted an ethnographic study in an urban afterschool program. This chapter discusses children's experiences with racism in both the school and community settings. It further explores how they and the adults charged with their care reacted to this racism. The adults often left the children feeling unprotected and vulnerable to racial conflict. The chapter posits that culturally responsive teachers are crucial to the well-being of children of color, and provides suggestions for improving cultural competency among professionals working with children in multiethnic environments.

INTRODUCTION

Keandra played the race card with me. She got an attitude, so I sent her home. (Staff Person, in reaction to an incident of racial conflict)

> She said, "Just drop it ... just leave it alone." (Keandra Johnson, age 12, describing the advice she received from an adult in response to a racial conflict)
>
> She didn't do nuttin'. (Fatimah Hoffmeier, age 12, describing a teacher's response to a racial conflict)

The statements above describe ways in which adults reacted to racial conflict. Adults often act in ways that seem unjust to the children in their care—by doing nothing, advising them to ignore it, or punishing the victim. This chapter discusses children's experiences with and reactions to racism, as well as the extent to which adults address racial conflict in formal and informal educational settings. I suggest that school teachers, administrators, counselors, and other youth workers need to increase their cultural competency. I suggest they do this through staff development to improve pedagogy, school climate and disciplinary actions, and to effectively manage racial conflict thereby protecting the children in their care.

In 2003, I conducted an ethnographic study of nine non-White, multi-ethnic children living and learning in a low-income community. The children attended two local elementary schools and two local middle schools. They all attended the same afterschool program, The Connection, the setting of this study. While my study sought to understand how these nine children navigated their relationships as they related to race, this chapter discusses the impact of the adults in these children's lives, particularly their teachers, on their feelings of connectedness to school. The extent to which the children experienced racial conflict and the manner in which the adults managed the conflict profoundly affected the racial lives of these nine children.

While the research questions guiding this ethnography did not seek to understand the notion of adult protection of non-White children, this theme unfolded through the children's stories. As is common with qualitative research, unexpected findings emerged through the analysis of the data. Merriam-Webster (2005) defines protection as the act to cover or shield from exposure, injury, or destruction. For purposes of this chapter, the term protection is referred to as both an emotional and physical protection.

INFLUENCES ON RACIAL UNDERSTANDING: FAMILY COMMUNITY AND SCHOOL

The literature suggests that there are several influences on children's understanding of their racial identity and societal constructs of race: the family, the community, and the school. Often the messages children receive from these sources are contradictory complicating their understanding of their racialized lives.

Family

When cultural components in one world are viewed as inferior to those in another world, sociocultural borders are created (Phelan, Davidson, & Cao Yu, 1993), making the transition between home and school culture very difficult for children of color. Many young children live two everyday realities; one at school and one at home (King, Chipman, & Cruz-Janzen, 1994). For example, in contrast to school ideals of education, in Mexican-American homes, *buen educado* (well educated) indicates a child with good manners (Delgado-Gaitan, 1992). Possessing good manners is the measure of a child's academic achievement, although parents in Delgado-Gaitan's study (1992) also had high aspirations for their children and taught them to value education. When the transitions are maneuvered with relatively more ease than would be expected, it is often because students have mastered the requirement of becoming bicultural, and are capable of demonstrating competence both in the larger society and within their own ethnic community (Spencer, Kim, & Marshall, 1987; Spencer, Swanson, & Cunningham, 1991). Yet, this often gives rise to an intrapersonal struggle.

Community

Research into low academic performance and school dropout rates among minority students often indicates the "presence of numerous contradictions between educational beliefs (values spoken) and actual academic behavior (values-lived)" (Philipsen, 1993, p. 420). While students often speak of the importance of education, frequently they do not witness its value in their everyday lives. Involuntary minorities, as Ogbu (1992) has classified African Americans, Native Americans, and some Latinos, have difficulty crossing cultural boundaries from their world to the world of school. Consequently, secondary cultural differences, such as teaching and learning style, cause extensive and persistent problems for these students. Involuntary minorities have less motivation to overcome these barriers between home and school culture because they do not see a payoff (Ogbu, 1992; Philipsen, 1993). They often lack role models of people for whom education has paid off (Philipsen, 1993), especially if they are living in a poor community. In response to this problem, The Connection provided college scholarships to students who grew up in the surrounding neighborhood. These scholarship students volunteered once a week as tutors and homework helpers in the afterschool program. Consequently, these older students served as role models in their communities for the younger children who attended The Connection, with the hope that the children view college as an option—that they see the payoff of education.

Additional discrepancies between values-spoken and values-lived include the pronounced goal of good grades. While making good grades is strongly verbalized by students, parents, and the community as a desirable outcome (values spoken), rarely is there any stigma attached to being a poor student (values lived) (Philipsen, 1993). There is little or no community gossip criticizing a poor student or his or her family (Ogbu, 1992; Philipsen, 1993). In a study of Mexican American families, Delgado-Gaitan (1992) found that parents "insulated any evaluation of academic performance from [extended family]; they usually did not discuss their children's grades" (p. 504).

Schools

All families are concerned about the quality of the schools their children attend and the treatment their children are given in school. In particular, African Americans have historically wrestled with the problems of quality education and integrated schooling (Ladson-Billings, 1994). Often, involuntary minorities do not believe that schools can be trusted to educate their children (Ogbu, 1998). American educational ideals have created a contradictory world—"an 'education-obsessed' society that nevertheless fails to ensure that education is easily available, makes sense, or pays off for all its members" (Philipsen, 1993, p. 424). This phenomenon is described by Spencer et al. (1991) as "societal inconsistency, which is more closely aligned with the experience of chronic frustration" (p. 369), or the disparity between what is said and what is actually done in societies. Schools are established on White, middle class values—the values of the majority (Delpit, 1995). For students who hold the same values, beliefs, expectations and normative ways of behaving, the transition between home and school is maneuvered with ease (Phelan et al., 1993). However, this illuminates the difficulties with double stratification for poor students of color and emphasizes the lack of a good match between the self and the environment (Spencer et al., 1987).

Viadero (1996) emphasizes that schools are not culturally neutral. She argues that schools teach children in the dominant culture of America, in which students who have the cultural capital excel and students of color spend their time trying to catch up (Viadero, 1996). To combat this phenomenon, cultural context is an important factor in teaching. A culturally responsive teacher, defined as using student culture in order to maintain it and transcend the negative effects of the dominant culture, is crucial for students of color (Ladson-Billings, 1994). For some students, classroom conditions, including a culturally responsive teacher, can mean the difference between staying in school and dropping out. School failure germinates in classrooms in which the norms and behaviors are not only different from the students' own backgrounds, but in opposition to those they encounter with family and friends (Phelan et al., 1993) Poor teacher-parent contact only exacerbates the problem (Delgado-Gaitan, 1992).

Davis and Jordan (1994) examined the context of the school and teacher in relation to achievement of African American males. They found factors such as an urban school setting, a focus on discipline, as well as an inability of teachers to motivate their students contributed to poor academic performance. Additionally, when high school teachers' perception of accountability for the success or failure of their students was low (locus of control), Black male performance dropped (Davis & Jordan, 1994). A Hawaiian study of at-risk youth found that "one factor that is likely to cause a disproportionate amount [sic] of Polynesian youth to become 'lazy' and more disinterested in school is negative interaction with teachers" (Mayeda, Chesney-Lind, & Koo, 2001, p. 112). Some of these factors are a product of school structure, teacher bias, or even geographical location, but many can be affected by pedagogy.

With a focus on pedagogy, "responsive teaching combines pursuit of the learning goal with the development of sensibilities that respond to the social ecology of the classroom" (Murrell, 1994, p. 565). In an article on culturally competent teaching in math classrooms, Murrell (1994) states that responsive teachers must be continuously aware of the relationship African American male students construct with their teachers as well as the subject matter. Additionally, teachers must be cognizant of the fact that this relationship is shaped by the degree to which discourse routines and speech events promote interest, social participation, a sense of efficacy and industry, and purpose (Murrell, 1994). As Delpit (1995) argues, it is essential for teachers to make explicit the rules, codes, and expected performances of classroom discourse in order to aid nonmainstream students in developing reasoning competence. She further maintains that these strategies contribute to the empowerment of these students. "The school provides their children with discourse patterns, interactional styles, and spoken and written language codes that will allow them success in the larger society" (Delpit, 1995, p. 29). In addition to a multicultural curriculum, all of these traits contribute to the cultural competence of the classroom teacher.

METHODS

By utilizing ethnographic methodology, I attempted to capture the subtleties of the children's relationships and share their perspectives to gain deeper meaning of the function of race in their daily lives. "Ethnographic research requires attentive observation, empathetic listening, and courageous analysis" (Ely, Anzul, Friedman, Garner, & Steinmetz, 1991, p. 41). As an ethnographic researcher, my activities can be described as "watching, asking, and ... reviewing" (Wolcott, 1992, p. 19). In collecting data, I was a participant-observer. More specifically, I was a privileged observer (Ely et al., 1991) because my relationship with the children at The Connection was well established, as I was also the site director, and knew most of the children in this study for 5 years. As I strived to adopt an insider perspective, I was cognizant of my role in the study and was reflexive at all stages of the research process.

Data Collection

I was a participant-observer at The Connection for one academic year, while I collected and analyzed the data for this study. I observed the children in the environment of the afterschool program, interacting with their peers, their tutors and mentors, and the adult staff at the site. I also interviewed the children, three times each (Seidman, 1998)—once individually and twice in a small focus group setting. In these interviews the children told me about their experiences with their teachers and other adults at their schools. I collected artifacts of the children's writing and drawings, as well as information about the afterschool program.

"Every fieldworker has to achieve some workable balance between participating and observing" (Wolcott, 1995, p. 95). I attempted to balance just "being there" to watch my participants, with being aware of my presence and how it might influence the study (Wolcott, 1995). Observing and interviewing are closely connected under the umbrella of fieldwork; however, observation lends itself to "experiencing" (Wolcott, 1995). I recognized there were no guarantees of what I would find going into the study, and while I developed an observation protocol to guide my observations, I was committed to also being flexible in what I would "see" and experience.

The purpose of the interviews was to obtain participant meanings, and more specifically, to learn how the children conceived of their world (McMillan & Schumacher, 2001), and how they made sense of their interactions relating to race. Through the interviews, I was able to see how the children perceived the role of adults in their educational settings as it related to race.

The first interview centered on racial identity, the second on racial perceptions, and the final interview, which was the main source of data for this chapter, was about their family, their neighborhood, their school, and The Connection, and their respective influence on the children's perceptions of and relationships around race. I audiotaped these interviews, had them transcribed, and use their verbatim language throughout this chapter.

Data Analysis

"The significant element of ethnography is the analysis of the data, a venture in 'thick description'" (Bodkin, 2003, p. 18). In ethnographic research, data collection and analysis happen simultaneously. These processes are flexible and dependent on each prior strategy and the data obtained from that strategy (McMillan & Schumacher, 2001). Analysis is a cyclical process that is interactive, inductive and overlapping (McMillan & Schumacher, 2001), iterative (Creswell, 2002) and which requires constant clarification.

I analyzed my data to search for meaning in the participants' stories, and the parallel nature of data collection and analysis continued to drive the research toward clarity. I began writing vignettes at the beginning of the data collection stage and developing analytic memos (Creswell, 1998; Ely et al., 1991; Miles & Huberman, 1994). This helped me recognize and develop themes relevant to answering my research questions. The analytic memos were notes to myself about how the data could be mapped into categories and themes, which highlighted any "shared [or dissimilar] patterns of behavior, thinking, or talking" (Creswell, 2002, p. 493) of the participants. Furthermore, I displayed the data visually to aid my interpretation (Creswell, 2002). I copied each transcript on a different color paper, assigned each ethnicity a color, and members of that ethnic group shades of that color. For example, the color assigned to the African American children was pink, and the three shades designated to each of the three African American participants were neon pink, pale pink, and salmon. Then I cut and sorted quotes from the children into specific categories. This method enabled me to visually determine if one theme was specific to one ethnic group, or if the experiences were shared among ethnicities. Furthermore, this method of data organization and analysis allowed me to triangulate the data for verification (Creswell, 2002; McMillan & Schumacher, 2001). The result was four large charts that I brought to the children to review and verify my discernment of their words.

The data were coded hierarchically, first by identifying topics, then categories, and finally themes. Emic and etic categories helped me to examine the perspective of the participants' insider views, and my views as the outsider (Creswell, 2002; Lancy, 1993; McMillan & Schumacher, 2001). As the data were interpreted, I engaged in selective coding that led to the development of the participants' stories (Creswell, 1998). The analysis moved from the broad, big picture, to the specific details of the research, and finally back to a broad spectrum for naturalistic generalizability purposes. I related "both the description and the themes back to a larger portrait of what was learned" (Creswell, 2002, p. 493). I found that even when analysis demands "micro-focus most of the time, it is important to zoom out occasionally" (Lancy, 1993, p. 241) to make sure the sight of the bigger picture is not lost.

Validity

"In qualitative research, claims of validity rest on the data collection and analysis techniques" (McMillan & Schumacher, 2001, p. 407). I employed several interrelated strategies to ensure validity. I pursued prolonged and persistent fieldwork, spending over 6 months in the field collecting data. This lengthy data collection period allowed me to conduct interim data analysis, develop preliminary comparisons, and obtain corroboration from my participants to ensure that there was a match between my interpretation and their reality (McMillan & Schumacher, 2001). Due to my immersion in the community and my prolonged time in the field, the participants did not exhibit contrived or forced behaviors for my benefit. My historical relationship with the children enabled me to identify whether their behaviors were typical or not. Further, by utilizing multimethod strategies in data collection, I was able to triangulate the data across techniques and participants, which increases the credibility of the study (Creswell, 2002; McMillan & Schumacher, 2001). I conducted frequent member checks and participant review of data synthesis to ensure accuracy (Creswell, 2002; Ely et al., 1992; McMillan & Schumacher, 2001). Additionally, I searched for discrepancies in the data that were an exception, or that directed the data analysis in a different direction, and have reported all findings (McMillan & Schumacher, 2001). Furthermore, I used low-inference descriptions, meaning the descriptions are void of my opinions, in order to be precise with displaying the data (McMillan & Schumacher, 2001).

Finally, in relation to the writing of this article, Clifford and Marcus (1986) caution that ethnographies are texts, like all literary works; they should be viewed not as representations of cultural truths, but as partial truths or interpretations of truths. This research is a product of my interpretation of the children's stories, the children's truths, and the ways in which adults at school and at The Connection contribute to the children's racialized lives.

THE PARTICIPANTS

I employed purposeful sampling (Creswell, 2002) in selecting the children to participate in the study. I chose the participants based on several criteria: family stability within the community, ethnic background, gender, age, relationship with myself as the researcher, and having a personality that is open to sharing feelings. My participants were representative of both genders and all racial groups who attended The Connection. Although White families lived in the community, none of them attended The Connection; thus there were no White participants in my study. Several of my participants were immigrants who faced additional stresses of immigration, such as language difficulties, economic marginality, and coping with parenting practices that were customary and effective in the parents' country of origin, but were often contradictory with American cultural norms (Mayeda et al., 2001).

To ensure confidentiality, the children chose pseudonyms for themselves. We agreed on the criteria for choosing pseudonyms: their choice had to reflect their cultural origin, and could not be a complete name of someone famous. The children both enjoyed this task and took it very seriously. Some chose a name immediately, while others took months to do so. While there were nine children who participated in the study, relevant demographic information of the eight participants discussed in this chapter is contained in Table 14.1.

Table 14.1. Participant Demographics

Name	Age	Gender	Ethnicity
Leon "Blackie" Brown	10	Male	African American
Fatimah Hoffmeier	12	Female	Asian Indian/Anglo
Keandra Johnson	12	Female	African American
Veronica Montano	11	Female	Latina
Antoine Moore	11	Male	African American
Jun Pham	11	Male	Cambodian
Chanta Than	11	Female	Vietnamese/Cambodian
Nga Tran	13	Female	Vietnamese

In the next part of this chapter, I describe the children's reactions to racism and how the adults in their schools and at The Connection reacted to racial conflict.

REACTIONS TO RACISM

The children discussed the racism that they experienced in their lives and identified several different ways in which they coped with the phenomenon. They identified their tendency to ignore it—"be the bigger person," or to talk to someone about it—either their friends, typically of the same ethnicity, or to an adult, in general a parent or grandparent. They described their emotional state as hurt or angry.

Hurt and Anger

Chanta described feeling angry when people teased her about her Asian ethnicity: "It makes me feel mad … or it makes me want to stand up there in their face and tell them not to call me that." Antoine also described feeling angry and empowered to "stand up to them":

> Sometimes I just din't do nothing 'cause I just let it go … and I feel so angry about it I just felt kin'a sad. But other times I would feel angry and it would make me wanna say something back.

The hurt feeling was not described as empowering, like the feeling of anger was. Rather, the sadness seemed to keep the person isolated within their emotions. Nga believed that Asians tend to react with hurt feelings, whereas her African American counterparts are more likely to express anger. As we see in the following interview passage, she felt that these differing responses indicated that African Americans experienced racism to a lesser magnitude.

> Nga: (describing how other Asians can relate better than other ethnicities to her experiences with racism) African American and those people like that, I think they don't have to go through it that much and so if I tell them they probably would be like "Oh," and that's it.
>
> Researcher: So you think that you get teased and made fun of more than Latinos and African Americans?
>
> Nga: (nods head) [Yes.]
>
> Researcher: Really?
>
> Nga: (nods head) [Yes]

Researcher: What do you think ... So, you think ... Do you think African Americans don't get teased?

Nga: Well, um, I know they get teased sometimes but for some reason we get teased the most because I think they know how to defend themself because, like, people make fun of them and then they yell at the people and stuff like that and then we don't do nothing. So then we get our feelings all hurt.

Nga's comment suggests that she interpreted yelling, or responding with anger, as a sign that there was no pain or hurt present, only anger. However, Keandra believed that the idea that racism does not hurt African Americans was a misconception:

[They think] they could, um, just like call us names and it won't hurt us... They think that we don't got feelings.

These two excerpts illustrate alternative interpretations that Nga and Keandra place on differing responses to racism. Nga believed that anger is not an indication of hurt feelings, and viewed it as an empowering emotion or reaction to racism. "To name oneself a victim is to deny agency" (hooks, 1995, p. 58). Nga interpreted the anger she sees in her African American peers in opposition to victimization. She viewed the anger as agency, and believed that non-Asian minorities experience less racism than Asians because by yelling back, or standing up to the perpetrators, they send the message to the perpetrators to leave them alone. In comparison, she believed that Asians tolerate this mistreatment and, due to cultural timidity are less likely to yell or fight back. However, for Keandra, her perception that others believe that she does not have feelings may provide the reason that others are racist toward her.

Talk to Someone

Contrary to suppressing their feelings about racist comments, the children also discussed talking to someone about how they feel. Antoine, Chanta, Keandra, and Leon stated they turn to their mothers and other family members, whereas Nga and Veronica talk to their friends. Veronica also uses her diary as a medium to cope with racism.

Ignore It

A strategy that the children often employed was to ignore racism—to be the bigger person. In fact, Chanta ignored it so fervently, she said, "I ignore them. I just pretend I can't hear them talking to me. Like they're dogs barking." Other children chose to ignore racist comments or actions purposefully. Antoine said,

> You know, some people can make me mad, and I will wanna say something, but I hold it in and I keep it to myself 'cause they don't need to hear what I wanna say 'cause that makes them think that they're hurting me and they're gonna think that they're doin' something, so I just keep it to myself.

Antoine's comment showed his resolve to not let racists win. His logic went something like this: He believed that if they thought they hurt him, then they would win. If he ignored their racism, then they would not think that they had succeeded in hurting him, which he believed was their ultimate goal.

The children also ignored racism to keep the situation at bay. Antoine recalled a peer's racist comment: "He said a lot of things that hurt my feelin's, but I stayed strong and I tried not ta say nothin' back to him because that would just make the problem worser." Leon agreed, "Even if it gets to me ... you just ignore it and walk away. [Fighting] don't get [you] nowhere." The reasons that Antoine and Leon provided for ignoring racism were to prevent the situation from escalating, possibly even to a physical level.

In the following section I discuss adult responses to racism that the children face, one of which is advice to ignore it. It was common for adults to advise children to ignore the racism or to be "the bigger person." As we will see, it is possible that the children have internalized this advice, and perceive racism as something that does not warrant a reaction; as something to ignore.

THE IMPORTANCE OF ADULT PROTECTION

When the children were faced with racism, they looked to the adults in their lives to protect them. They told countless stories of what adults did or did not do when they witnessed or were told of acts of racism. These adults included school principals, teachers, and staff at The Connection, and their action (or inactions) can be categorized into three areas:

1. The "leave it alone" response that adults often gave to children who experienced racism.
2. The "no response" or inaction that adults imposed in situations of racial conflict.
3. The "one word against another" response, which ultimately resulted in "no response."

The children identified school personnel as responding in all of the above manners at different times. However, they identified, and I observed that the staff at The Connection always responded to racism that they saw or were told of. While they always responded, they did not always do so effectively.

Leave It Alone

I described the following situation that occurred at The Connection in another paper, which focused on psycho-cultural effects of racism (Masko, 2004). I feel it is necessary to share this incident again in this context to examine the role of the adult in handling this situation. It was a poignant incident for Keandra Johnson, and clearly illustrates the role of adults in the protection of the racial lives of the children in their care. Keandra's description and my recollections of an incident that happened on the public bus while on a Connection-sponsored field trip provide an illustration of the "leave it alone" response. After the children returned to The Connection, one of the staff members chaperoning the trip informed me about this incident, saying, "Keandra played the 'race card' with me. She got an attitude, so I sent her home." This staff member's comment came during a busy evening at The Connection, so I was not able to probe more deeply at that time. As a researcher, I chose not to interview the staff person for two reasons: (1) this study is limited to the children's perceptions, and (2) I did not have institutional human subject approval to interview anyone but the nine children in my study. However, several days later, during an interview for this study I asked Keandra about the incident. Her voice cracked as she began to tell the story, and within a few minutes she was crying profusely. Her crying continued sporadically throughout the 45-minute interview. The portion of the transcript that includes her account of the incident was 18 pages. The following is a summary of this interview together with my reflections:

> Keandra described how she and her best friend (who is also an African American preteen) were standing toward the back of the bus. All The Connection's children and the two staff members were standing and spread out the length of the bus. She recalled that there was a man, who looked like "he was from India or something. The people from Afghanistan, like them people," sitting in the back reading a book that had a picture of a burning cross on the cover. Keandra and her friend looked at the cover and whispered to each other. The man became agitated and started saying things to them, including insulting their ethnicity. While certain aspects of this story were not entirely clear, I do know that the man insulted their ethnicity, but I am uncertain of his specific remarks, and the aspect of danger related to his

remarks. But it was clear to me that Keandra felt threatened by the man's response. When the bus stopped in the neighborhood, and the children and staff got off, Keandra and her friend were angry. She told me that the Connection staff person told them to calm down and ignore it: "She said, 'Just drop it. You're off the bus. The bus is gone. Just leave it alone.'" However, this reaction infuriated the two girls, even though other children, including Jun and Antoine, told them to "drop it, drop it, there ain't nothin' to it." The staff person, recognizing that there was some level of fear through their anger, told them she had a cell phone with her for situations such as this. Keandra was exasperated and responded, "What's a cell phone gonna do?" In her interview with me, Keandra reported that she was angry with the staff person because she felt she did not understand her. "I have felt mad 'cause of what she said: to stop, to leave it alone."

In analyzing this long section of the interview, I still cannot determine precisely what happened. It is possible that the girls provoked this man's response by looking at him. It is possible that they had a heightened fear because this incident took place during the American conflict in Afghanistan, and Keandra noted that he looked like "he was from India or something. The people from Afghanistan, like them people." However, I believe that Keandra did not feel protected by the adult responsible for her protection on the bus, and adding insult to injury, she did not feel understood, either.

There are three other issues that emanate from this excerpt. First, the staff person's belief that Keandra and her friend "played the race card," supports the notion that White people do not understand the perspective of people of color (Delgado & Stefancic, 2001), which also provides another illustration to add to the body of literature on the disparity between home and school. Racism is something that parents of children of color understand, yet their teachers (who are typically White) do not.

The limitation of this particular analysis of Keandra's story is that I was unable to interview the staff person. As the director, I would have pursued further explanation of the incident; however, as a researcher I did not want the staff person's viewpoint to color my understanding of Keandra's perspective, so I chose not to pursue such an explanation. Simply analyzing the staff person's comment that Keandra "played the race card" in combination with Keandra's report that she was told to "drop it," leads me to suggest that the staff person failed to understand the seriousness of the situation from Keandra's perspective. By indicating that she had a cell phone, the staff person possibly recognized that on some level Keandra felt physically threatened by this man, and was attempting to assure her that she would have been able to protect her. Keandra's reaction "What's a cell phone gonna do?" indicates her belief that a cell phone was not a suitable protection, which possibly further contributed to Keandra's belief that the staff person didn't understand her.

Second, the staff person's response to "leave it alone," indicated her discomfort in dealing with racial issues. Joyce King (1991) refers to this as dysconscious racism: the uncritical acceptance of racist attitudes, values, and behaviors. By advising Keandra to ignore the racism she experienced, the staff person was teaching her, and the other children present, that racist attitudes are acceptable.

Third, the fact that the other children were advising her to "drop it" as well, including children of color, presents a further concern. By giving her such advice, these children seem to have internalized the notion that racism is not an oppression that should be discussed, and their anger should be suppressed. This idea is supported earlier in this chapter where the children identify "ignoring it" as a mechanism for coping with racism, which may be an internalized notion that racism should not be confronted. hooks (1995) posits that people of color are taught to repress their rage. Quite the opposite occurred in this case; the advice escalated Keandra's anger and did not effectively end the dispute. West (1993) states, "Our truncated public discussion of race suppresses the best of who and what we are as a people because they fail to confront the complexity of the issue in a candid and critical manner" (p. 4). When we advise our children to ignore racism, we may be suppressing the best of who they are.

No Response

The children described that on occasion adults provided no response to their concerns of racism. Fatimah recalled an incident at school where a Latina girl told an African American girl that she should stop drinking so much chocolate milk, a commentary on her skin tone. When the African American girl complained to a White teacher, Fatimah stated that, "she didn't do nuttin'." However, the child received a different response when she approached an African American teacher: "She got offended by it and then, that girl [the Latina girl] got in a lot of trouble. So it seemed like that [White] lady was just being racist because she didn't even really care ... she took her [the Latina girl's] side." Fatimah's comment suggests that she recognized the racism present in the act of doing nothing. By not responding to the African American girl's complaint, the White teacher sent the message that racism is not worth her comment. To Fatimah, that was a racist act in and of itself.

One Word Against Another

A child's tendency in response to adult intervention in racist acts is to deny any racist behavior when faced with disciplinary action. Keandra said, "Sometimes if they's like, if we are havin' an argument, they'll just say it, but when it comes to we going to the office, they say they don't mean it, but they do." She reported that if the perpetrators deny the racist act, the authority (whether a staff person at The Connection or a teacher at school) does not impart any disciplinary action at all, based on the reasoning that it is one child's word against another. When I talked to Keandra and a Vietnamese boy about a fight they had at The Connection, the Vietnamese boy denied having said anything racist (or anything about her mother). I consulted a third party, the Vietnamese boy's Latino friend, whom I trusted to be honest, to verify what happened. He confirmed that they both commented on each other's mothers and that they both "called out each other's color."

Anyone who has been in a disciplinary role with children knows that it is often challenging to mediate a conflict between children and identify the nature of the offense. However, the children's stories about the frequent inaction of adults are poignant. The manner in which the adults 'brush off' racial conflict has sent these children the unintended messages that racism is not an important offense, the victims of racism are not valued and will not be protected, and most clearly that they are not understood. With most other types of conflict, such as a physical altercation, the authority typically investigates the conflict and takes disciplinary action as warranted. However, the children's comments in this chapter suggest that racism was not treated with the same vigilance.

How does this action, or inaction, affect the children's relationships with adults? I asked Keandra, who was so angry with the staff person who advised her to ignore the racism she experienced on the bus, to describe her overall relationship with that staff person. She said, "I like her and she likes me, but I know she'll protect us if she would have [understood]." While Keandra was angry with the staff person for not protecting her, she still described their relationship as positive. The lack of protection and understanding provided by adults presented a barrier to their relationships with the children, as illustrated by the previous examples; however, on an individual level, Keandra was able to navigate that barrier.

SUMMARY

The children's stories indicate they have a considerable amount of experience with racism. Their stories illuminate the multitude of issues related to experiences with racism, and provide examples of how our system, in this case schools and The Connection, have difficulty redressing the wrongs (Delgado & Stefancic, 2001), which leaves the children feeling unprotected. The children's experiences with racism often led to poignant emotional reactions and coping mechanisms. While the children looked to adults for help on occasion, the adults failed to protect them. School teachers and administrators sometimes chose to ignore racism, and when they did not, or could not ignore it, they disregarded the victims' feelings and advised them to ignore it, as did the staff at The Connection. These findings have implications for pedagogical practices in schools and other informal educational settings.

IMPLICATIONS FOR PRACTICE

Creating an environment where every student feels respected and safe is imperative for children's learning and connectedness with schools. I suggest that this can be done proactively to decrease the frequency of racial conflict, as well as retroactively to improve the types of adult response. This issue is important for schools, and I suggest that capacity building around issues of cultural competency among school personnel deserves allocation of staff development resources.

Teachers' pedagogical practices can foster respect, and hence decrease the frequency of interracial conflict. "We have a lot of evidence that shows that good teaching is only good teaching with respect to a particular cultural context" (Viadero, 1996, p. 40). If children do not feel understood, respected, and protected by their teachers, their learning can be negatively impacted. Murrell (1994) describes the necessity of a positive relationship between African American students and their teacher in learning mathematics, as well as the "social ecology of the classroom" (p. 565) that is culturally responsive. These aspects of teaching are reflected in a teacher's pedagogy, which I argue must take into consideration the racial realities of the particular context (classroom, school, or after school program). A culturally responsive teacher is crucial for students of color.

A further implication of this research for practice relates to how teachers, school administrators, and other youth leaders retroactively handle racial conflict when it occurs. I have developed a training using many of the children's stories in this article as case dilemmas that educators and other professionals working with youth contemplate and discuss. When these professionals work through these dilemmas with time and collaboration, they make better choices for managing the racial conflict than the teachers and after school personnel in this article. I believe training that brings educators together to examine their own pedagogy and other informal and disciplinary interactions with children has the power to transform schools for children of color. Staff development is crucial to furthering cultural competency in educators, and should be given greater emphasis within educational contexts.

Professionals working with children and youth should consider the consequences of utilizing empathy in their disciplinary approaches to racial conflict. Further, they should regard racial conflict with the same level of seriousness as other conflict experienced in schools and other youth settings, such as after school programs. The children in this study indicated that when an adult failed to intervene in and/or advised them to ignore a racist incident, they were sending the message that they (the adults) did not understand how they felt, which in turn, indicated that they were not able or willing to protect them. This lack of protection resulted in children feeling physically and emotionally unsafe. Adults have the responsibility to protect children, and when they fail to do so they risk limiting, and possibly even damaging, children's personal and intellectual growth and development.

REFERENCES

Bodkin, S. (2003). *Being musical: Teachers, music, and identity in early childhood education in Aotearoa/New Zealand.* Unpublished doctoral thesis, Otago University, Dunedin, New Zealand.

Clifford, J., & Marcus, G. E. (1986). *Writing culture: The poetics and politics of ethnography.* Berkeley, CA: University of California Press.

Creswell, J. W. (1998). *Qualitative inquiry and research design: Choosing among five traditions.* Thousand Oaks, CA: Sage.

Creswell, J. W. (2002). *Educational research: Planning, conducting, and evaluating quantitative and qualitative research.* Upper Saddle River, NJ: Merrill/Prentice Hall.

Davis, J. E., & Jordan, W. J. (1994). The effects of school context, structure, and experiences on African American males in middle and high school. *Journal of Negro Education, 63,* 570-587.

Delgado, R., & Stefancic, J. (2001). *Critical race theory.* New York: New York University Press.

Delgado-Gaitan, C. (1992). School matters in the Mexican-American home: Socializing children to education. *American Education Research Journal, 29,* 495-513.

Delpit, L. (1995). *Other people's children: Cultural conflict in the classroom.* New York: The New Press.

Ely, M., Anzul, M., Friedman, T., Garner, D., & Steinmetz, A. M. (1991). *Doing qualitative research: Circles within circles.* New York: The Falmer Press.

hooks, b. (1995). *Killing rage: Ending racism.* New York: Henry Holt.

King, E. W., Chipman, M., & Cruz-Janzen, M. (1994). *Educating young children in a diverse society.* Boston: Allyn & Bacon.

King, J. (1991). Dysconscious racism: Ideology, identity, and the miseducation of teachers. *Journal of Negro Education, 60,* 133-146.

Ladson-Billings, G. (1994). *The dreamkeepers: Successful teachers of African American children.* San Francisco, CA: Jossey-Bass.

Lancy, D. F. (1993). *Qualitative research in education.* White Plains, NY: Longman.

Masko A. (2004, April). *"I think about it all the time": A 12-year-old girl's crisis with racism.* Paper presented at the meeting of the American Ethnological Society, American Anthropological Association, Atlanta, GA.

Mayeda, D. T., Chesney-Lind, M., & Koo, J. (2001). Talking story with Hawaii's youth: Confronting violent and sexualized perceptions of ethnicity and gender. *Youth & Society, 33,* 99-128.

Merriam-Webster. (2005). *Merriam-Webster Online.* Retrieved March 5, 2005, from www.webster.com

McMillan, J. H., & Schumacher, S. (2001). *Research in education: A conceptual introduction* (5th ed.). New York: Addison Wesley Longman.

Miles, M. B., & Huberman, A. M. (1998). *Qualitative data analysis: A sourcebook of new methods.* Beverly Hills, CA: Sage.

Murrell, P. (1994). In search of responsive teaching for African American males: An investigation of students' experiences of middle school mathematics curriculum. *Journal of Negro Education, 63,* 556-569.

Ogbu, J. U. (1992). Understanding cultural diversity and learning. *Educational Researcher, 24,* 5-14.

Ogbu, J. U. (1998). Voluntary and involuntary minorities: A cultural-ecological theory of school performance with some implication for education. *Anthropology & Education Quarterly, 29,* 155-188.

Phelan, P., Davidson, A. L., & Cao Yu, H. (1993). Students' multiple worlds: Navigating the borders of family, peer, and school cultures. In P. Phelan & A. L. Davidson (Eds.), *Renegotiating cultural diversity in American schools.* New York: T. C. Press.

Philipsen, M. (1993). Values-spoken and values-lived: Female African Americans' educational experiences in rural North Carolina. *Journal of Negro Education, 62,* 419-426.

Seidman, I. (1998). *Interviewing as qualitative research: A guide for researchers in education and the social sciences.* New York: Teachers College Press.

Spencer, M. B., Kim, S. R., & Marshall, S. (1987). Double stratification and psychological risk: Adaptational processes and school achievement of black children. *Journal of Negro Education, 56,* 77-87.

Spencer, M. B., Swanson, D. P., & Cunningham, M. (1991). Ethnicity, ethnic identity, and competence formation: Adolescent transition and cultural transformation. *Journal of Negro Education, 60,* 366-387.

Viadero, D. (1996, April 10). Culture clash: When white teachers and students come from different backgrounds, researchers say, they may not end up speaking the same language. *Education Week,* 39-42.

West, C. (1993). *Race matters.* New York: Vintage Books.

Wolcott, H. F. (1992). Posturing in qualitative research. In M. D. LeCompte, W. L. Millroy & J. Preissle (Eds.), *The handbook of qualitative research in education* (pp. 3-44). New York: Academic Press.

Wolcott, H. F. (1995). *The art of fieldwork*. Walnut Creek, CA: AltaMira Press.

ABOUT THE AUTHORS

Chara Haeussler Bohan is assistant professor in the School of Education at Baylor University. She earned her doctoral degree at The University of Texas at Austin. She is the author of *Go to the Sources: Lucy Maynard Salmon and the Teaching of History*.

Hsuan-Jen Chen is assistant professor of educational and school psychology at the Indiana State University. She teaches in the areas of multicultural education and qualitative research methods.

Sara McCormick Davis taught preschool through fifth grade for 18 years. She is currently an assistant professor of early childhood education at Portland State University's Graduate School of Education. Her research interests include documentation of children's learning and how critical reflection supports the development of teachers.

Violet Dickson has taught for 18 years in the public school system. She is currently a doctoral student at the University of North Texas in Denton, Texas.

Marilyn J. Eisenwine is an associate professor in the School of Education at Angelo State University in San Angelo, TX. She teaches undergraduate reading and early childhood courses and a graduate course in curriculum.

David J. Flinders is an associate professor of education at Indiana University, Bloomington. He has published six books on education, the most recent of which is *The Curriculum Studies Reader, Second Edition*, co-edited with Stephen Thornton. His most recent research examines how adolescents think about the war in Iraq. He is also the American Educational Research Association's Vice President-elect for Division B (Curriculum Studies).

Edie S. Gaythwaite is a graduate student in the College of Education, Curriculum and Instruction at the University of Central Florida. Her interests include communication, distance education, and self-regulated learning in higher education.

Nancy J. Hadley is an associate professor in the School of Education at Angelo State University in San Angelo, TX. Over the past 6 years she has analyzed teacher certification exam questions and worked closely with students to discover problems encountered in this specific standardized testing environment.

Judy Luckett is an instructor in the University of Central Florida College of Education. She teaches courses in methodology, educational psychology, critical issues in education, and strategies for success in college. Her current research interests are foreign language education, bilingual education, and the effects of the 1970 Orange County, Florida school desegregation on the lives of teachers and their students.

Amy L. Masko is an assistant professor of English education, preparing teacher candidates to teach elementary literacy. Dr. Masko's research interests are in urban education, after school programs, and multicultural education. She is also an educational consultant in the areas of diversity in education and literacy.

John Mihelich teaches sociology, anthropology, and American studies at the University of Idaho along with teaching an interdisciplinary Core Discovery course titled "Time Warps: Religion, Science, Technology, and Cultures of Time." He is interested in innovative pedagogy with the goals of cultivating students' curiosity and critical thinking capacities, expanding interdisciplinary understandings and fostering relationships between course material and students' life experience.

James R. Moore is an assistant professor of social studies education at Cleveland State University. Professor Moore taught world history for 21 years in the Miami-Dade County public schools.

Christy M. Moroye is a PhD student and admissions coordinator for teacher education at the University of Denver. Her research interests include the practice of ecologically minded teachers and ecological perspectives in teacher education.

David W. Nicholson is an assistant professor of education at Concord University in Athens, West Virginia, where he teaches courses in educational psychology, technology, research, and action research.

J. Wesley Null is assistant professor in the School of Education and the Honors College at Baylor University. His areas of research and study include pedagogy and the history of teacher education curriculum.

Steve Purcell is an assistant professor in the College of Education at James Madison University. There he teaches a variety of graduate and undergraduate courses in such areas as technology integration and implementation, media development, instructional design and technology, and human-computer interaction.

Teresa W. Russell teaches English, Advanced Placement, and critical viewing classes at Princeton Senior High School in Princeton, West Virginia.

Mary G. Sanders is an assistant professor in the School of Education at Angelo State University in San Angelo, TX. She teaches reading, special education and an educational diagnostics course.

Printed in the United States
35949LVS00010B/5-42